TODAY IS A GOOD DAY TO FIGHT

About the Author

Dr Mark Felton is the author of more than two dozen history books, including several bestsellers, and regularly appears on television and radio. He holds a PhD in Native American–white relations in nineteenth-century North America. In 2011, *Today is a Good Day to Fight* was used as a central source for Melvyn Bragg's BBC *In Our Time* documentary 'Custer's Last Stand'. He lives in Norwich.

Today is a Good Day to Fight

THE INDIAN WARS AND THE CONQUEST OF THE WEST

MARK FELTON

The History Press

'For Fang Fang, my inspirational wife'

Cover illustrations: Top: Geronimo (right), leader of the Chiricahua
Apache, his son and two braves on the occasion of his final surrender to
American forces, Tombstone, Arizona, 1886. Glenbow Museum. *Bottom:*
Brigadier General Nelson A. 'Bearcoat' Miles (second left), photographed
'viewing hostile Indian camp' at Pine Ridge Reservation, 1891. Library
of Congress.

First published 2009
This paperback edition first published 2018

The History Press
The Mill, Brimscombe Port
Stroud, Gloucestershire, GL5 2QG
www.thehistorypress.co.uk

© Mark Felton, 2009, 2018

The right of Mark Felton to be identified as the Author
of this work has been asserted in accordance with the
Copyright, Designs and Patents Act 1988.

British Library Cataloguing in Publication Data.
A catalogue record for this book is available from the British Library.

ISBN 978 0 7509 8890 2

Printed and bound in Great Britain by TJ International Ltd

CONTENTS

ACKNOWLEDGEMENTS

The author would like to extend his thanks to many individuals, institutions and organisations. A great many thanks to my editor Simon Hamlet and the staff at The History Press. Some of the topics in this book stem from original research undertaken during my MA and PhD study at the University of Essex, and I would like to extend my thanks to Dr Colin Samson, Dr Mary Ellen Curtin and Dr Edward Higgs, and also to the staff at the Albert Sloman Library. I should like to acknowledge the kind assistance of the following individuals: Dr Karen Jones at the University of Kent; Dr Sarah Carter of the University of Calgary; Dr Faye Hammill of the *British Journal of Canadian Studies*; Carmen Harry of the Royal Canadian Mounted Police Museum in Regina; and Dr Joy Porter of the University of Wales Swansea. Many thanks to the following institutions and organisations: the British Library; the British Museum; The National Archives (Public Record Office), Kew; the National Archives (NARA), Washington DC; the National Archives of Canada, Ottawa; the Museum of Civilisation in Hull, Quebec; the Museum of Anthropology, University of Cambridge; the Royal Historical Society; the International Council for Canadian Studies; Idaho State Historical Society; and the British Association for Canadian Studies. Finally, I owe a great debt of thanks to my wife, Fang Fang, who has tirelessly encouraged me in my writing over the years, and whose belief is so appreciated.

INTRODUCTION

'I am a red man. If the Great Spirit had desired me to be a white man he would have made me so in the first place. He put in your heart certain wishes and plans, in my heart he put other and different desires. Each man is good in his sight. It is not necessary for Eagles to be Crows. We are poor ... but we are free. No white man controls our footsteps. If we must die ... we die defending our rights.'

Sitting Bull, Hunkpapa Sioux

Sun-blackened and bloated corpses lay spread across the dusty hillsides over several square miles. Colonel John Gibbon's infantry column had arrived on the banks of the Little Bighorn River in Montana Territory. It was 27 June 1876, and officers and men of the 7th Infantry, accompanied by survivors of the more famous 7th Cavalry, walked slowly among the prostrated bodies. Many were clustered together, others lay in stark isolation. All around the sun glinted off thousands of expended cartridge casings clustered in little piles in the short dry grass, and every so many yards a dead horse lay on its side, its legs stiff in the air. Some horses were still alive, an animal standing here and there, black flies swarming over their bleeding wounds, heads down and bridles trailing on the ground.

The human bodies were unrecognisable, both from lying out in the hot sun for two days, and for the furious assaults they had sustained from their enemies, both in life and after death. Heads were missing from some, arms and legs from others. Some were missing noses, eyes or ears, others a finger or a hand. Most had been scalped, many had cut throats, and most had been gutted from sternum to crotch, stinking guts lying in fetid piles beside their bodies. Many of the soldiers' bodies were shot so full of arrows that they resembled porcupines. All were naked, save for scraps of

9

blood-soaked underwear or an odd sock, their uniforms and equipment long since carried off the field as trophies and spoils of war.

Atop a conical hill above the river valley the corpses were particularly thick, many lying in tight groups beside dead horses, marking a long retreat from the river to high ground. A ring of six dead horses atop the hill marked the final redoubt in what had evidently been a grim fight to the death, and behind the horses lay seven more corpses in various states of undress and decomposition. Gibbon's men and the cavalry officers went from body to body with handkerchiefs clamped over their faces to ward off the stench of decay, vainly attempting to find friends and colleagues. This battle, and its bloody aftermath, has come to symbolise the struggle for the American West. Its legacy was used as a reason to eradicate the Indians from their ancestral lands, lands the Indians had inhabited for millennia.

A Lakota Sioux story tells of two men who were on a hunting trip when they noticed a beautiful young woman walking towards them across the prairie. She was dressed in white buckskins and carried a bundle on her back. One of the men had bad thoughts about her and threatened her with his bow, but the moment he approached her he was suddenly surrounded by a white mist. When the mist dispersed, nothing of the man remained but his skeleton. The beautiful woman turned to the other warrior and told him to go home and prepare a big tepee for her. The man ran home and did exactly what she had told him to do. When the woman walked into his village, he had already completed his task. She then told the people of the village that she came from heaven and was here on earth to teach them how to live and what their future would be. She gave the people maize, showed them the use of the pipe and taught them the seven sacred ceremonies. Furthermore, she gave them colours for the four winds or directions. When she was finished she turned into a white buffalo calf, then turned its colour black, then red, then last she turned yellow, representing the colours of the four directions. Then she disappeared.[1] This story explained to the Sioux how their society was formed in the past. It was a creation story. At the centre of that society was the buffalo, the symbolic animal of the American West that white people almost made extinct, along with the Indians who depended upon it to survive.

The American West can mean many things to many people: it can be the story of hardy pioneers going west in covered wagons; it can be the 'Frontier' culture of cowboys, one-horse towns and range wars; it can be the Gold Rush and the intrepid 49ers with their picks and pans; it can be hunters, fur trappers and backwoodsmen living with nature and overcoming immense physical challenges. It can be any of these and more. In the case of this book it is the wars that ceaselessly ravaged the American West throughout the second half of the nineteenth century, as white Anglo-American culture clashed with the indigenous culture of the region's original inhabitants, the American Indians.

'Cowboys and Indians,' a children's game and a euphemism for the 'American West,' has entered the consciousness of generations around the world. Hollywood has wholeheartedly embraced it, and recycled the story of Indian–white interaction and reaction endlessly, losing the original history along the way and supplanting a new history in the minds of the watching public. In the Hollywood version of the American West the whites represent righteousness, progress and civilisation, while the Indians are the bogeymen waiting in the shadows to do foul deeds to the settler or soldier, a people trapped in a prehistoric world of sun worship, ritual mutilation and subsistence hunting and gathering. The Indians are mysterious, other-worldly and dangerous, more akin to wild animals than to human beings. Their cultural destruction, though unfortunate, was necessary, according to the old history of the American West, to save them from themselves. It would allow Americans to complete their national Manifest Destiny of controlling the whole landmass of North America from the Atlantic to the Pacific, or 'from sea to shining sea' as the founders of Virginia termed it.

The real history of the American West is not nearly as noble, courageous or glorious as Hollywood movies and generations of Americans have portrayed it. The real history is the story of white people imposing their will upon the Indians by whatever means at hand in order to gain control over the Indians' land and resources. In order to subjugate the Indian, whites stooped very low indeed. Every treaty that the Americans made with Indian peoples, 371 in total, was fraudulent and subsequently broken by the US Congress. The US Army was regularly unleashed to attack peaceful villages and butcher men, women and children in cold blood, and other methods, such as killing off the Indians' food sources to induce starvation, were also practiced very effectively on the orders of the American Government. In various combinations these methods, allied to the spread of epidemic diseases to which the Indians had no natural resistance, were hugely successful strategies for the United States and by 1891 the last gasps of Indian resistance had been swept aside at Wounded Knee in South Dakota: the usurpation of the American West from its rightful occupiers was virtually complete.

It is not possible to encapsulate the entire bloody and brutal history of the American West in a single book, but what this account tries to do in an intentionally limited way is to highlight some of the more prominent campaigns the United States undertook against Indians during its march to the West, and to show how the Americans overcame Indian resistance. These are only glimpses into a dark and violent history, and of course ignore the steady Americanisation of the West by generations of white settlers who prospered between the storms of war. Think of American expansion into the West in terms of a gradual erosion of 'Indianness' until only little islands of aboriginal culture remained in the form of today's reservations.

There was nothing intrinsically special about Native Americans. They were humans that had adapted their lifestyles to meet the particular challenges of their existence, and the cultures that sprang up throughout the continent of America were diverse and unique mainly because of geography, climate and resources. No-one knows for certain how long Indians have been in North America, and current thinking suggests anywhere from 9,000 to 35,000 years. It is believed that their ancestors crossed the frozen Bering Strait from Asia, but even this theory has been contested. They had prospered and multiplied, creating multitudes of languages, tribes, nations and modes of living long before the first Europeans tentatively began exploring the eastern seaboard, the first known white visitors being a small group of Vikings who arrived in Newfoundland in AD 1000. After the arrival of Columbus and the Spanish in 1492, contact between the Indian inhabitants of North America and Europeans was sporadic for over a hundred years, as the Spanish turned their attention and energy to plundering the great Indian city-building civilisations in Central and South America, like the Aztec and the Maya. The first European settlement in the West came not from the east, but from the south, when a Conquistador named Juan de Onate led a group of settlers north from Mexico across the Rio Grande in 1598. Onate established the first European settlement in North America at Santa Fe a few years later. Spanish soldiers, settlers and missionaries pushed farther north into southern Arizona in the 1690s, south-eastern Texas in 1716 and finally into California in 1769, with the establishment of a settlement they named San Diego.

As the Spanish moved north, French settlers and fur traders moved southwest from Canada's St Lawrence Valley. Beginning at Quebec in 1608, by 1718 French settlements stretched thinly along the Great Lakes and the

Mississippi River to New Orleans, but numbered fewer than 50,000 people. All of this was achieved long before English or American colonial explorers began to range west of the Appalachian Mountains. The English colonies in the east had begun at Jamestown, Virginia, in 1607. By 1700 the colonial population was only 250,000 people, but boomed in the decades that followed, pushing forward expansion into the West. By the 1740s there were a million English-speaking settlers stretching from Maine to Georgia, and by the time Thomas Jefferson penned the Declaration of Independence in 1776 that figure had reached 2.5 million. This huge population began to spill over the old colonial boundaries into Indian lands across the Appalachians in Kentucky, Tennessee and the upper Ohio Valley. The settlers followed long-established practices in trading with Indian peoples, forming alliances with them to use their manpower in the incessant struggle with France for control of eastern America, and when Indians outlived their usefulness they ruthlessly killed them, infected them with diseases or pushed whole tribes further west at the point of a musket. Indians were not to form a significant part of the new English-speaking landscape east of the Mississippi; they would disappear almost entirely from the future southern states and almost cease to exist in New England.

From 1710 the English-speaking population of America would double every twenty-one years, while the Indian population that had stood at perhaps 2 million in North America when Columbus had arrived continued to decline. The unsettled lands of the West appeared limitless to Americans and full of opportunity for those hardy, brave and resourceful enough to abandon the overcrowded east. The peace treaty that ended the American War of Independence in 1783 generously awarded the new United States control over all lands east of the Mississippi, and the Louisiana Purchase of French territory in America from a cash-strapped Napoleon in 1803 doubled that area. By 1848 the United States had annexed the Republic of Texas, the entire south-west after defeating Mexico in a short war and all of present-day Oregon as well. Hundreds of thousands of Indians had already perished since the whites had first arrived, most wiped out by European diseases, and the survivors had either been enslaved by the Spanish (later the Mexicans) or herded onto reservations by the Americans. The West, however, remained a barely touched island surrounded by white lands, and settlers contented themselves with merely passing through the Great Plains to get to California and Oregon. Conflicts arose over the emigrant trails, and the United States moved to control the Indian peoples who lived on the Plains and remove their power to impede settlement. Soon, whites began to settle upon the Plains themselves, bringing railroads, towns, military posts, ranching and gold prospecting with them from the 1850s onwards. Above all, the whites wanted land upon which to thrive, and the American government was ruthless in the methods it employed to rid the vast lands of the West of their aboriginal inhabitants. What was at stake was the development of the United States from an under-populated agricultural society into a vast, industrial world power, a transition that was made extremely quickly in comparison with the old countries of Europe.

It was not difficult for Americans to justify to themselves removing Indians from their tribal territories. Whereas white Americans seemed to stand for progress, technology and science, American Indians appeared to hail from entirely different millennia. Their cultural practices were extraordinary and disagreeable to nineteenth-century whites. The nineteenth century was the high point of imperialism across the globe and the Americans, like the British and the French, were no less prone to labelling anyone who was not white as a 'savage' or a 'heathen'. The American West was the great experiment in 'backyard imperialism' for the United States, and we tend to forget today that the Indian tribal groups that America attacked, subjugated and stole land from were as independent as African tribes subjugated by the British or Pacific islanders whose atolls were usurped by the French. In all these cases for one group of people to take the lands of another by force or deception did not make it right, moral or legal. The United States was founded on the ideas of freedom, equality and the rule of law. When America sallied westwards in the mid-nineteenth century these principles were largely abandoned or ignored in the quest for wealth and hegemony. America confronted a dizzying variety of Indian nations who had spent perhaps 30,000 years or more migrating around the continent, fighting with each other over resources and developing specialised modes of living to suit their geographical circumstances. The Americans looked hard and saw peoples who were not 'civilised,' that reminded the industrial-agricultural progressive people of the east of their own humble beginnings millennia before as hunter-gatherers. It seemed fair and reasonable to most Americans that the more advanced should supplant the ignorant and backward as masters of the land, and that the 'savage', no matter how noble he might be, give up his right to the bountiful lands of the West to the white man. It was not only a clash of cultures – it was race war.

The United States followed a clear agenda with regard to the Indian peoples it encountered as it expanded west. When the great Sioux leader Sitting Bull was only an infant in the 1830s:

> white attitudes in the time of Andrew Jackson ... centered on the idea of progress, a conception rooted in the Renaissance and the Enlightenment but given a distinctly American cast by the westward expansion. Progress demanded the conquest of the wilderness, an imperative fortified by God's command to 'be fruitful and multiply, and fill the earth and subdue it.[2]

Americans viewed Indians as part of that wilderness, merely as something else to be tamed or eradicated. Human history, according to whites of the time, was a linear path of progress from 'savagery', as demonstrated by Indian society, to ultimate Christian civilisation embodied in the United States. The Indians had no right to the land they occupied because they had not improved it, and therefore their societies must give way to a higher civilisation. It was an idea originally espoused by John Locke, and had been brought to America by the Pilgrims in the seventeenth century.

This book is essentially the story of how Americans tried to make good on God's command to 'fill the earth and subdue it.' The wars against the Indians were not unique to nineteenth-century America. Wherever white men trod they sought to bring the purported benefits of Western 'civilisation' with them, and everywhere they labelled indigenous peoples 'savages' or worse. The plight of the Aborigine in Australia, the Maori in New Zealand and the Zulu in South Africa are excellent examples. But perhaps nowhere else has a nation succeeded so succinctly in making glorious the dark deeds of the past. The 'Hollywood history' of the American West that has been current for several generations is a lie. It took the United States about forty years to fully subdue Indian resistance in the West and cost the lives of thousands of people on both sides. It would also leave a legacy of pain, anger, hatred, mistrust and sadness among the Indian peoples of the region who were crushed in a struggle that remains raw to this day. The conflict would lead many on both sides to question the morality behind the methods used to solve the 'Indian Problem.' Occasionally, the painful wounds of conquest and subjugation were reawakened in modern America. The last time gunfire was exchanged between Indians and the forces of the American government was at the time of writing only thirty-five years ago in 1973 at a place called Wounded Knee. And in a sense the 'Indian Wars' have never really ended, the fighting instead having been transposed to the courtroom, the rifles exchanged for lawsuits and statute books. In the new battlefield of the law the Indians remain the losers, and the United States remains implacable in refusing to address the wrongs of the past.

Notes

1. James R. Walker, *Lakota Belief and Ritual* (Lincoln: University of Nebraska Press, 1980).
2. Robert M. Utley, *The Lance and the Shield: The Life and Times of Sitting Bull* (London: Pimlico, 1993), 42.

1

THE LONG WALK

'You have deceived us too often, and robbed and murdered our people too long, to trust you again at large in your own country. This war shall be pursued against you if it takes years, now that we have begun, until you cease to exist or move. There can be no other talk on the subject.'

Brigadier General James H. Carleton to the Navajo, 1863

March 1864. A long line of Indians stretched away across the broken terrain for miles. Many were women and children. Bundled in blankets and carrying their few possessions the line shuffled along slowly, led by a group of warriors wearing distinctive headbands that marked them out as Navajo. Along the flanks of the great column, so long that it would take several hours for it to pass a single place, soldiers, their blue uniforms covered in a thick layer of dust, rode slowly on equally dirty horses, many carrying Navajo women or children behind them on their saddles. Grinding along the dusty trail the occasional army covered wagon drawn by a team of horses bounced on its crude springs, the box stacked high with provisions and overflowing with Navajo who were too exhausted, pregnant, sick or lame to walk.

There were insufficient soldiers to guard the long column from the predators that congregated to the rear, waiting for an opportunity to swoop down on hapless victims. Many of the Navajo, hungry and exhausted, fell behind the footsore column, and each day a few more people disappeared. The predators were Ute Indians, closely trailing the column armed with rifles and hatchets, and Mexicans. Both groups would accost those who left the column and sell these unfortunates into slavery or kill them where they stood and rob them of their few possessions, like wolves trailing a wounded buffalo. This great column of defeated and disillusioned Indians was the culmination of a concerted American campaign to rid the south-west of the bigger and more troublesome Indian tribes. A few months earlier the destruction of the Navajo way of life had reached a terrible and terminal crescendo.

July 1863. Colonel Kit Carson sat on his horse and stared blankly at the scene of destruction unfolding around him. Hither and thither ran his soldiers with torches blazing, igniting the fields of crops that stretched away along the canyon floor. Beneath the brim of his campaign hat Carson's face was deeply tanned after forty years on the Frontier, his eyes narrowed, around which deep crow's feet stood out after years of squinting in the harsh south-western sunlight, hair parted on top and worn below the collar of his blue officer uniform. Carson was in his fifties and a living legend. In the pre-movie era he had become the equivalent of today's Hollywood celebrity – a genuine all-action hero whose exploits had been retold countless times in the most lurid prose by eastern journalists and hack writers. There would be other 'heroes' of the West, men like Buffalo Bill Cody and Wyatt Earp, but Carson's exploits had been largely genuine and his reputation well earned. Hence he was now overseeing a scorched-earth policy in New Mexico Territory in the midst of the terrible Civil War in the east, aimed at solving the Navajo Indian problem once and for all. Denying the Navajo their food supplies by destroying their crops inside the sheltered and fertile canyons was one method for ridding the south-west of Indians. Carson determined to starve them out and force their surrender.

The traditional homeland of the Navajo stretched from north-western Arizona through western New Mexico, and north into Utah and Colorado. They had lived in bands for generations, cultivating crops and raising livestock in the numerous canyons. Inter-tribal warfare and trading was common in the south-west, and the Navajo rubbed along uneasily with the Apache, Pueblo and Comanche peoples, as well as Spanish and later Mexican settlers who came up from the south. After 1846 contact with Americans suddenly and dramatically increased after the United States and Mexico went to war. America was victorious, gaining the former Mexican territories of California, Arizona, New Mexico, Texas, Utah and Colorado as the spoils of that victory in the 1848 Treaty of Guadalupe Hidalgo, including an extension of the border down to the Rio Grande. All Mexicans living in these territories automatically became American citizens, but the Indians did not. For the region's Indians victory in the Mexican–American War signalled a new and aggressive master quickly attempting to control them through treaties and military force. The Americans wanted nothing less than the corralling of the Navajo and the other tribes onto reservations as quickly as possible, where they could no longer interfere with the orderly settlement of the new territories. They ordered that the Navajo immediately cease all raiding on Americans and Mexicans. The Navajo method of raising livestock, primarily sheep, would be pushed aside by white cattle and horse ranchers moving in from the east and from Texas. The American government had quickly identified the Navajo and the Apache as the strongest and best-organised Indian groups that had to be conquered before real progress could be made in turning the wild territories into new states.

The Navajo had signed their first treaty with the Americans in 1846, and this had swiftly been followed by an agreement in 1851 permitting the United States to construct military posts on Navajo land in return for promised peace and presents from the Indian Department. In 1855 Colonel Edwin Sumner boldly led military forces into the centre of Navajo lands at Canyon de Chelly, Arizona Territory, and constructed the first post there, which he appropriately named Fort Defiance. The Navajo elders signed another treaty that same year which decreased their lands to 7,000 square miles, of which only 125 square miles was actually cultivatable. The upshot of such American short-sightedness was a food supply problem for the Navajo which could only be satisfied by warriors making periodic raids on other Indian or American settlements. Armed conflict followed, as American greed for Navajo land drove the Indians into armed resistance merely to secure the basics of life.

Fort Defiance was located amid some of the best Navajo grazing areas. Indian horses and sheep lived contentedly upon these ancient lands, most of which were under the control of a band led by Chief Manuelito. In 1858 Major William Brooks, the post commander, decided to graze his command's horses on the local Navajo lands, and Brooks arrogantly issued instructions to Manuelito to remove his animals or see them shot. When Manuelito refused Brooks sent out a party of troops who proceeded to kill sixty Navajo horses and over one hundred sheep. Manuelito's band was furious at their leader's treatment by the Americans. In retaliation the Navajo killed Brooks' black slave, who had recently raped a local Indian woman. Brooks' response was to order the Navajo to turn in the murderer for punishment or the soldiers would attack them. Manuelito's band and others suffered several months of intermittent fighting with American troops from Fort Defiance after failing to heed Brooks' instruction. Eventually, having grown tired of the disruption to their economic life the Navajo chieftains went to Fort Defiance and signed another treaty promising to remain on their assigned lands in the future. The army could claim a victory, of sorts.

The Navajo simmered with anger and resentment at the high-handed and unfair treatment dished out to them from the fort, and they bided their time. Then, quite suddenly in 1861, the soldiers began to leave the fort and New Mexico and Arizona. The outbreak of the Civil War in the east witnessed a sudden drawing down of American military strength west of the Mississippi as regular troops were desperately needed by the newly constituted Union Army. The Navajo immediately spotted the great opportunity that the Civil War offered their people. It appeared simple. Strike at Fort Defiance now and wipe the army from their lands while the Americans were occupied with killing each other thousands of miles away in the east.

The Navajo and the Mescalero Apache rose in a huge revolt aimed at driving the whites out of the southwest. They stole livestock, killed settlers, attacked settlements, raided mining camps, and even attacked a Union Army column sent by Washington to defeat General Henry Sibley's Confederate forces. The region's settlers were joined by Mexican-Americans, Ute and Zuni Indians in demanding that action be taken at once against the Navajo and Apache and the attacks ended. At the beginning of the Civil War Kit Carson had immediately resigned from his post as federal Indian agent for northern New Mexico and joined the locally-raised New Mexico Volunteer Infantry. New Mexico had thrown its support behind the Union, even though slave ownership was legal throughout the territory. The commander of army forces in the Territory after the withdrawal of regular forces east was Lieutenant Colonel Edward Canby of the 19th Infantry, based at Fort Marcy, Santa Fe. Carson was commissioned a Colonel of Volunteers, a temporary emergency rank for the duration of the war, and he took command of two battalions of the 1st New Mexico Volunteers numbering about 500 men.

In 1862 General Henry Sibley, commanding Confederate forces in Texas, invaded New Mexico, adding further to the complicated situation already existing there as under-strength and ill-trained Union volunteer forces tried to control the Navajo and Mescalero. Sibley's aim was to push on through New Mexico into Colorado and capture the rich goldfields there to aid the Confederate economy. Advancing confidently up the Rio Grande, Sibley's force clashed with Canby's troops at the Battle of Valverde on 21 February 1863. The Confederates won, forcing Canby across the river with sixty-eight killed and 160 wounded. Following this Canby was promoted and recalled east. Although the Confederates had been victorious, and would go on to occupy Albuquerque and Santa Fe, a lack of supplies eventually drove Sibley's army out of New Mexico and back into Texas. The situation with the Indians remained tense and the populace of the Territory was on edge after the invasion and constant Indian raiding. A new commander was dispatched from back east.

Fortunately for the settlers and friendly Indians the new commander of the Department of New Mexico who replaced Colonel Canby was just the man to crush the rebellious natives, a hard man who would use the harshest of methods to achieve his goal. Brigadier General James H. Carleton was a decorated hero of the Mexican-American War. He disliked the Navajo and the Apache, based on twenty years of fighting them in New Mexico and Arizona, and he believed that trying to negotiate with them was a waste of time. Carleton delivered a simple message to the Navajo: surrender and agree to go to a new reservation that he had picked for them at Bosque Redondo beside the Pecos River, or be exterminated. Carleton passionately believed that the Navajo were the reason for New Mexico's 'depressing backwardness,' and he decided to tap into the fear and anxiety caused by Sibley's invasion, and turn that collective civilian ill feeling onto a problem they could actually solve – the destruction of the Navajo and Mescalero. Carleton believed that gold existed somewhere on Navajo land and he also wanted rid of the Indians so New Mexicans could exploit any potential riches for themselves.

For the Apache, relations with the United States had long been strained and difficult. When America had claimed the former Mexican territories making up the southwest the Apache had maintained an uneasy peace with the new masters. A great Apache leader named Mangas Coloradas had signed a peace treaty with the Americans in 1846 recognising the United States as conquerors of Mexican lands. The peace held until the discovery of gold in the Santa Rita Mountains led to an influx of white miners. In 1851, near Pinos Altos, a group of miners accosted Mangas Coloradas, tied him to a tree, and beat him severely. Similar incidents led to Apache reprisals. In December 1860 thirty miners launched a surprise assault on a Bedonkohe Apache encampment on the west bank of the Mimbres River. They killed four Indians, wounded several others and captured thirteen women and children. Retaliatory raids by the Apache became more widespread. In February 1861 Lieutenant George N. Bascom lured the principal chief of the Chokonen Apache, Cochise, his family and several warriors into a trap at Apache Pass in south-eastern Arizona. Cochise managed to escape but everyone else was captured and imprisoned. The 'Bascom Affair' ended with Cochise's brother and five other warriors being hanged from a tree by the soldiers. Later in 1861 Cochise allied his people with his father-in-law Mangas Coloradas, and a unified Apache group agreed to try to drive all of the Americans out of their territory. The alliance was shortly after joined by chiefs Juh and Geronimo and only came about because of American attacks. Worse was to come.

Throughout 1862 Mangas Coloradas tried to broker a peace deal with the Americans, and in January 1863 he decided to meet personally with American military leaders at Fort McLane, near present-day Hurley, New Mexico. Mangas Coloradas arrived under a white flag of truce to meet Brigadier General Joseph Rodman West of the California Militia and future senator for Louisiana. Rodman ordered Mangas Coloradas arrested and executed. That night Mangas Coloradas was cruelly tortured by the troops and then shot dead. On the following day the chief's head was cut off, boiled clean of flesh and muscle, and then sent to the Smithsonian Institution in Washington DC as an exhibit.

In dealing with the Navajo issue General Carleton ordered Kit Carson to kill all of the men of the Mescalero Apache tribe as a prelude to forcing all Apache and Navajo onto a new reservation. Carson was appalled at such an order and refused to obey. Instead, Carson accepted the surrender of over one hundred Apache warriors and dispatched them to the new reservation at Bosque Redondo. After breaking the Mescalero, Carson was ordered to turn his forces onto the much more numerous Navajo. Carson tried to resign, but Carleton managed to talk him around to continuing with his task, which Carleton clearly saw as almost a messianic mission to rid the southwest of Indians. Carson was instructed to deliver to Navajo of the following message:

> You have deceived us too often, and robbed and murdered our people too long, to trust you again at large in your own country. This war shall be pursued against you if it takes years, now that we have begun, until you cease to exist or move. There can be no other talk on the subject.

The Navajo traditionally conducted raids so Carson knew it was unlikely that they would fight any pitched battles with the soldiers that would lead to their defeat and subjugation. Instead, Carleton and Carson hit on the idea of turning Navajo lifestyle against them. Why not destroy the Navajo crops that they depended upon for food, and run off or kill their livestock? Why not find their villages and burn them also? Such a 'scorched-earth' policy would deny the Navajo the means to continue their resistance and quickly bring about their surrender. Carson also exploited regional tribal enmities by recruiting many Ute Indians to his cause as scouts, and they did a sterling service killing their traditional Navajo enemies and burning Navajo fields and houses with alacrity.

Bringing the Navajo under American control was a gruelling task for Colonel Carson and his men. Twelve thousand Navajo were scattered over a vast and rugged country that included the Grand Canyon in Arizona. Carson spent months riding across this territory burning crops and Navajo villages, destroying stocks of grain, rounding up sheep and hacking down Navajo peach orchards. Starvation soon became widespread among the Indians. Winter followed. The cold weather carried off old people and young children who were weakened by hunger. Carson's men entered the Navajo heartland at Canyon de Chelly where they wrought more destruction and looting while the Indians watched helplessly from the canyon walls. The scorched-earth policy eventually drove many Navajo to surrender. A hardcore of about 4,000 scattered into the remote western parts of their territory, moving into the Grand Canyon with the Chiricahua Apache and into parts of Utah. They held out for two years before starvation also ended their resistance. Carson had achieved his objective. The majority of the Navajo had surrendered, and the army prepared to march them 300 miles across New Mexico to the barren new reservation at Bosque Redondo. It was a forced march that came to be called the 'The Long Walk'.

The Long Walk was actually three 'walks', as the Navajo were divided into three large parties to make the 300-mile trek. The great march began in January 1863 and would last for eighteen days as the Navajo made the journey by easy stages to the new reservation. However, many died along the route as they were already weakened by hunger and disease after Carson's successful 'scorched-earth' policy that had compelled their surrender. They travelled east by the present-day settlements of Gallup, Churbbito and Fort Wingate. If the three processions had been combined into one long column the marching Navajo families would have stretched for ten miles. As it was, each of the three columns was enormous, escorted by armed troops who made sure that none of the Indians broke ranks and attempted to escape. The attitude of the soldiers was quite relaxed towards their charges, and the compassion of many of the young troopers towards the defeated Indians was mystifying to the Navajo, who in common with most Indian tribes did not show mercy towards defeated opponents but rather killed or enslaved survivors. A Navajo elder, Very Slim Man, recalled of the march:

> If there was room the soldiers put the women and children on the wagons. Some even let them ride behind them on their horses. I have never been able to understand a people who killed you one day and on the next played with your children?[1]

Of the 8,500 Navajo who made the Long Walk, about two hundred died en route. Some were killed by Ute Indians along the way, while others who fell behind were snatched by the Utes or local New Mexicans and subsequently sold into slavery. Many were swept away and drowned trying to cross the Rio Grande when it was in full spate.

When the footsore and ill Navajo arrived at their destination what they found at Fort Sumner was the ill-prepared Bosque Redondo Reservation. The army had only expected 5,000 Navajo, but over 8,500 made the trek. Already resident were 500 Mescalero Apache who hated the Navajo and were intimidated by their enemies' much greater numbers. Having these two Indian groups in such close proximity to one another on a forty-square-mile reservation was a disaster from the get go. The reservation itself was devoid of wild game, most of the land was infertile and what little crops the Navajo did manage to plant were soon destroyed by parasites or heavy rain storms. There was no wood for cooking or heating, and the water source was so alkaline as to be undrinkable. Water taken from the Pecos River caused stomach problems, and people soon began to sicken with various water-borne diseases and die. General Carleton had declared that in his opinion Bosque Redondo would become 'the happiest and most delightfully located pueblo of Indians in New Mexico – perhaps in the United States,'[2] but his optimism was ill-placed. To exacerbate the already alarming problems faced by the Navajo the government failed to issue enough food to them, largely because of arguments between the army and the Indian Bureau, and corruption and theft by Indian agents. During the winter the Navajo were issued with inadequate clothing so they froze. The Indians were permanently half-starved, sick and under attack as constant raids occurred between the Navajo and the Apache over limited resources. The local Comanche also raided the reservation searching for food, and the dire problems caused gangs of Navajo warriors to raid nearby white settlements in search of food for their starving family members.

As mentioned, one group of Navajo had avoided surrendering to the Americans following Kit Carson's destructive campaign. Led by Chief Manuelito they had disappeared into the Grand Canyon. General Carleton sent a group of surrendered Navajo chieftains led by Herrero Grande to locate Manuelito and give him a straightforward message. Carleton warned Manuelito and his followers to surrender or be hunted down and killed. Manuelito was unimpressed by the warning, commenting to the chiefs sent to find him:

> My God and my mother live in the West, and I will not leave them. It is a tradition of my people that we must never cross the three rivers – the Grande, the San Juan, the Colorado. Nor could I leave the Chuska Mountains. I was born there, I shall remain.

Regarding Carleton's threat Manuelito cared little: 'I have nothing to lose but my life, and that they can come and take whenever they please, but I will not move.' But starvation would eventually compel Manuelito and his last twenty-three followers to surrender at Fort Wingate in September 1866. They too were sent to Bosque Redondo.

In 1865 most of the Mescalero Apache simply abandoned the reservation and fled back to their own country, and eventually in 1868 the American government admitted defeat and allowed the Navajo to return to a sizeable reservation in their former territory. The captivity of the Navajo at Bosque Redondo, known as the 'Fearing Time' to the Indians, had cost them more than one quarter dead from starvation, disease or warfare, equating to over 2,000 men, women and children. In 1868, in a replay of the earlier trek east, the surviving Navajo formed into a huge column that stretched for miles and walked slowly all the way back to Canyon de Chelly and onto a new and livable reservation. Today that reservation covers sixteen million square miles and is the largest in the United States. Chief Manuelito spent the remainder of his life fighting for better rights for his people, and it was partly his eloquence that persuaded the Americans to abandon the Bosque Redondo experiment and allow the Navajo to return to their own country. Although latterly Manuelito became a heavy drinker after whites introduced whisky to the reservation and was frequently imprisoned, he also became convinced that the Navajo would have to adopt some white ways in order to survive and prosper after his death. Shortly after visiting the World's Fair in Chicago, Manuelito said: 'The white men have many things we Navajo need but we cannot get them unless we change our ways. My children, education is the ladder to all our needs. Tell our people to take it.'[3] Manuelito died shortly afterwards in 1893.

Notes

1. Richard van Valkenburgh, *Desert*, April 1946, 23
2. Geoffrey C. Ward, *The West: An Illustrated History*, (New York: Little, Brown And Company, 1996), 198
3. Marie Mitchell, *The Navajo Peace Treaty, 1868*, (Mason & Lipscomb, 1973), 136

2

THE GREAT SIOUX UPRISING

'So far as I'm concerned, if they are hungry, let them eat grass or their own dung.'

Andrew Myrick, Lead Trader
Lower Sioux Agency, Minnesota

A light wind gently stirred the hanging bodies, each suspended by the neck from a long rope attached to the scaffold. The ropes creaked eerily, the faces of the thirty-eight dead Sioux warriors constricted into violent masks of death. Army surgeons moved quietly among them with stethoscopes examining each and pronouncing death. A large crowd of white onlookers watched the spectacle impassively, filling Mankato's dusty main square, a cordon of armed soldiers guarding the place of execution. It was 26 December 1862 and the United States, on the orders of President Abraham Lincoln, had just conducted the largest mass execution in the nation's short history. The white citizenry of Mankato, Minnesota did not feel any pity for the dead warriors, believing that justice had been served on men who had committed a string of vile and terrible outrages against the settlers in a bloody conflict they had labelled 'The Great Sioux Uprising.' Few, if any, in the audience understood that the men now twisting in the wind were victims of a government that had actively driven the Sioux to war in order to steal their land. Soldiers cut the bodies down and piled them unceremoniously onto wagons for the short drive to the Minnesota River. Beside the river a large trench had been excavated, and into the hole the Indian bodies were thrown, and the grave filled in. The Sioux menace in Minnesota had finally been ended.

Minnesota was the point of origin of all the Sioux peoples, beginning in the forests around Mille Lacs, roughly 100 miles north of Minneapolis.[1]

The Sioux were a powerful confederation of different tribal peoples united by a common language, customs and origin stories. Broadly, the Sioux were divided into three large groups. The Santee Sioux consisted of four large bands (Mdewakantonwan, Wahpekute, Wahpetonwan and Sisseton) and generally these people are called the Dakota Sioux. The second distinctive group was the Nakota Sioux, divided into two large bands called the Yankton and Yanktonai. The last, and biggest, group was the Titonwan (Camping on the Plains), or Teton Sioux, known today as the Lakota and divided into seven large and distinct groups.[2]

From the mid-seventeenth century large bands had begun to move west onto the plains after the reintroduction of the horse in America by European settlers, and these bands had evolved into full-time buffalo hunting nomads of the northern plains, becoming known as the Lakota or Plains Sioux. Not all of the Sioux bands had abandoned their woodland home in the forests of Minnesota, and sizeable groups of Santee remained. But the territories of the various Sioux bands were contiguous, a massive hunting range they had created through driving less strong and numerous Indian peoples off the plains. This meant, in reality that 'Each [Sioux] tribe usually occupied a separate area of land, although the boundaries between them were overlapping and were not exclusive.'[3]

The proximate cause of the Sioux Uprising was, unsurprisingly, American greed. As happened on countless occasions, the American government failed to fulfil its promises to the Indians. The old Indian saying about a white man speaking with a forked tongue was never truer than in the case of the Santee Sioux. The Santee had first ceded vast stretches of their homeland to the United States in 1851 at the treaties of Traverse des Sioux and Mendota. In exchange for money and goods necessary for their subsistence the Santee had accepted a reservation twenty miles wide and 150 miles long beside the upper Minnesota River. But when the Senate came to ratify the treaties they deleted a portion of the agreements, and much of the promised compensation was never paid. Most of the supplies that had also been promised never turned up at the reservation, being withheld, lost or stolen by corrupt officials of the Bureau of Indian Affairs and local white traders. The government cared little for the plight of the Santee, as the spurious treaties were only designed to relieve the Indians of as much land as possible without causing a war.

Considerable white settlement in Minnesota resulted in the territory being admitted to the Union in 1858 as a state, and there were calls to reduce still further the Santee reservation to make way for state development and immigration. Representatives of the several Santee bands, led by Chief Little Crow, travelled to Washington DC at the government's invitation, but ended up being pressured and threatened into parting with the northern half of their reservation along with rights to a valuable quarry at Pipestone.

The newly opened land was soon settled by eager whites who began a deforestation campaign to clear the land for farming. The Santee still lived largely by limited agriculture, hunting, fishing and gathering, and the furs they collected were an important source of revenue for the bands. Whites over-hunted the native fauna, drastically reducing the population of fur-trade animals like buffalo, elk, whitetail deer and bear. With the outbreak of the Civil War, the cash subsidies negotiated by Little Crow and other chieftains were not paid. The remaining reservation lands were not suitable for widespread agriculture and this led to crop failures, and when combined with reduced hunting, famine among the Santee.

On 4 August 1862 the leaders of the northern Sisseton and Wahpeton bands met at the Upper Sioux Agency and asked the agent there for food. Supplies were released shortly afterwards, and a confrontation defused. However, when representatives of the southern Mdewakanton and Wahpekute Santee asked for supplies at Lower Sioux Agency they were rebuffed. The meeting was arranged between the Indians and the government and local traders. The Santee leaders asked top local trader Andrew Myrick to help them press their claims for supplies against the government. Myrick, in a display of incredible arrogance, replied: 'So far as I'm concerned, if they [the Santee] are hungry, let them eat grass or their own dung.' Myrick's reply was met initially by a stunned silence by those gathered at the meeting, but this quickly turned to anger as Santee chiefs shouted insults and threats at the whites in a crescendo of disapproval. The meeting broke up and Myrick's words were circulated throughout the Santee bands, providing a catalyst to violence for people already deeply embittered and resentful towards the whites.

On 17 August some Santee warriors decided to take matters into their own hands. Four young warriors, who had been out hunting, had wandered into the small settlement of Acton, near present day Grove City, Minnesota. The Indians had stolen some food and when challenged they had murdered five white settlers. The murders proved the trigger for a widespread outbreak of violence aimed at ridding Santee lands of the white invaders.

The following day Little Crow and other chiefs led hundreds of warriors in attacks on white settlements and the Lower Sioux Agency. Among the first to die was Andrew Myrick, who body was later discovered with grass stuffed into its mouth. The agency was looted and several of the white-washed wooden buildings torched by the jubilant Santee. Major John S. Marsh and Company B, 5th Minnesota Infantry headed towards the scene of the attack on the Agency. As Marsh and his men were boarding the Redwood Ferry to cross the river opposite the smouldering agency they were ambushed by a Santee war party that opened a vigorous fire. The ferry grounded on the Indian side of the river, and the soldiers piled off the boat, taking cover and returning fire at the Indians. The soldiers soon began to run out of ammunition and, outnumbered and with their backs to the river, the situation looked grim. Marsh ordered his men to swim the river to safety. Marsh drowned, along with many of his company, the final death toll being twenty-four soldiers killed by Santee rifle fire or lost in the river. Five wounded and sixteen unharmed soldiers managed to make it to safety on the opposite bank. Only one Santee warrior was killed during the battle.

The defeat of Marsh encouraged the Santee to attack the small town of New Ulm on 19 August. About 900 whites lived and worked in the settlement, and it was the largest town near the Santee reservation and a natural target. Forewarned of the Indians' approach, the settlers barricaded the streets in the centre of town and packed their women and children into the few brick structures, most of the town being built of wood. The Santee fired into New Ulm from nearby bluffs, and the settlers returned their fire as best they could. A thunderstorm that afternoon drove the Indians away, the day's fighting having resulted in the deaths of six settlers, with five more wounded. Local state militia managed to get through to the town commanded by Charles Flandrau, numbering about 300 men. On the morning of 23 August the Santee returned to New Ulm in greater numbers. The militia burned down many of the buildings on the outskirts of town to clear fields of fire, and the civilian soldiers fought offensively, sallying forth several times to engage the Santee warriors and drive them off the heights. On the 24th the Santee seemed to lose interest in the town and withdrew. The next day the settlers and militia abandoned New Ulm and headed to Mankato, twenty miles to the east.

Whilst New Ulm was under fire Santee warriors attacked nearby Fort Ridgely on the 22 August. The fort was the army's sole military post between the Santee and the city of St Paul. The garrison was already much reduced after the rout of Major Marsh and his company at Redwood Ferry. Lieutenant Thomas P. Gere commanded the remaining forces, assisted by a militia unit called the Renville Rangers under Major Thomas Galbraith, an Indian-hating Minnesota state senator. The fort was a fort in name only as it lacked a stockade, and was simply a collection of wooden clapboard buildings. However, it was well-supplied with artillery pieces, having six guns ranging from 6- to 24-pounders, and an experienced gunner to direct their fire, Sergeant John Jones. Jones had the guns dug in at strategic points around the fort's perimeter, and their fire would prove the determining factor in the battle that followed.

On the first day groups of Mdewakanton warriors were held off by a combination of canister shot and another violent thunderstorm. The next day over 800 warriors were involved in assaulting Fort Ridgely as war parties from the Sisseton and Wahpeton bands joined in the assault. As well as laying down heavy rifle fire on the fort, peppering the wooden buildings with bullets and musket balls, the Santee shot dozens of fire arrows in an attempt the burn the defences down. They were unsuccessful, as mobile fire-fighting parties were quickly onto the blazes before they could take hold, assisted by the wet weather conditions. The artillery proved to be the deciding factor, preventing the warriors from using their numerical advantage to storm the fort. The Santee withdrew having lost only two men killed, and the army licked its wounds. Thirteen soldiers had been killed and three wounded, but the majority of the garrison had survived due to Sergeant Jones and his guns.

Minnesota governor Alexander Ramsay made repeated appeals for help in quelling the violence to President Lincoln, but because of the raging Civil War Lincoln could not spare any regular regiments for the task. Lincoln sent professional army officers who raised a series of militia regiments throughout the state. The final battle occurred at Wood Lake on 23 September 1862 when Lieutenant-Colonel William R. Marshall and men of the 6th and 7th Minnesota Volunteers, aided by a 6-pounder gun, defeated the Santee in a sharp fight. One soldier was killed and three wounded, while seven Santee warriors fell. The Santee began to surrender in large groups three days later. Six weeks later the 'war crimes' trial of 303 Sioux warriors was convened, most of the defendants receiving less than five minutes on the stand before their guilt was pronounced. It was a show trial of the type later favoured in Nazi Germany and Stalinist Russia. Thirty-eight Sioux men were condemned to death and hanged in December.

It was perhaps natural that the many of the Santee chose to go to Canada instead of surrendering to the vengeful Americans. Relations between the Santee and the British had deep historical roots. When the first Santee bands crossed the border and headed for Wood Mountain in what was then known as Rupert's Land in pre-Confederation Canada (later Manitoba) they came fully prepared to demonstrate that they had a right to seek British protection. When the original discussions were conducted between British officials and the Santee Sioux leader Chief Little Crow shortly after his arrival in May 1863, Little Crow said that he and his followers 'were really British Indians who merely hunted in the United States but considered their first loyalty to be to the Queen.'[4] Another Santee chief, Standing Buffalo, produced sixteen silver peace medals at a meeting in Canada in 1865, the medals having been distributed to Sioux leaders at Montreal on 18 August 1778 to recognize the assistance they had rendered to British forces in the Kentucky and Illinois campaigns of the Revolutionary Wars. Standing Buffalo claimed that the Santee Sioux were 'British Indians.' Little Crow said to British officials that 'the elders of the tribe had been told during the War of 1812 that if they ever got into trouble with the Americans they should appeal to the British, and the "folds of the red flag in the north would wrap around and preserve them from their enemies".'[5] The British allowed them to settle around Wood Mountain on condition that they remained peaceful. Eventually, these Santee refugees were accepted as a part of Canada itself, and came to be called the 'Canadian Sioux', severing forever their ancestral links to Minnesota.

Congress had already declared all the treaties signed with the Santee Sioux null and void before many fled to Canada, and the Minnesota reservations were forfeit. A large section of the Santee attempted to escape to their Nakota Sioux cousins but Sibley overtook and defeated them with great loss to the Indians at Big Mound, Dakota Territory on 24 July 1863. The conflict now spread to the Lakota Sioux, as the survivors fled to them. On 3 September Brigadier General Alfred Sully struck the main Santee camp led by Chief Inkpaduta at Whitestone Hill, near modern-day Ellendale, North Dakota. The troops killed 300 Indians and captured almost the same number.

On the Little Missouri the Santee had found allies with the Lakota and some Yanktonai Dakota bands. On 28 July 1864, Sully struck at the large pan-Sioux camp at Kildeer Mountain, and during this battle Sitting Bull led the Lakota warriors against the army. Unfortunately, the Sioux were heavily defeated, and the Santee were forced onto two new reservations in Dakota Territory and Nebraska. In effect, the Santee peoples were forever split by the war, beginning new lives hundreds of miles apart in Canada and America, their ancestral lands largely illegally taken from them. It was a salutary warning for Sitting Bull and the Lakota, and they knew that sooner or later the whites would try to do the same to them. The only question was when this would happen?

Notes

1. Alexander Adams, *Sitting Bull: An Epic of the Plains*, (New York: G.P. Putnam's Sons Ltd, 1973), Edwin Denig, *Five Indian Tribes of the Upper Missouri*, (Norman: University of Oklahoma Press, 1961), and Robert M. Utley, *The Lance and the Shield: The Life and Times of Sitting Bull*, (London: Pimlico, 1998)
2. J. Walker, *Lakota Society*, (Lincoln: University of Nebraska Press, 1982)
3. Ibid: 194
4. James Howard, *The Canadian Sioux*, (Lincoln: University of Nebraska Press, 1984), 25
5. Ibid: 27

3

WADING IN GORE

'Kill and scalp all, big and little; nits make lice.'

Colonel John M. Chivington
Sand Creek, 29 November 1864

The buffalo, iconic animal of the West, was found in enormous migrating herds all across the northern and southern plains. It provided a subsistence hunting culture for tens of thousands of people who had come to dominate the animal's migration routes to the high plains in the upper valleys of the South Platte, Republican, Smoky Hill and Arkansas rivers. To the west the snow-capped Rocky Mountains marked the end of the plains, a great geological barrier that stretched like a jagged backbone through the American West. Out on the rolling grasslands wandering bands of nomadic hunter-gatherers scoured the land for prey, and lived in tepee villages beside tranquil rivers and woods. Sometimes these equestrian peoples fought one another, raiding parties descending suddenly upon the impermanent villages to steal horses, carry off women or settle old scores. In the harsh winter months the people bundled themselves up in brown buffalo robes, and ate dried meat, berries and root vegetables until the spring thaw.

It was a lifestyle followed by perhaps thirty different peoples, speaking many different languages, across the length and breadth of the plains, north and south, and although the peoples were dissimilar in dress, customs, beliefs and languages, they nonetheless shared one thing in common – the survival of their culture was based entirely upon the continued migration of the buffalo. It was the reason these people had first come to the plains. After trading horses off tribes further to the south and east, some woodland Indians had rapidly transformed themselves into efficient equestrian hunters by the eighteenth century, and for the first time the horse gave these people the ability to live permanently upon the plains. The horse had come from the Spanish, so the plains tribal lifestyle was very much influenced by contact with whites. A contact based upon trade had begun, by the 1850s, to turn increasingly tense as the Americans to the east began to demand more and more from the southern plains peoples. Four tribes, the Kiowa, Comanche, Arapaho and Cheyenne, would feel the pressure most greatly, for these peoples dominated the southern buffalo ranges and had the most to lose from agreeing to American demands.

The Kiowa and Comanche had only migrated onto the plains from the eastern woodlands in the late eighteenth century, and the Arapaho and Cheyenne perhaps fifty years before them. In terms of history, these four peoples had only been on the plains just over a hundred years before conflict erupted with the United States, but in that short time they had all established themselves as distinct and strong peoples who believed themselves to be the legitimate occupiers of the land they hunted and warred over. They would not meekly stand by and watch these lands invaded and settled by alien peoples from the east.

Representatives of the United States concluded a treaty with the Cheyenne and Arapaho at Fort Laramie in 1851, the object being to assert American rights over aboriginal lands by having the tribes agree to accept designated hunting grounds on the eastern plains between the South Platte and Arkansas rivers. The agreement made no difference to the lives of the Indians in the beginning, as the only whites who visited the region were occasional small parties of settlers passing through what they dismissed as the 'Great American Desert' on their way to California or Oregon Territory, and small military units. The buffalo was still numerous, and the Indians were happy to accept the Great White Father's gifts from Washington and let him draw his lines on maps. All that changed quite suddenly in 1859 when gold was found in the Rockies in Colorado. Within a few short and distressing months the Cheyenne and Arapaho witnessed grubby little tent cities flourish like poison mushrooms around the goldfields, as thousands of prospectors and settlers flooded the land. Soon the once pristine buffalo ranges were criss-crossed with wheel ruts left by hundreds of prairie schooners, as the covered wagons were called, sailing in great white flotillas across the waving green grasslands. To the north the Sioux began to resist the influx of white settlers as best they could, and with increasing success as America slid towards a civil war in the east. In the south the trails were having an unwelcome effect on the buffalo. Because the trails were now so heavily used, the buffalo, always shy of human contact, split into two enormous herds. One was in the north and one in the south, their migratory patterns permanently affected by the white influx.

In autumn 1860, following the shrill demands of the new white population to remove all Indians from Colorado, the government concluded a new agreement with the Cheyenne and Arapaho, both tribes keen to avoid trouble with the Americans. At the council the tribes agreed to give up vast areas of land that had been granted to them in 1851 and instead move onto a smaller triangular-shaped reservation between the Arkansas River and Sand Creek. In return for surrendering their lands, the Americans promised to help the Indians become farmers, to abandon the 'uncivilised' pursuits of hunting and nomadism, and the reservation would be surveyed and each adult would receive forty acres to farm. At a stroke, the Americans would introduce the purported benefits of private ownership over collective tribal ownership, a major step in removing what many Americans perceived to be the greatest barrier to assimilating the Indians, tribalism. The government promised instructors and tools to turn the Cheyenne and Arapaho into farmers, as well as mills and schools, and a $30,000 subsidy for fifteen years to each tribe to assist with the transition. Unfortunately, what the Americans promised and what the Indians actually received was often not the same thing. Once the Americans had the land, honouring their promises made to encourage the Indian leaders to give up the land in the first place often became a secondary consideration.

The Indian agents appointed by the Department of the Interior to oversee the Indians during their transition were often criminally negligent and deeply corrupt. Soon the Cheyenne and Arapaho discovered that agents were stealing from them, and often making large sums of money selling goods and supplies meant for the reservation in the local white settlements instead. The Kiowa, a tribe with little time for whites, aggravated the situation that was rapidly unfolding by frequently striking at the trails, killing white settlers, burning their wagons, and attacking stage coaches. In their ignorance, local whites blamed all local Indians for the attacks, and the Cheyenne and Arapaho lived in considerable fear of retaliatory attacks by the troops sent to guard the trails. The peaceful Cheyenne and Arapaho were quite literally caught in the crossfire when the shooting started.

Colonel John M. Chivington, a thick-set, middle-aged Methodist minister and volunteer army officer, was a man who believed himself to be headed for better things. He wore a full beard, trimmed short, and his receding hair was swept straight back from his wide forehead. By 1864 the Civil War had been raging for three years, and Chivington had managed to become a bone fide hero earlier in the war, nicknamed 'The Fighting Parson.' His exploits at Glorieta Pass in Texas, when he and his men had single-handedly turned the tables on the Confederates and thrown 'Johnny Reb' out of the south-west, had won him wide acclaim back home in Colorado. It was now November 1864, and Chivington, his eyes set firmly on a seat in Congress, needed another military victory, but one that was directly relevant to the good voters of Colorado. In Chivington's opinion, the surest way to ensure an easy victory was an Indian war, and there was plenty of fighting already occurring in Colorado as local tribes launched raids on the trails. Territorial Governor John Evans of Colorado was in agreement with Chivington, and he appointed him military commander of the district with orders to suppress the Indians. Only two months before, in September 1864, fearing an all-out war, several senior chiefs of the Cheyenne and Arapaho, including a man called Black Kettle, had travelled to Denver for the Camp Weld Meeting with Evans. It was an effort launched by the Indians to avoid war, but Evans spurned them and referred the 'Indian Problem' to Chivington to solve.

Colonel Chivington's solution was firstly to raise more troops. Already there was a specially-raised Indian fighting unit, the 1st Colorado Cavalry, in the territory, formed from a pair of local volunteer infantry units in November 1862. It was thought that cavalry were more effective against Indians, and the 1st Cavalry was tasked with protecting the territory and its gold mines from a Confederate invasion and the rapidly expanding white settlements from Indian raids. In 1863 the regiment had participated in isolated skirmishes with the Utes in present-day Wyoming, and the Kiowa and Comanche in Kansas. Chivington's efforts led to the raising of a second Indian fighting regiment, the 3rd Colorado Cavalry, in late 1864.

Chivington's recruiting methods were unusual to say the least. He plastered Denver with posters inviting men to come on an Indian killing party, the term of enlistment to be only one hundred days. The 'Fighting Parson' gave several rabble-rousing recruiting speeches, and also managed to have martial law imposed on the city, leading to saloons being shut down and a steady supply of sobered-up 'recruits' to fill the new regiment's ranks. The regiment's nickname was 'The Bloody Third,' though it had yet to spill any blood in defence of the citizenry of Colorado – something Chivington was very keen to rectify.

The 3rd took the field at the instigation of Governor Evans, who had asked Chivington to pacify the Indians and protect the trails. Some months previously in July, Evans had issued a proclamation to the Indians that stated that any of the bands that did not want war were to come in to the various military posts in the region and place themselves under the 'protection' of the army. Having invited the Indians to place themselves within easy striking distance of the forts, Evans had then issued a contradictory proclamation to the white citizens of the territory, all but inviting settlers to kill Indians, declaring that 'most of the Indian tribes are hostile and at war.' Following Evans' snubbing of the Cheyenne and Arapaho peacemakers who had come to Denver in September, the way was now open for an Indian war in Colorado Territory. Many of the Indians were unaware of Evans' trickery and began to move closer to the various army posts. Black Kettle of the Southern Cheyenne moved his band close to Fort Lyon, and he flew a large Stars and Stripes flag from his tepee as a symbol of peace and amity.

Moving through the snow towards Fort Lyon was Colonel Chivington, riding along with what many locals had re-christened 'The Bloodless Third.' The regiment had yet to prove itself in combat, and Chivington was under considerable pressure to give his men the opportunity to kill some Indians before their enlistment expired. He was also worried lest his new victory should not be realised, and with his future political career in jeopardy Chivington was prepared to do anything to achieve his goals. Chivington accompanied the column as district commander; actual command of the 3rd was vested in Lieutenant-Colonel George Shoup. At Fort Lyon the 3rd was joined by 125 men forming several companies of the 1st Colorado Cavalry and a small artillery unit.

Riding into Fort Lyon on 28 November, Chivington knew that time was running out, for within a few short days the enlistment period would expire and the 3rd Colorado Cavalry would cease to exist. Chivington outlined a plan to fellow officers at the fort that day, explaining that he had decided to attack the Southern Cheyenne encampment of Chief Black Kettle some forty miles from the fort. Many of the officers were outraged and disgusted by Chivington's half-baked idea. Since Black Kettle had settled his people along Sand Creek there had been no trouble with the Indians, and many scouts, soldiers and traders regularly visited the camp of buffalo-hide tepees arranged in neat circles on a flat of land beside the river. Furthermore, Black Kettle flew a large Stars and Stripes flag from the top of his lodge so that no soldiers could confuse his people for 'hostiles'. Some regular officers inside the fort were concerned that any attack on Black Kettle's village would betray the pledge of safety the army had made to the Indians. The entreaties and arguments of his fellow officers were silenced by the large Chivington, who bellowed:'I have come to kill Indians and I believe it is my right to use any means under God's heaven.' Only days before Chivington had been heard to remark ominously:'I long to be wading in gore.'

At 8pm that cold, frosty evening, the 3rd rode out through the gates of Fort Lyon two abreast, with companies C, D, E, G, H and K of the 1st Cavalry under Major Scott J. Anthony, and the artillery section of two howitzers following on behind. Out into the snow-covered landscape they rode, disappearing into the darkness as they began a night march to bring them upon Black Kettle's village at dawn the next day.

Most of the people in Black Kettle's village were women and children, along with the elderly and a handful of warriors whose job was to protect the camp. The bulk of the warriors were away hunting. When the Indians saw the blue-clad column moving towards them they were not thrown into panic immediately, for they believed that they were under army protection. The American flag flew clearly from Black Kettle's tepee, so no mistake could be made. Inside the camp that day were several mixed race scouts employed by the army, who were married to Indian women and even Indian wives of soldiers from the fort. It seemed inconceivable that they were to be attacked without warning by the people who had pledged to protect them.

In his subsequent reports on the fighting Chivington exaggerated the number of Indians in the camp considerably.[1] He claimed that there were at least 130 tepees, and 900 to 1,000 warriors, including eight tepees of Arapaho under Chief Left Hand. In fact, subsequent testimony from his officers and men and from many army scouts and Indians put the true figure closer to 100 tepees, and perhaps 500 men, women and children, the majority being females with young children. Chivington exaggerated the numbers of warriors faced by his expedition for several reasons, primarily to demonstrate that the 'Bloody Third' had won a great victory against overwhelming odds, and to conceal the extent of the massacre he and his men perpetrated against unarmed and defenceless civilians.

Chivington's companies deployed preparatory to launching the assault, the soldiers eyeing the dozens of tepees with contempt, their hands nervously fingering their carbines and pistols. Lieutenant Wilson, 1st Cavalry, and his battalion was deployed on the right, with Colonel Shoup's 3rd Cavalry in the centre and Major Scott. F. Anthony's battalion of 1st Cavalry on the left. About 600 soldiers now prepared to attack. Chivington ordered the Indians' horse herd to be run off first, and Wilson and his men charged around the side of the village and cut out the hundreds of horses corralled there. Chivington did not want the Indians to escape the coming slaughter. By now, hundreds of people had come out of their tepees and were standing watching the soldiers, unsure of what to do. Black Kettle stood with members of his family and watched with growing unease as the first companies of cavalry advanced on his village menacingly. Chivington wheeled his horse around to face the ranks of cavalrymen and shouted in his loud preacher's voice: 'Kill and scalp all, big and little; nits make lice.' On hearing this, his men, their blood up, gave out a ragged yell, and with a wave of his arm Chivington signalled the attack, carbines were readied and a steady aim was taken at the milling groups of Indians. By companies a heavy volley was fired and then the companies charged forward.

As the cavalrymen's horses came thundering across the open ground towards the village, women and children screamed in terror and warriors hastily plunged inside their tepees to fetch arms and ammunition, intent on protecting their families as best they could. George Bent, a mixed race army scout who had been ordered at gunpoint to lead Chivington's troops to Black Kettle's village, recalled: 'In the camps ... all was confusion and noise – men, women, and children rushing out of the lodges partly dressed.'[2] As the first shots began to thud into tepees and running people, Black Kettle stood by the American flag, beneath which he had raised a smaller white flag. Black Kettle 'kept calling out not to be frightened; that the camp was under protection and there was no danger ...'[3]

A group of warriors, heavily outnumbered, charged on foot towards the mounted soldiers, recalled Major Anthony. 'I never saw more bravery displayed by any set of people on the face of the earth than by these Indians. They would charge on the whole company singly, determined to kill someone before being killed themselves.' Anthony added: 'We, of course, took no prisoners.'[4] Soon the soldiers were riding through the camp firing at anything that moved as hundreds of terrified Indians ran about trying to find cover from the onslaught. Some soldiers dismounted and entered tepees, shooting the occupants, and others knelt in the snow taking careful aim at fleeing Cheyenne before gunning them down. Major Anthony discharged his revolver at fleeing Indians, all the time encouraging his men to kill. In his report on the action Anthony was happy to have taken such a leading part in the butchery, writing: 'The evidence is most conclusive that these Indians are the worst that have infested the routes on the Platte and Arkansas', adding 'The massacre was a terrible one and such a one as each of the hostile tribes of the plains richly deserves.'[5] No-one was spared, no matter how old. Another army scout, Robert Bent, later recalled:

> After the firing, the warriors put the squaws and children together, and surrounded
> them to protect them. I saw five squaws under a bank for shelter. When the troops
> came up to them they ran out and showed their persons to let the soldiers know
> they were squaws and begged for mercy, but the soldiers shot them all.

Colonel Shoup recalled that Captain John McCannon's Company I attacked
the village from the south and 'opened a terrible and withering fire on
the Indians, completely checking them, killing many and causing them
to retreat up Sand Creek.'[6] Company G, under the command of Captain
O.H.P. Baxter was dispatched to reinforce McCannon, and then the two
companies fought the Indians on the south side of the creek for about
two miles. According to Shoup, these soldiers killed about fifty Indians,
including twenty-six who were sheltering in a large pit dug out of the sand.
Baxter and Lieutenant Templeton then pursued fleeing Indians to the south
and west, and their troopers gunned down another twenty.

Lieutenant W.E. Grinnell with a detachment of twenty-one men from
Company K fought part of the engagement on the south-west side of the
battlefield, and lost several men killed and wounded. Shoup himself, leading
four hundred men, advanced up the north side of the creek and attacked
the main Cheyenne camp and a large body of Indians who were fleeing to
the west. He dismounted his men, and they killed dozens of Indians who
were attempting to shelter from the firing under the creek bank.

Captain Nichols and Company D charged after another group of fleeing
Cheyenne who were running north-east, overtook them and butchered all
of them numbering between twenty-five and thirty individuals. It was a
confused action that took place over five miles in all directions from the village, with most of the killing occurring between 6.30am and 1pm. Colonel
Chivington, in his official report of the action, described the massacre as
if it had been a respectable battle: 'The commands of Colonel Shoup and
Major Anthony pressed rapidly forward and attached the enemy sharply,
and the engagement became general, we constantly driving the Indians,
who fell back from one position to another for five miles.'[7] The carnage
was appalling. Not only did soldiers deliberately target non-combatants,
but they seemed to take pleasure in killing infants and women. No mention was made of the atrocities committed by both regiments when the
official reports were made, Chivington's only reference being an ominous
line that read: 'It may perhaps be unnecessary for me to state that I captured
no prisoners.'[8]

Although the officers and men of the 1st and 3rd Colorado Cavalry produced reports on the action which made no mention of a massacre, and in fact were at pains to point out the gallantry and heroism of the command in confronting so many warriors, when officers stationed at Fort Lyon discovered the true extent of the crimes they began to speak out. Reports, such as that submitted by Captain Theodore G. Cree of the 3rd Cavalry, were fabrications, containing lines such as: 'As for the bravery displayed by any one in particular, I have no distinctions to make. All I can say for officers and men is that they all behaved well and won for themselves a name that will be remembered for ages to come.'[9] The officers at Fort Lyon had attempted to dissuade Chivington from launching the attack on Black Kettle's peaceful village when he had outlined his diabolical plan, and their revenge was to generate enough doubt over Chivington's official reports to cause an army investigation. Major Edward W. Wynkoop of 1st Colorado Veteran Cavalry, a different unit from the 1st Cavalry involved in the massacre, investigated the affair and produced dozens of witness statements proving that Chivington had committed a terrible outrage.

The findings of Wynkoop's investigation were horrific. 'Women and children were killed and scalped,' wrote Wynkoop, 'children shot at their mother's breasts, and all the bodies mutilated in the most horrible manner.'[10] Babies were dragged from their mothers and clubbed to death with rifle butts. Pregnant women were either shot down, or attacked by soldiers who first hacked the foetuses out of their bellies with their bayonets before dispatching the mother. The tiny foetuses were carried away as trophies. Chivington had ordered his men to 'scalp all,' and whether they were alive or not, dozens of men, women and children were roughly scalped with bayonets and knives, and the bloody trophies carried from the field by jubilant American soldiers. Wynkoop continued: 'Numerous eye-witnesses have described scenes to me coming under the eye of Colonel Chivington of the most disgusting and horrible character. The dead bodies of females profaned in such a manner that the recital is sickening.'[11]

Wynkoop demonstrated that Chivington incited his troops to commit these outrages. 'Previous to the slaughter commencing he [Chivington] addressed his command, arousing in them by his language all their worst passions, urging them on to the work of committing all these atrocities.'[12] Wynkoop wrote that in his opinion Chivington was an 'inhuman monster'. In the affidavit of Lieutenant James D. Cannon, 1st New Mexico Volunteer Infantry, who had been ordered by Major Anthony to accompany the expedition as battalion adjutant, 'In going over the battle-ground next day I did not see a body of man, woman, or child but was scalped, and in many instances their bodies were

43

mutilated in the most horrible manner – men, women, and children's private parts cut out, &c.'[13] Many body parts were subsequently carried from the field by soldiers. 'I heard one man say that he had cut a woman's private parts out,' wrote Cannon, 'and had them for exhibition on a stick.'[14] Another man was heard to state 'that he had cut the fingers off of an Indian to get the rings on the hand.'[15] Young children were not immune from extreme barbarism, Cannon writing: 'I heard of one instance of a child a few months old being thrown in the feed box of a wagon, and after being carried some distance left on the ground to perish.'[16] The soldiers' mutilation of Indian women was extensive during and after the massacre. Lieutenant Cannon went into more detail than Major Wynkoop on this subject: 'I also heard of numberless instances in which men had cut out the private parts of females and stretched them over the saddle bows, and wore them over their hats while riding in the ranks.'[17]

When the killing stopped twenty-five Indian men, including chiefs White Antelope, One Eye, Little Robe and Knock Knee, lay dead. Ninety-eight Indian women and children lay sprawled in the snow, shot, scalped, disembowelled, their brains bashed in and their private parts ripped out. Black Kettle survived. Under Chivington's orders, the tepees were ransacked, the soldiers carrying away vast amounts of Cheyenne property as souvenirs, and the entire village was torched, condemning the survivors who had managed to flee far away from the soldiers to homelessness during the harshest time of the year.

Although Chivington was effusive in his praise for the men under his command, he singled one officer out for approbation for his refusal to take part in the massacre. Captain Silas S. Soule, officer commanding Company D, 1st Cavalry, was, in Chivington's opinion, 'at least ill-advised, he saying that he thanked God that he had killed no Indians, and like expressions, proving him more in sympathy with those Indians than with the whites.'[18] Although Soule disapproved of Chivington's actions, he had been unable to constrain some of his men who had run amok like all the other soldiers killing and mutilating the Cheyenne.

Chivington's casualties were nine killed and thirty-eight wounded, and within days the 'Bloody Third' was, for the first time, able to truly live up to its self-imposed moniker, riding into Denver with 100 Cheyenne scalps proudly displayed. Along with women's vaginas, men's penises, scrotums and dead foetuses, all were displayed to great acclaim in a local theatre and the men congratulated on a successful campaign against the 'savages.'

Following Major Wynkoop's investigation, the army was forced to convene a formal court of inquiry into the alleged 'massacre'. Captain Soule was one of the most outspoken critics of Colonel Chivington's actions at Sand Creek, and he was instrumental in bringing on the later army investigations that led to an enquiry. Chivington was a civilian by 1865, and was therefore not bound by any ruling made by the army court. He denounced Soule as a liar, but the affidavits collected by Major Wynkoop from Soule's troopers, army scouts and officers from Fort Lyon proved conclusively that a massacre had taken place. The army judge publicly declared that Sand Creek was 'a cowardly and cold-blooded slaughter, sufficient to cover its perpetrators with indelible infamy, and the face of every American with shame and indignation.' Such was the level of public outcry and media indignation when people learned the truth about what had occurred, particularly the mutilation of Indian corpses, some historians have suggested that it led Congress to shelve plans for a general Indian war in the Midwest.

The Sand Creek Massacre is important in the history of the American West because for the first time ordinary American citizens criticised the behaviour of their government and army. Most still believed that the Indians were 'savages,' but most also believed that the government was supposed to help these people to become 'civilised,' and not to behave like savages themselves. There would be many more massacres and acts of cruelty and injustice committed by American soldiers against the Indians over the next twenty-five years, but none ever matched the brutality and sadism of Sand Creek.

John Chivington's dreams of a political career were left in tatters following the 1865 court of inquiry. Afterwards, he left Colorado Territory and moved to Nebraska, where he unsuccessfully ran a freight haulage business. After a brief period in California, Chivington moved to Ohio and farmed, and was the editor of a local newspaper. In 1883 he tried once more to get into politics, running for a seat in the Ohio State Legislature, but withdrew when his opponent raised the spectre of Sand Creek. Increasingly embittered, but still firmly believing that his actions were justified at Sand Creek, Chivington went back to Denver where he worked as a deputy sheriff until his death from cancer in 1892 at the age of seventy-one. In 1887 the state of Colorado had honoured him by naming a town after him. Chivington was abandoned in the early 1930s during the Great Depression, and today just a few ghostly shells of buildings remain in memoriam to Colonel Chivington, the 'inhuman monster.' Some historians now believe that Chivington may have had a hand in killing again after Sand Creek, as he may have been involved in the murder of Captain Soule, killed by a former soldier under Chivington's command at the massacre. Chivington certainly must have blamed Soule for beginning the process that witnessed the 'Hero of Glorieta Pass,' the 'Fighting Parson,' reduced to a figure of loathing and hatred in the eyes of the American public.

The survivors of Black Kettle's village had fled in disorder up the Republican River towards friends and relatives in a much larger Cheyenne encampment. When the Cheyenne and their leaders were told by the survivors of Sand Creek about what the Americans had done to their kith and kin they were furious. Chiefs who had once proposed peace and cooperation with the whites now turned away from that path, and the war chiefs were asked to prepare the warriors for battle. Indians scalped and mutilated dead opponents primarily to incapacitate them in the spirit world, but the Cheyenne knew that the white soldiers did not fight in this way and abhorred the ways and traditions of the Indians. Making war on women and children, and mutilating non-combatants was not the Cheyenne way. The whites would be made to pay for their arrogance and their brutality. Many chiefs proposed a loose alliance with the Lakota Sioux further to the north, who were encountering similar problems with white emigrant trails appearing across their hunting grounds, and with the Arapaho, whose close relationship with the Cheyenne was legendary.

Messengers took gifts of tobacco to the Sioux and Arapaho chiefs who smoked it as a sign of their willingness to fight alongside the Cheyenne, and messages of solidarity were passed between the bands. In early January 1865, just as the army was beginning to gather information concerning a possible massacre at Sand Creek the previous November, around 2,000 Cheyenne, Sioux and Arapaho warriors moved their camps further south, closer to the South Platte Trail where it cut through the northeast corner of Colorado. Although each nation's warriors would fight under their own war chiefs, the chiefs cooperated in joint councils to decide upon a common strategy against the Americans. It was decided to try to lure a sizeable group of soldiers out of one of their forts and annihilate them. On 6 January a party of warriors fell upon a wagon train on the trail and killed twelve white men. Throughout the night of 6–7 January a large party of allied warriors, numbering in the several hundreds, began to conceal themselves in the sand hills close to Fort Rankin, a small military post on the Platte River protecting the settler community of Julesburg. The honour of springing the trap was given to Chief Big Crow and a party of Cheyenne Dog Soldiers. At first light on 7 January these warriors suddenly burst from cover and cut down a handful of soldiers on guard duty outside the fort. The astounded soldiers inside Fort Rankin managed to fire a few straggling shots as Big Crow and his men ran off towards the sand hills whooping and hollering and shouting insults at the whites. Inside the fort hasty preparations were made to pursue the Indians, and minutes later the front gates swung open and two companies of cavalry, numbering sixty men, came thundering out, pistols and carbines at the ready, determined to ride the Cheyenne warriors down and kill them.

The Indians' decoy and ambush plan worked perfectly, the cavalrymen falling straight into the trap. Suddenly, the 'Long Knives,' as the Indians called the cavalry after the sabres they sometimes carried, were confronted with hundreds of screaming Cheyenne, Sioux and Arapaho warriors streaming down the hillsides all around them, firing arrows and rifles as they came on. The confused soldiers managed a few ragged shots before they began to die, shot from their saddles or dragged from their horses and beaten to death by mobs of vengeful warriors armed with stone clubs, axes and clubbed rifles and muskets. A few managed to escape the encirclement and flew back into the fort on lathered mounts, wild-eyed and terrified.

The Indians now surged up the river past the fort and into the streets of Julesburg. The remaining troops at the fort had barricaded the gates and manned the palisades, but they were too few in number to sally forth once more and try to save Julesburg. The Indians went wild, killing many of the inhabitants, and looting and pillaging the town completely before moving off to make camp. The troops at the fort fired an occasional howitzer shell towards them, but it was ineffective to deter the Indians from continuing to pillage.

A few days later the Indians returned to Julesburg. On 2 February hundreds of warriors looted the town again and then torched the wooden buildings in a replay of what Chivington had ordered done to the camp at Sand Creek. To demonstrate their power and their lack of fear of the soldiers, the Indians held a huge victory dance within sight of the fort, dancing and drumming continuing for hours into the night before the Indians struck camp the following morning and melted into the hinterland. Sand Creek permanently poisoned relations between the United States and the Cheyenne and the other tribes. Many years of periodic warfare and raiding were the result.

Notes

1. *Report of Colonel John M. Chivington, First Colorado Cavalry, commanding expedition, in The War of Rebellion: A Compilation of the Official Records of the Union and Confederate Armies*, Series I – Volume XLI, Part 1 – Reports, (Washington DC: Government Printing Office, 1893), 972
2. *The West, Episode Four – Death Runs Riot 1856–1868*, http://www.pbs.org/weta/thewest/program/episodes/four/whois.htm, accessed 29 August 2007

3. Ibid.

4. Ibid.

5. *Reports of Maj. Scott J. Anthony, First Colorado Cavalry, 1 Dec. 1864, in The War of Rebellion: A Compilation of the Official Records of the Union and Confederate Armies,* Series I – Volume XLI, Part 1 – Reports, (Washington DC: Government Printing Office, 1893), 974

6. *Report of Col. George L. Shoup, Third Colorado Cavalry, 7 Dec. 1864, in The War of Rebellion: A Compilation of the Official Records of the Union and Confederate Armies,* Series I – Volume XLI, Part 1 – Reports, (Washington DC: Government Printing Office, 1893), 980

7. *Report of Colonel John M. Chivington, First Colorado Cavalry, commanding expedition, in The War of Rebellion: A Compilation of the Official Records of the Union and Confederate Armies,* Series I – Volume XLI, Part 1 – Reports, (Washington DC: Government Printing Office, 1893), 949

8. Ibid: 949

9. *Report of Capt. Theodore G. Cree, Third Colorado Cavalry, 6 Dec. 1864,* National Park Service, Department of the Interior, http://www.nps.gov/sand/history-culture/people.htm, accessed 10 August 2007

10. *Report of Maj. Edward W. Wynkoop, First Colorado Cavalry, of an investigation of Indian Affairs in the vicinity of Fort Lyon, Colo. Ter., 15 Jan. 1865, in The War of Rebellion: A Compilation of the Official Records of the Union and Confederate Armies,* Series I – Volume XLI, Part 1 – Reports, (Washington DC: Government Printing Office, 1893), 960–961

11. Ibid: 961

12. Ibid: 961

13. *Affidavit of Lieut. James D. Cannon, First New Mexico Volunteer Infantry, 16 Jan. 1865, in The War of Rebellion: A Compilation of the Official Records of the Union and Confederate Armies,* Series I – Volume XLI, Part 1 – Reports, (Washington DC: Government Printing Office, 1893), 960–961, 994

14. Ibid: 994

15. Ibid: 994

16. Ibid: 994

17. Ibid: 994–995

18. *Report of Colonel John M. Chivington, First Colorado Cavalry, commanding expedition, in The War of Rebellion: A Compilation of the Official Records of the Union and Confederate Armies,* Series I – Volume XLI, Part 1 – Reports, (Washington DC: Government Printing Office, 1893), 974

4

THE WAR FOR THE TRAILS

'They [the Americans] made us many promises, more than I can remember, but they never kept but one; they promised to take our land, and they took it.'

Red Cloud, Oglala Sioux

A pair of blue eyes lay on a snow covered rock staring up at crazy angles towards the leaden sky. Nearby, a human brain, grey and blood-streaked, squatted atop another rock, and at the foot of each the owners of these gruesome trophies lay naked and broken. The relief force stood open-mouthed and stared at this and dozens of other sights of incredible carnage that covered the frozen valley before them. Sounds of retching and gasps of disbelief erupted at each new grisly find. A body here with its penis protruding indecently from a mouth where all the teeth had been hacked out, a body there with its arms carved out of their sockets and carried away, another corpse yonder minus a chin that had been excised from its owner's face, a mess of guts coiled on the floor like rancid sausages at Hell's banquet. The stricken field marked the Indians' greatest victory yet over the US Army, a day that would not be surpassed until a decade later when another body of American soldiers would lie naked and broken upon bloodstained prairie grass.

The Fetterman Massacre occurred on 21 December 1866 and it raised the level of violence between Indians and whites to new and perhaps unimagined levels of brutality, and the dismembered bodies that littered the frozen earth beside the Bozeman Trail were mute testimony to the Plains Indians' determination to defend their lands against all comers by whatever means to hand. It also marked the first Indian victory of Red Cloud's War.

Chief Red Cloud was the only Indian to win a war against the United States. His victory did not end white expansion across the plains, but it managed to buy the Lakota Sioux and their brethren a few more years of peace, and a chance to live the old life free of American interference. But ultimately Red Cloud's victory was to prove pyrrhic, the Americans regrouping for a bigger campaign to wrest the buffalo hunting grounds from the Sioux in a bloody final showdown on the northern plains.

As mentioned, the Lakota Sioux were the largest of the three Sioux tribal groups in America, the others being the Santee or Dakota peoples who still occupied the tribal ancestral woodlands of Minnesota, and the Yankton and Yanktonai Nakota peoples inhabiting territory between the Santee and the Lakota. The Lakota consisted of seven distinct groups that were almost independent tribal peoples, but bound together by a single unifying language, common cultural practices and beliefs and a collective unity of purpose and identity. The groups were the Sicangu or Burnt Thighs, later known by the French word Brule; Oohenonpa or Boil-Twice, named for their habit of cooking their food twice and who came to be called the Two-Kettle; Minikanyewozupi or Plant-Near-Water, later the Minneconjou; Oglala or Cast-On-Own; Itazipco or No-Bow, who name was also transliterated into the French Sans Arc; Sihasapa or Black-Foot; and the Hunkpapa or End-Of-Horn. All of these names followed the Sioux practice of naming people or groups for a characteristic or peculiarity. Particular bands identified themselves as belonging to one of these seven groups, sometimes called 'divisions.' The divisions were formed by these many interrelated and similar bands, and by around 1850 the Lakota numbered 15,000 people.[1]

The Lakota have come to represent the classic 'Plains Indian' in Westerns and popular culture. They lived in animal hide tepees, hunted buffalo, worshipped at the annual Sun Dance, subjugated many other Indian peoples and were great horsemen and respected warriors. They conquered a vast territory on the plains, the expansion of which was only stopped by the arrival of whites. For example, Sitting Bull's Hunkpapa division, numbering less than a thousand people, controlled a territory of 30,000 square miles, slightly smaller than modern Hungary. The Indians were peoples who had adapted their lifestyles to suit the landscape they inhabited, and this was why American Indians were so diverse in appearance, custom and language. 'The American Indian is of the soil, whether it be the region of forests, plains, pueblos, or mesas,' wrote famous Sioux warrior and writer Black Elk. 'He fits into his surroundings, for the hand that fashioned the continent also fashioned the man for his surroundings. He once grew as naturally as the wild sunflowers, he belongs just as the buffalo belonged ...' Indians lived alongside nature and used it without altering it, while the white settlers tried to harness and overcome nature. That was the essential difference between the two groups. As Black Elk wrote: 'Once we were happy in our own country and we were seldom hungry, for then the two-leggeds and the four-leggeds lived together like relatives, and there was plenty for them and for us.'

Red Cloud was born in 1822 near the fork of the Platte River in modern-day Nebraska. His mother was a member of the biggest and most warlike Lakota clan, the Oglala, and his father, who died when Red Cloud was a young boy, was from one of the smaller Sioux clans, the Brule, or Burnt Thighs. When Red Cloud was born the Plains was 'a checkerboard of more than thirty different societies and six distinct language families.'[2] The Sioux spoke Siouan, but so did many semi-agrarian peoples the Sioux regularly attacked, including the Osage, Kansa, Oto, Omaha, Iowa, Ponca and Missouri peoples. Other tribal peoples spoke Caddoan, Algonquian and Uto-Aztecan languages that were incomprehensible to the Sioux, and 'in some cases more dissimilar than English and Chinese.'[3] The whole plains region had been successively settled by tribal peoples from all over North America, hence all the different languages that they spoke and customs that they followed.

After his father's death, Red Cloud's mother took the boy to live with her brother, an Oglala chief named Smoke, and it was amongst the Oglala that Red Cloud was raised as a warrior. Much of his teenage years and his twenties were spent winning honours in the ceaseless intertribal fights between his clan and the Pawnee and Crow, sometimes even against other Oglala bands, for the Lakota were by no means totally unified. Warriors like Red Cloud rode from camp in small war parties to lay claim to buffalo ranges and land, to uphold honour and to settle scores. They fought with bow and arrow, war club, lance, axe and knife, and took the scalps of their foes, stole horses and counted coup on their enemies with long feathered sticks. It was bloody, brutal and tough work, and it soon made men out of boys, warriors who applied all their skill as hunters to fighting their human adversaries. They fought for the group, their band, to protect the economic livelihood of their relatives and loved ones – and they were terrible when roused.

The ceaseless round of intertribal fighting never abated, even when the Americans came rolling through the prairies, redrawing boundaries and arrogantly building their houses in the midst of the Indians' lands. No united Indian front was ever possible, for although loose alliances of tribes formed and dispersed, the language, cultural practices, and different religions between the thirty or so Indian nations who called the Great Plains home were irreconcilable.

In 1841 Red Cloud first came to prominence among his own people when he killed one of his uncle's chief rivals. It was an event that split the Oglala into two factions for half a century. His rise to prominence continued as he became a leader of warriors, and a member of various fraternal warrior societies within the Oglala and wider Sioux nation, winning honour upon honour for his cool-headed leadership in fights with the Pawnee, Ute, Shoshone and Crow. In 1851, the United States convened a meeting at Fort Laramie in Wyoming with the Indians of the region (including the Southern Cheyenne who were brutally massacred at Sand Creek), and they declared that the area of land between the Powder River and the Bighorn Mountains was Crow territory, while also recognising the right of other tribes to move through it and hunt upon it. The whites had little understanding of the tribal dynamics of the region, or of how the Indians viewed territory and land ownership. The treaty was pleasingly legal to the Americans, but nonsense to the Indians.

Within four years, the inexorable expansion of the Lakota was irresistible, and the Crow soon found themselves being pushed off the very lands the Americans had just declared were theirs forever. Three hundred years of Crow occupation of this pristine buffalo hunting range was ended by 1860, as the Lakota, with their Cheyenne allies, sent large war parties to fight the Crow and force their migration further west. As we have seen with the Navajo and Cheyenne, the ability of the Americans to enforce treaty obligations was severely tested by the outbreak of the Civil War in the east, and the necessity to strip the west of regular troops. In their place were raised local volunteer regiments from the small white settler communities that had mushroomed across the plains over the last twenty years, poor quality troops led by ill-trained officers serving home-grown territorial interests rather than national ones. Colonel John Chivington's 'Bloody Third' at Sand Creek in 1864 had exemplified this trend.

The Sioux were strong, well organised and well led. Since arriving on the plains in the mid-eighteenth century 'the Lakota, the Cheyenne and others had to be more or less permanently on a war footing, as more and more tribes crowded onto the Plains, increasing pressure on the people already there.'[4] The arrival of whites in large numbers only added to the pressure.

In 1862 a gold strike was made on Lakota territory, leading to the rapid development of two Frontier mining towns, Bannack and Virginia City.

Emigrants travelled to Salt Lake City in Utah before turning north and making for Montana until an enterprising frontiersman named John M. Bozeman discovered a route through the last and best remaining Indian hunting grounds on the northern plains in 1863, 500 miles from Fort Laramie to Virginia City. Settlers would have to cross territories belonging to the Lakota, Northern Cheyenne and Crow, but the risk appeared worth it for the new trail reduced the journey by 400 miles.

By April 1864 widespread hostility towards settlers had flared up among all of the tribes who watched in disbelief the arrogant Americans running prairie schooners, horses and cattle through the heart of their buffalo ranges, scaring away the herds upon which the Indians depended for their very survival. 'The Great Spirit raised both the white man and the Indian,' said Red Cloud, 'I think he raised the Indian first. He raised me in this land, it belongs to me. The white man was raised over the great waters, and his land is over there.' The bloodbath at Sand Creek stiffened Indian resistance, and over fifty raids were launched on settlers using the Bozeman Trail until it became a hell's highway of broken wagons and bleached bones strewn about the prairie. The United States had hoped that the 'Indian problem' on the northern plains could have been settled diplomatically, but the disastrous Sand Creek Massacre had naturally increased Indian hostility, and war had become inevitable.

Responsibility for the Bozeman Trail rested with the Department of the Platte, headquartered in Omaha, Nebraska under Brigadier General Philip S. Cooke. The entire department only contained 2,000 troops, completely inadequate for policing the massive trail. Although possessing limited manpower, the government was nonetheless determined to act against the Indians who were obstructing the nation's development with their incessant guerrilla warfare, and act it did. In 1865, Major General Grenville M. Dodge assumed command of the Department of the Missouri, the army's most significant command in the West. Dodge ordered a punitive expedition mounted to suppress the Sioux, Cheyenne and Arapaho. Tactical command was given to Irish-born Brigadier General Patrick E. Connor, commander of the District of Utah, and would consist of 400 men. Colonel Henry M. Carrington, with 1st Battalion, 18th Infantry, was ordered to begin progressing along the Bozeman Trail building forts and dropping off companies to garrison them. It was to prove an extremely arduous task for the Sioux never let up in their constant attacks on the Trail. Carrington reported to headquarters at the end of

July, requesting more men. 'I need officers, and either Indian auxiliaries, or men of any regiment' wrote Carrington. 'I can resist all attacks, and do much active fighting, but I have a long line to watch and cover. The Indians are aggressive to stop the new route.'[5]

Much was expected from Connor's expedition, but it proved to be an anti-climax. Connor encountered only light skirmishing with small groups of Indian warriors, the Indians wary of engaging so many troops in open combat. Connor had constructed a rough log stockade 169 miles north of Fort Laramie at the forks of the Powder River which was subsequently named Fort Reno. In the meantime, Connor's scouts had located a large Arapaho encampment along the Tongue River in north central Wyoming. Consisting of about 500 people, the camp was made up of bands under the leadership of chiefs Black Bear and Old Devil, who had erected their tepees on land where the Tongue makes a bottleneck with the river on three sides. It was a perfect position for Connor, because the location of the Arapaho camp inhibited their easy escape when the soldiers attacked. On the morning of 29 August, the blue-uniformed troops leapt from their concealed positions and charged by companies towards the Indian village, firing as they came on. Warriors spilled out of tepees half-dressed and clutching whatever weapons they had, and met the charge before the village. Fierce fighting ensued, but the warriors, outnumbered as they were, only gave up ground slowly, intent on giving their women and children time to ford the Tongue and escape to safety. Connor's troops eventually forced most of the warriors out of the village, and they were then ordered to ransack and burn the whole camp to prevent reoccupation by the Arapaho. When the warriors saw what the soldiers were doing, as they watched their tepees burst into flames and everything they owned going up in smoke, they counter-attacked into the village with great determination. Connor just managed to hold them with the assistance of a pair of howitzers, which lobbed high explosive shells among the warriors for the rest of the day.

By nightfall, painfully lit by the burning village, the fighting had died down as the warriors disengaged and tried to locate their families. Sixty-three Arapaho lay dead or wounded around the village, and Connor had captured eighteen women and children, but he released them soon afterwards. Most of the village's pony herd was also captured by the troops, and Connor ordered over 1,000 horses and ponies to be shot to prevent their recapture by the Indians. Connor hoped that by doing this he would remove the Indians' mobility, and he was right. For many months after the

Battle of the Tongue River the Arapaho were unable to support the Lakota and Cheyenne in their raids on the Bozeman Trail.

At the end of the summer the United States concluded nine treaties with the Lakota Sioux in an effort to prevent further warfare. The chiefs who signed the agreements did not really understand what the documents meant, and most of the warrior chiefs such as Sitting Bull and Crazy Horse were away, preying on the Bozeman Trail, and they would not have signed anyway. Fort Reno was a source of aggravation to the Sioux, sitting as it did in their territory. In response to continued Indian attacks, despite the treaties, Colonel Carrington, with 1st Battalion, 18th Infantry, had been ordered to begin progressing along the Bozeman Trail building forts. Many Sioux leaders were present at Fort Laramie when Carrington and his command arrived, and the Indians correctly inferred that if the Americans could not obtain the passage they sought along the Bozeman Trail without fear of Indian attack through negotiation they would take it by force. Carrington's arrival was a blatant American challenge and Red Cloud and his followers would have nothing more to do with negotiations.

The sounds of axes on wood soon filled the air along the length of the Bozeman Trail as Carrington's forces progressed with their construction programme, building Fort Phil Kearny on the bank of Piney Creek near present-day Banner, Wyoming, in July 1866. The new fort would be the main garrison for the Trail and Carrington's headquarters. A single company had been left behind at Fort Reno, and two companies garrisoned the newly-built Fort C.F. Smith ninety-one miles north of Phil Kearny near present-day Yellowtail, Montana in August. The idea of building a chain of forts to protect settlers using the Trail had seemed sensible enough on paper. The reality was somewhat different, for the forts were too widely spaced to support one another's operations against the Indians. Fort Laramie to Fort Reno was 100 miles; Fort Reno to Fort Phil Kearny sixty-seven miles; and Phil Kearny to C.F. Smith ninety-one miles. They were also too lightly garrisoned to take the fight to the Indians or aggressively patrol the country between the posts, and they lacked mobility and firepower. The troopers sent to garrison the forts were also indifferently armed with muzzle-loading Model 1858 Springfield muskets, only Carrington's twenty-five bandsmen carrying modern seven-shot Spencer carbines.

Red Cloud feared that the forts were the first stage leading to complete American domination of the Lakota Sioux, and counselled resistance at all costs. He was supported in this belief by the Hunkpapa Sioux leader Sitting

Bull and many others from across the entire Lakota confederation. Many, including Red Cloud, were aware of what had befallen their Santee Sioux cousins in Minnesota in 1862, an event the whites had named the Great Sioux Uprising. The decision was taken, along with their Cheyenne and Arapaho allies, to strike at the new forts. Red Cloud's offensive attitude was in direct contrast to Colonel Carrington's defensive inclinations, and would give the Sioux and their allies an enormous psychological advantage over the army.

Henry Carrington had been a successful lawyer until just before the Civil War. When war was seen as inevitable Carrington had used his political connections to obtain for himself the colonelcy of the 18th Infantry, which he himself had raised in July 1861. The regiment had performed well throughout the war, joining Sherman during his march through Georgia and fighting at Missionary Ridge, Kenesaw Mountain and Atlanta. But the regiment had gone into battle without its colonel, as Carrington had been permanently detached on staff duties. By 1866, out on the wild and dangerous frontier lands between the white and the Indian worlds Carrington's lack of combat experience left him with little in common with his battle-hardened subordinate officers. Carrington, described as a man of 'patience, forbearance and common sense,' failed to impose discipline on these officers, who mostly held their commander in contempt and were frequently insubordinate. Carrington's subordinates formed two cliques, and this had disastrous consequences for the garrison.

Fort Phil Kearny sat on a plateau slightly higher than the surrounding terrain, with excellent fields of fire in all directions. But the vital timber required for its construction, maintenance and cooking and heating tasks had to be cut from a stand five miles west, at the foot of the Bighorn Mountains. The woodcutting parties were constantly traversing a route called the Wood Road that was overlooked to the north by the Sullivant Hills. Northwest of the Sullivants across the Big Piney River lay a parallel range of broken mountains named Lodge Trail Ridge rising to 5,000 feet. South of the fort across the Little Piney River was 4,900-foot Pilot Hill. Carrington established an observation post atop this feature to keep watch on the woodcutters using Wood Road.

While Carrington was busy building Fort Phil Kearny the Sioux struck the length of the Bozeman Trail. They attacked wagon trains, killed settlers and ran off stock. Carrington reported the deteriorating situation to the Department of the Platte. 'Major Haymond, with four companies, halted to burn charcoal and repair wagons, at Crazy Woman's Fork,' wrote

Carrington. 'The next day Indians drove off his herds. All but seventy head were recovered. He lost two men killed and five wounded in pursuit.' That same night, wrote Carrington, 'a small train camping with Cheyennes, were attacked by Sioux and all whites were murdered.' Any whites travelling the Trail were at risk of Sioux attack.

> Colonel Sawyer arrived with train and sixty men, but, for one hundred miles had been constantly threatened and compelled to camp on hills away from water. Six officers and one officer's wife, with an escort of fifteen men, coming to join me, were attacked at Crazy Woman's Fork. Lieutenant Daniels, a little in advance, was shot, scalped, and barbarously tortured with a stake inserted from below.'[6]

Carrington knew he could not respond effectively, so he simply ignored the raids and concentrated instead on completing his fort building programme. On 3 August he detached two companies under Captain Nathaniel Kinney, who was to march north and begin the construction of Fort C.F. Smith. Carrington's dispersed forces were now effectively prisoners behind their wooden walls. Carrington sent a messenger to Brigadier General Cooke requesting a detachment of cavalry, modern breech-loading rifles and more ammunition. In November Cooke sent reinforcements, an additional forty-five infantry and a sixty-man detachment from the 2nd Cavalry under Lieutenant Horatio Bingham. But all of the reinforcements were raw recruits who could barely manage a horse, and all were armed with antiquated muskets.

Captains William Fetterman and James Powell arrived at Fort Phil Kearny in November. They led the anti-Carrington clique, and both were experienced Civil War officers with the kinds of distinguished combat records their colonel could only envy. Fetterman had been brevetted a lieutenant-colonel during the Civil War, and had bragged on arrival at Phil Kearny: 'Give me eighty men and I'll march through the whole Sioux nation!' Powell was a much older man, with thirteen years experience in the West before the war, and he was very much aware of the realities of fighting Indians. These two infantry officers were joined in mutual contempt for Carrington by the fort's quartermaster, Captain Frederick Brown, Carrington's adjutant, Lieutenant William Bisbee and a company commander, Lieutenant George Grummond. The pro-Carrington clique was very small, and consisted of Captain Tenodor Ten

Eyck and famous Frontier scout Jim Bridger who said to Carrington of Fetterman and his friends: 'Your men who fought down South are crazy. They don't know anything about fighting Indians.' Bridger's words were to prove prophetic.

It didn't take the Indians long to work out that the army's main weakness was the woodcutting parties sent miles out from Phil Kearny. The Sioux launched constant small raids on these groups, and Carrington quickly developed a drill to protect the cutters. The observation post atop Pilot Hill would signal the fort using semaphore the moment the woodcutters came under attack. Carrington advised the cutters to form a defensive circle when attacked and to hold out until relieved by a force from the fort. This process was repeated dozens of times, and the Sioux always broke off their skirmishing when the relief force showed up. Fetterman and Brown, both eager to get at the Indians, suggested a 100-man sweep against the numerous Sioux camps along the Tongue River to the north, but Carrington dismissed the idea as impractical and foolhardy.

By December, Carrington began to realise that the effective besiegement of Phil Kearny by marauding bands of Sioux had reduced morale to rock-bottom. He had to mount active operations to restore the troops' confidence in his ability to command, and punish the Sioux for their boldness. The idea was simple: wait until the Sioux attacked the wood train once again, but this time trap the warriors between two strong converging forces quickly dispatched from the fort.

On 6 December Pilot Hill signalled that the wood train was under attack. The plan had already been decided upon. Fetterman and Lieutenant Bingham, with thirty cavalry, would relieve the wood train and pursue the Indians along their usual line of retreat round the western end of the Sullivant Hills, across the Big Piney and up and over Lodge Trail Ridge to Peno Creek. Carrington would lead Lieutenant Grummond and thirty-five mounted infantry up the Bozeman Trail and cut the Sioux line of retreat at Peno Creek. It appeared to be a sound plan, but one with a disastrous outcome for the army. When the Sioux, who numbered around one hundred warriors, realised that they outnumbered Fetterman's relief force by three to one, instead of running away they turned around and charged. In the ensuing melee Bingham was killed. Carrington was held up by the broken terrain on Lodge Trail Ridge and became involved in a confused fight with another party of Sioux until Fetterman and some of the cavalry joined him and the Indians disengaged and withdrew. Grummond reined his horse in beside Carrington's and virtually shouted at his commander, asking him whether he was a fool or a coward to allow his men to be cut to pieces without offering help. Characteristically, Carrington let this gross insubordination pass without comment. Overall casualties were two soldiers killed and five wounded.

Carrington's ill-conceived attempt to trap the Sioux gave his foes an idea. The Sioux were delighted that so large a force of soldiers could be coaxed to travel so far from the wooden walls of the fort. The Sioux decided upon an ambush of their own, Crazy Horse of the Oglala being the brains behind the proposal. Carrington also realised how vulnerable his tiny force had been miles from the fort, and he forbade any pursuit of Indians beyond Lodge Trail Ridge in the future. The Sioux made their first attempt to ambush a force of Carrington's men on 19 December. They attacked the wood train, and then tried to lure Captain Powell's relief force further from the fort by feigning retreat, but Powell wisely refused to play along and follow them out of sight of Pilot Hill. Two days later the Sioux tried again. The day was bright and cold, with huge patches of partially melted snow lying in hollows shaded from the sun. At 10am the wood train left the fort, and an hour later the signal flags waved atop Pilot Hill indicating the train was under attack once again. The garrison was stood to, and Carrington detailed Powell to once more lead out the relief force. However, Fetterman appeared and demanded to take command on account of his seniority to Powell, and Carrington backed down and gave Fetterman permission. Carrington's orders to the vainglorious Fetterman and equally ambitious Grummond were explicit, and repeated several times to both men before they were clear of the fort: 'Support the wood train, relieve it and report to me. Do not engage or pursue Indians at its expense. Under no circumstances pursue over the ridge [Lodge Trail Ridge].'[7] Fifteen minutes later the relief force, forty-nine dismounted infantry led by Fetterman, marched out of Phil Kearny. At 11.30 Carrington dispatched Company C, 2nd Cavalry numbering twenty-seven men, armed with the fort band's modern carbines, under Grummond's command. Grummond, though only a lowly subaltern, had served as Lieutenant-Colonel of the 14th Michigan Volunteers and been brevetted Brigadier General of Volunteers during the Civil War. Captain Brown, who was due to be posted shortly, was given permission to join the column so he could experience combat at least once, along with two civilians who were both former Civil War officers. James Wheatley and Isaac Fisher carried sixteen-shot Henry repeating rifles. Carrington ordered Grummond to report to Fetterman, obey his orders, and never leave him. The warning about not crossing Lodge Trail Ridge was repeated to Grummond as well.

Once out of the fort, Grummond's cavalry soon overtook Fetterman's marching infantry. Grummond was trying to catch up with a group of mounted Sioux who were acting as decoys for the larger body of warriors concealed ahead. The infantry had no way of keeping up, and soon a 400-yard gap opened up between Grummond and Fetterman. Fetterman, much to Carrington's chagrin, appeared to change his route, moving away from the wood train and across the Big Piney and along the Bozeman Trail behind the Sullivant Hills. Carrington was soon busy directing the fire of the fort's howitzers against another party of Sioux who were sitting on their horses near the Bozeman Trail to the west. When he looked back in Fetterman's direction with a naval telescope he could see the infantrymen slowly climbing the slopes of Lodge Trail Ridge in skirmish order, puffs of smoke snatched away in the wind indicating that they were engaging the enemy. Soon Fetterman and his men disappeared from sight beyond the crest.

Laying in wait on the reverse slope were hundreds of Sioux, Cheyenne and Arapaho warriors, some of whom had buried themselves beneath the snow wrapped in buffalo robes, while others hid behind bushes and large rocks. Some were mounted and waited behind more rocky ridges further down the valley. The trap was set and Fetterman was about to walk straight into it.

Grummond's cavalry swiftly pursued the Sioux decoys down the northern head of the ridgeline towards some snow covered grass flats below the banks of Piney Creek. Here the Indian decoys subdivided into two groups and rode a figure '8' formation – the signal for the assault to begin. At about 12 noon heavy and sustained firing was heard in Grummond's and Fetterman's direction and Carrington dispatched Captain Ten Eyck and fifty-four infantry and dismounted cavalry to relieve Fetterman.

Ten Eyck followed a different route from Fetterman and after fording the Big Piney north of the fort he climbed the high ground to obtain a clear view of the battlefield beyond the crest of the ridgeline. Looking down the reverse slope, the icy wind stinging his eyes, Ten Eyck could discern hundreds of Indians drifting about the valley or moving away north. Strewn around the patches of grass and snow were ghastly white lumps that looked from a distance to be stripped bodies. When the Sioux spotted Ten Eyck and his men silhouetted against the sky as they stood impassively on the ridge, they yelled out taunts and insults, gesturing for the soldiers to come down and fight them. Ten Eyck knew that to attack such a huge force would only result in his annihilation, so he stood firm and dispatched an urgent message to Carrington that read: 'The valley on the other side of the ridge is filled with Indians who are threatening me. The firing has stopped. No sign of Fetterman's command. Send a howitzer.' On receipt of this message Carrington dispatched forty more men at 12.45pm, along with an ambulance and two ammunition wagons but no field gun. There were simply not enough fit horses at Phil Kearny to haul the heavy artillery piece across the broken terrain to Ten Eyck.

As Ten Eyck and his men stood motionless atop the ridge, their blue greatcoats flapping wildly in the wind, the Indians grew bored of trying to lure these new soldiers into the valley and dispersed amid much hollering and screaming. Once it was safe, Ten Eyck ordered his command to gingerly descend into the valley and look for Fetterman and his men. What they discovered shocked and revolted them. When the white men had all been killed the Indians had assaulted their corpses, stripping off the soldiers' uniforms and performing horrific mutilations. All were scalped, slashed with knives, gutted or dismembered. Some bodies were decapitated or emasculated, the Indians in their fury reducing their enemies to butchered carcasses to be left bristling with arrows upon the red stained frozen earth. Such was the level of dismemberment that it was impossible to correctly identify which body part matched which body. 'We walked on top of their organs and did not know it in the high grass,' recalled John Guthrie, 2nd Cavalry. 'Picked them up, that is their internals, did not know the soldier they belonged to, so you see the cavalryman got an infantryman's guts and an infantryman got a cavalryman's guts.'[8] Fetterman and Brown fell together at the base of the ridge. Brown's body was covered with hatchet wounds and he was scalped. A bullet hole in his left temple, scorching around the wound indicating that the firearm was pressed to the skin when it was discharged, suggested suicide. Fetterman's skull was broken and caved in and his throat cut. Both officers bodies were shot full of arrows. The Indians had lost about 200 killed and wounded during the brief but fierce battle, but they had in turn inflicted a great defeat on an arrogant and overconfident enemy. Eighty-one hated 'Bluecoats' had been expunged from Sioux lands, and the Indians were only just beginning their campaign to kill as many white soldiers as possible until the whites left them in peace and gave up their attempts to enter Sioux territory uninvited.

For Colonel Carrington was left the task of trying to work out what had happened to Fetterman and Grummond, and the grisly job of collecting their scattered remains for burial. Over many decades of research the truth about the so-called 'Fetterman Massacre' is relatively clear. Grummond pulled his small cavalry force way ahead of Fetterman's slower moving infantry, and both units found themselves inside the valley that ran alongside the Bozeman Trail, lured there by Indian decoys. When the decoys broke into two groups and began riding in a figure '8', the Indian signal to attack the soldiers, Grummond was no doubt intrigued – but his sudden curiosity was expunged in an instant as a chorus of unearthly cries and screams rose from all around, and Indians seemed to materialise out of the very earth in front of him. In an instant of dreadful clarity Grummond perhaps saw his own death minutes away, but determined to go down fighting he reined in his horse and shouting orders wheeled his company away from the charging warriors. Furiously spurring their mounts forward, the terrified troopers began to climb the steep, rock strewn valley side towards the Bozeman Trail, their escape route if they could reach it. It was a hopeless manoeuvre, for the charging warriors were soon almost on top of Grummond's men, arrows thudding with sickening regularity into exposed blue-coated backs and black cavalry horses, their riders pitching backwards out of their saddles in agony. The pair of civilians riding with Grummond, Wheatley and Fisher, knew that to run from Indians was only to hasten one's death. They quickly dismounted and took cover behind some big rocks, several young troopers around them doing the same, while they all opened a devastating fire on the mass of advancing warriors. Bullets zipped among the charging warriors like angry hornets, hurling many to the ground, but still they came on screaming and chanting like madmen. The valley soon filled with dense blue smoke as heavy firing reverberated across the hills. Grummond managed to lead some of his panicked troopers to a lone tree, beside which was a natural trench in the earth into which many piled, priming their muskets with cold-numbed fingers. Sergeant Augustus Lang had remained mounted, slashing at the warriors with his cavalry sabre, decapitating one before arrows toppled him from his horse and he was finished off by club-wielding Indians. Grummond had unsheathed his sabre as well, killing several warriors before being overwhelmed and partially decapitated by a hatchet. The remaining cavalrymen fought it out with the Indians among the rocks in vicious hand-to-hand engagements until they fell. Wheatley and Fisher and the few troopers with them fought like demons, killing a great many warriors before their ammunition began to give out and they were slaughtered.

Fetterman saw the mass of warriors rising up before his footsore and frozen infantrymen, and witnessed the panicked movement of Grummond and his cavalry towards high ground. Suddenly, from Fetterman's rear a mounted Sioux warrior came charging in amongst his men wielding a war club, and was quickly dispatched by the nearest soldiers. Then another came storming in on foot like some crazed Viking berserker and was also shot down. But soon hundreds of Indians were closing rapidly on Fetterman's little command, preceded by a storm of arrows that knocked many of his men down, who lay writhing and groaning on the frozen ground while their comrades tried to reload their old muskets. Brown, Carrington's quartermaster, who had ridden along with Grummond for the experience, had somehow managed to get clear of the destruction of the cavalry and had joined Fetterman.

Fetterman attempted to fight his way out of the encirclement towards higher ground, but his command was soon overwhelmed by sheer weight of numbers and the slow rate of fire of his musket-armed soldiers. In a hacking and slashing melee Fetterman's men were killed. Those who lay wounded on the ground were granted no quarter by the Indians, who went from man to man caving in skulls with their war clubs and cutting throats before the mutilations began. Fetterman, who had once claimed he could ride through the whole Sioux nation with only eighty men, now lay dead alongside exactly eighty American soldiers.

Reaction in the east to the Fetterman Massacre was muted. The United States had only just passed through the most bloody war in its history, and the deaths of eighty soldiers in some God-awful outpost in the far west was unfortunate but relatively insignificant in the grand scheme of things. It was more seriously received in army circles, and the major participants who remained alive came in for some serious, career destroying criticism. Carrington was an easy target, and most of his contemporaries merely thought that he had been the wrong man for the job. Carrington, in turn, spent the rest of his life justifying his actions in 1866, and he left the army when his best-selling author wife Margaret died in 1870. He became professor of military science at a college in Indiana and later in Boston, and briefly returned to the west to take part in treaty negotiations with the Flathead Indians and the Cherokee. Made a doctor of letters in 1873, Carrington wrote ten books before his death in 1912. He and his wife had been very good to Grummond's widow Frances after her husband's untimely death, and after the death of his wife Carrington and Frances became close. Eventually she became the second Mrs Carrington, an interesting match knowing that Lieutenant Grummond had held Carrington in considerable contempt. The real victim of the whole mismanaged affair was Captain Ten Eyck. Soon after the massacre rumours began to circulate that Ten Eyck could have saved Fetterman if he had marched directly to his aid instead of taking a longer route to a vantage point from where he conducted a reconnaissance. If Ten Eyck had done as his detractors had wished, in all likelihood the army's death toll would merely have been augmented. Suggestions of cowardice levelled against Ten Eyck caused him to seek solace inside a whiskey bottle. He was eventually court-martialled and found guilty of conduct unbecoming an officer and a gentleman, though a sympathetic President Grant had the verdict set aside. It did not help Ten Eyck however, and with his health broken he quit the army in 1871.

With Carrington removed from command at Fort Phil Kearney, the army attempted to put its house in order with a little reorganisation and re-equipment. A new regiment was formed from the old 18th Infantry and attached units, the 27th Infantry, and Lieutenant-Colonel Henry Wessells took command. One cause of the Fetterman Massacre so far as the army was concerned was the poor performance of the antiquated firearms they had issued to the soldiers garrisoning the forts, and immediate efforts were made to rectify this problem. The old Model 1858 musket was replaced by the issue of 700 new Model 1866 Springfield Allen .50-70 calibre rifles. The new weapons were a cheap modification of the old muskets, breech-loading, accurate and reliable. Importantly, the new rifles could be loaded very quickly, vastly increasing the amount of lead even a small outfit could generate against any attackers. One hundred thousand new bullets were sent to the Trail forts, and the Indians never knew a thing about it.

Throughout the spring and summer of 1867 the Sioux and their allies, emboldened by their amazing victory over Fetterman the previous winter, continued to launch sporadic raids all along the Bozeman Trail, effectively closing it to emigrant traffic. The Sioux and Cheyenne also struck repeatedly against the wood cutting parties out from Forts Phil Kearny and C.F. Smith, and the army remained completely on the defensive.

At the end of July the experienced Captain Powell, the officer who should have led the Fetterman force out to relieve the wood train in

December 1866, assumed command of Company C of the new 27th Infantry. His job, with only thirty-two men, was to escort and protect the wood cutting parties as they established a camp six miles from Fort Phil Kearny to feed the post's prodigious appetite for timber. Powell, along with his second-in-command Lieutenant Jenness, decided to create a proper defensive position close to the woodcutters' camp. A long line of fourteen wagons was driven out to the site under escort, and then the men set to work removing the wooden wagon beds, or boxes, from the iron axles and placing them on the ground to form an oval-shaped defensive perimeter measuring sixty by thirty feet. The wagon trolley, consisting of axles and wheels, was then used to haul the long logs more comfortably back to base. Each wooden wagon bed was ten feet long and four and a half feet wide. Each was two and a half feet tall, and loopholes were cut in the wooden sides and the sides double-lined with sacks of corn to absorb bullets. Blankets were spread over the tops of the boxes to conceal the firing positions of riflemen, and to absorb some of the impact of Indian arrows sweeping in on a high trajectory. The space between each box was plugged with logs or bundles of blankets and clothing, the entire effect being to create an extremely squat little fort with the soldiers laying down and firing from the prone position through the loopholes in the sides. The laager afforded all-round protection from attack.

Before his men had marched out of the fort Powell had drilled them hard on the new rifles, creating a corps of marksmen from the best shots in the company and detailing the rest of his men to act as loaders in the event of a fight with the Indians. The theory behind the wagon box fort was similar to the old British square that had been formed many times by Redcoats standing off French cavalry during the Napoleonic Wars, and was used successfully many times during the almost ceaseless colonial conflicts that engaged Britain's attention during the second half of the nineteenth century.

At Fort C.F. Smith a similar fortification had been erected to protect parties of haycutters working away from the fort. A stout log stockade had been built into which civilian workers and escorting soldiers could muster when threatened by warriors. On 1 August 1867 a party of six civilians was cutting hay three miles from C.F. Smith in Montana Territory. They were escorted by twenty soldiers from the new 27th Infantry under the command of Lieutenant Sigismund Sternberg. Mounted Sioux warriors were spotted approaching them in the morning. The warriors attempted to lure the soldiers into pursuing them into what was clearly a trap, but Sternberg ordered everyone into the log stockade instead, where rifles and revolvers were checked and an all-round defence posted.

It was just as well that Sternberg had moved with urgency, for within minutes some eight hundred Sioux warriors descended upon the stockade in a wild charge. Sternberg ordered rapid fire, and the stockade spat lead at a rate not seen by the Indians before. Unnerved by the sudden increase in firepower from the new pattern rifles the charge broke apart and the Indians rode or ran clear of the firing, leaving many dead and wounded in the hay. The Sioux changed their tactics and decided to use fire to wheedle out the few white men hiding behind the stockade. Warriors fired the hay-fields, and soon the men inside the stockade began to worry as the flames crawled inexorably towards their wooden fort, thick black smoke obscuring their fields of fire. Then, by a miracle the men were quick to praise, the wind abruptly changed direction when the flames were only twenty feet from the stockade and the danger passed. When the Sioux observed what was happening another strong attack came sweeping in against the stockade, hundreds of warriors trying again to swamp the defences and kill the motley collection of white men. Sternberg stood up as the mass of screaming warriors closed the distance to the perimeter and shouted above the din: 'Stand up, men, and fight like soldiers!' His men responded and opened a brisk fire into the sea of warriors before them, but suddenly Sternberg was struck in the head by an Indian bullet and fell dead against the stockade. Sergeant James Norton leapt to his feet and rallied the men, but he too was struck and killed within seconds, another bullet wounding Private Thomas Navin close by. Al Colvin, one of the civilians, took charge of the defence, and armed with a fifteen-shot Spencer repeating rifle, he was everywhere at once, firing, reloading and encouraging the men like a man possessed. The defenders fired their weapons until the barrels were almost white hot. The Indians backed off out of range for the moment. During the lull Private Charles Bradley of Company E bravely volunteered to mount his horse and ride to the fort to fetch a relief force. Colvin told him to go, and by sheer luck young Bradley was able to ride past the warriors and reach safety, though he was knocked from his saddle at one point by a pursuing Indian. Bradley arrived at the gates of the fort, his face, hands and uniform smudged with gun smoke, his eyes slightly wild and staring, and reported immediately to the commander, Lieutenant-Colonel Luther P. Bradley.

Bradley's efforts to organise and dispatch a relief force were remarkably slow considering the urgency of the situation out in the hayfields. It was not until 4pm that Captain Thomas B. Burrowes led Company G and a howitzer from the fort at the trot, closely followed by Lieutenant Reuben N. Fenton and Company H. Burrowes and Fenton arrived at the hayfield stockade just as the light was beginning to fade from the horizon. About half of the warriors had already left by this stage, and of the rest none showed any further interest in fighting the soldiers. Burrowes hastened the Indians' withdrawal with a few volleys from Company G and then relieved Colvin and the others. Casualties among the soldiers and civilians in the stockade had been remarkably light, amounting to only two killed and four wounded. At least eight warriors lay dead around the defences, with another thirty wounded. Many of the Indian dead and wounded were carried from the field by their relatives so no accurate count could be made.

On 2 August 1867 the 'wagon box' laager at Fort Phil Kearny was put to the test for the first and only time. A huge gathering of Sioux and Northern Cheyenne that included Crazy Horse descended upon the isolated wood cutting party protected by Captain James Powell's Company C, 27th Infantry, hundreds of warriors accompanied by their families, all believing that another easy victory over the soldiers was within their grasp. Red Cloud himself watched the action atop a hill some three miles from the battlefield flanked by a large group of senior chieftains drawn from across both nations. In the valley below Hunkpapa, Minneconjou, Oglala, Brule and Sans Arc Sioux, alongside Cheyenne Dog Soldiers, moved towards Powell's position, their families trailing close behind ready to strip the enemy dead and carry off any booty. The sudden appearance of such a dense mass of warriors dispersed the civilian woodcutters, who fled towards the sanctuary of the fort. The Indians burned the woodcutters' camp and ran off their livestock. Then they came for Powell's men. Powell ordered Company C into the prepared laager, and the men settled down inside the darkness of the boxes, their eyes scanning the horizon in all directions through the rough cut rifle loopholes, tense and sweaty. 'Men, find a place in the wagon boxes, you'll have to fight for your lives today!' Powell declared in a loud voice, and after what had happened to their comrades who had died with Fetterman, no-one considered taking to his heels. After all, the oft-repeated rule on the Frontier was never run from Indians as it was a death sentence. Powell also impressed on his men to need for them to stay quiet and not to open fire until he gave the order. The canny Powell wanted to lure the warriors close to the laager and then hit them with everything he had.

Mounted Indian warriors numbering perhaps as many as five hundred formed up in the distance intending to charge the soldiers' puny little defensive position and open up cracks in the defences by physically riding their ponies *through* the laager. Following behind the mounted warriors came hundreds more on foot who would wait until their brothers had created gaps in the soldiers' defences before they would storm in on foot and finish the business quickly as they had finished Fetterman and his soldiers up close and personal. As the mounted warriors wheeled closer the atmosphere inside the wagon boxes was electric with tension, as men nervously checked their weapons and squinted out through the loopholes. Suddenly, the bronzed and feathered mass let out a great cry and, kicking their ponies, a great wave of warriors came charging towards the laager. The thunder of hooves was loud inside the wagon boxes, and the vibration came up through the wooden floor, growing stronger and stronger as the distance between the Indians and the laager wound down. Captain Powell stared intently at the charging mass, his eyes keenly estimating the distance to the target, whilst he rhythmically repeated the words 'Steady boys, don't fire until I give the order.' Suddenly, at fifty yards, Powell yelled 'Fire!' and the wagon boxes gained a sudden ripple of fire and smoke along their lengths, the deafening crack of rifles overwhelming the thunder of charging hooves.

The effect on the Indians was stunning. Some warriors were blown clean off their mounts as sprays of blood lashed their comrades beside and behind them; horses twisted in the air as though stung by hornets, and then crashed to the ground whinnying in pain, their legs kicking helplessly in the air. The unwounded Indians rode their ponies over the fallen and charged on believing the worst was now past, for the white soldiers would now be desperately reloading their awkward old muskets. By the time they were ready to fire again the braves would be riding over their heads and shooting down upon them. But this did not happen. Seconds later the fire slits cut in the wagon boxes spat fire again, a wall of lead that blew great gaps in the attackers' ranks. This resembled more a European battlefield than a skirmish with Indians, and the attack was soon shot away. In their haste to get clear of the barrage of rifle fire many of the warriors swept past the laager, emptying their rifles through the flimsy cover of blankets before dispersing into the countryside. Lieutenant Jenness died instantly, an Indian pumping a single heavy slug into his head as the young officer tried to direct the fire of his men. But once the Indian riders were out of range, Powell was relieved and amazed that his casualties had been so light – only two killed and two men badly wounded. Around the makeshift little fort lay dozens of dead and wounded Indians and horses lying on their sides feebly twitching their legs or heads. The soldiers inside the laager carefully aimed their rifles and picked off any wounded warriors crawling around the battlefield, sparing none. They knew the Indians would give them no quarter should they break into the puny defences, and the Americans returned the courtesy. 'We had to kill them for self-protection,' recalled R.J. Smythe, a mule driver attached to the wood train.

The Indian warriors soon rallied from their initial mounted charge, and from the shock of encountering such unexpectedly strong resistance from the handful of whites. Several hundred warriors began to approach the laager on foot, utilising the broken terrain as cover. These warriors opened a tremendous firestorm of bullets, musket balls and arrows at the little fort, the near constant impact of heavy slugs in the wagon boxes deafening to the soldiers sheltering inside. Wood chips flew everywhere, but the grain sacks piled against the walls stopped the bullets from finding any victims. The high velocity arrows that thumped down through the thin blankets that provided head cover for the boxes were serious enough, but by a miracle none of the defenders was seriously injured. Powell ordered his men to hold their fire once more, and the warriors interpreted the sudden silence from the laager to indicate that they had been victorious. With a cry, hundreds of warriors leapt to their feet from cover and came charging across the open ground before the laager. Closer and closer they came, brandishing mean-looking hatchets and war clubs, their war paint and feathers adding a primeval terror to the fight. Suddenly, Powell gave the order to fire and from the loopholes a devastating barrage of rifle fire carved its way through the Indian ranks. Dozens were cut down as the soldiers pumped round after round into them, the attack quickly breaking up as the warriors scrambled for cover. Six times the warriors came on with suicidal bravery and determination, and six times their assaults were shot away. As they tried to recover their dead and wounded from the field a howitzer shell screamed in among them, detonating with an ear-splitting crack.

A small relief force was advancing cautiously towards Powell's besieged position. Major Smith led one hundred men from various companies, conscious that he was heavily outnumbered by the Indians. As he came in sight of the laager, gunfire continued to ripple along its sides, chasing many of the warriors off the battlefield. The vulnerable relief force was not molested; the mass of warriors had clearly had enough and were withdrawing. Powell and his men emerged after four hours of intense combat smoke-blackened, tired, and thirsty but relieved to shake Smith's hand and the hands of the relief. 'Thanks to God,' said Sergeant Sam Gibson, 'and Lieutenant General Sherman we were armed with the new weapon.' They went among the Indians dead, scalping the bodies with their knives and bayonets. Indian casualties were difficult to accurately assess, for the bands had carried many of their dead and wounded from the field, but Powell estimated that sixty-seven warriors had been killed and over 120 wounded. Army casualties amounted to only four men killed. The new rifle had certainly proved its worth. Without it there is no question of doubt that Sternberg's and Powell's commands would have been annihilated by the Indians. Although both the Hayfield Fight and the Wagon Box Fight were army victories, and the loss of so many warriors was keenly felt by the Sioux and Cheyenne, the Bozeman Trail remained practically impassable to travellers. The forts remained isolated, the garrisons too small to police the Trail. The Indians remained the masters of the surrounding country.

Colonel Wessells, Carrington's replacement as commander at Fort Phil Kearny, proved to be even less capable than his predecessor in taking the offensive against the Indians. The Sioux and their allies were too numerous, and the puny army garrisons only managed to cling to the Trail by their fingertips. The government had grown weary of financing the effort to break the power of the Lakota in their heartland, and by late 1867 Washington decided to abandon the effort for the time being and concentrate American resources into enabling the speedy completion of the transcontinental railroad then pushing through south-western Wyoming towards Salt Lake City. The Powder River country would be temporarily abandoned by the army.

Peace commissioners were sent to Fort Laramie in the spring of 1868. Red Cloud refused to discuss a peace settlement until Forts Phil Kearny and C.F. Smith were closed. He wanted these symbols of white arrogance erased from his people's territory, and the government was more than happy to oblige him. Both forts had proved expensive and had failed to yield a single positive result. In August the garrisons marched out towards the east, and even before the thin, blue-clad columns had disappeared over the horizon victorious Sioux warriors had torched both forts and erased them from their lands.

In November, Red Cloud and a collection of other Lakota chieftains arrived at Fort Laramie. The agreement which was eventually signed by the Sioux leaders created a vast Indian dominion named the Great Sioux Reservation, an area that included most of modern-day western South Dakota. The land grant included the Black Hills, sacred heartland of the Lakota world. The Powder River country was declared to be 'Unceded Territory' attached to the new reservation, and those Lakota who chose not to live on the reservation were free to remain unmolested in the unceded lands to the west, an area including many of the finest buffalo ranges left in North America. All Lakota had the right to hunt in the Unceded Territory, and no white man was allowed to enter Sioux lands without their permission. Red Cloud had scored an amazing and unique victory for his people, for it appeared that the Americans had caved in to Sioux military pressure, but no-one then knew how long the hiatus would last. 'I hope the Great Heavenly Father, who will look down upon us, will give all the tribes his blessing,' said Red Cloud at the time, 'that we may go forth in peace, and live in peace all our days, and that He will look down upon our children and finally lift us far above this earth.'

Red Cloud settled on the new reservation and he became a tireless campaigner for Sioux rights. The younger and more aggressive Sioux leaders such as Sitting Bull and Crazy Horse stayed out in the Unceded Territory disdaining life on the reservation. Red Cloud lived at Pine Ridge until his death in 1909 aged eighty-seven, outliving all of his contemporaries, Indian and white, and going to his grave having witnessed the final degradation of his people by the United States. As he remarked in later life: 'They [the Americans] made us many promises, more than I can remember, but they never kept but one; they promised to take our land, and they took it.'

But, in the late 1860s it appeared that the Sioux could live at peace for now. The Americans had not forgotten their inglorious reversal, and as the United States grew stronger new threats to the Lakota domain would materialise. 'I have listened patiently to the promises of the Great White Father,' commented Red Cloud of the President and the treaties years later, 'but his memory is short.'

Notes

1. Royal B. Hassrick, *The Sioux: Life and Customs of a Warrior Society*, (Norman: University of Oklahoma Press, 1964), 30

2. James Wilson, *The Earth Shall Weep: A History of Native America*, (London: Picador, 1998), 251

3. Ibid: 21

4. Ibid: 259

5. *Carrington to Adjutant General, US Army, Washington DC*, 29 July 1866
6. *Carrington to Major H.G. Litchfield, Acting Assistant Adjutant General, Department of the Platte*, 30 July 1866
7. *Carrington to Assistant Adjutant General, Department of the Platte*, 3 January 1867
8. Dee Brown, *Bury My Heart at Wounded Knee: An Indian History of the American West*, (London: Arena, 1990), 215

5

CONQUERING A PEACE

'The more we can kill this year, the less will have to be killed the next war, for the more I see of these Indians the more convinced I am that they all have to be killed or be maintained as a species of paupers. Their attempts at civilization are simply ridiculous.'

Lieutenant General William T. Sherman
September 1868

Just as Red Cloud was concluding his successful campaign against the United States that resulted in the 1868 Fort Laramie Treaty and the closure of the Bozeman Trail and its forts, on the southern plains a brand new conflict was brewing.

With the closure of the Bozeman Trail the Americans had shifted the emphasis of their campaign to open up the remaining Indian lands of the West to the great transcontinental railroad that was slowly snaking its way from east and west towards an as-yet undefined midway point. The Union Pacific Railroad was one of the greatest engineering feats undertaken by the United States, and its success would mean the final physical unity of the American West with the settled and industrial east. It would also mean the end of the wagon train and usher in a new influx of settlers from Europe and the eastern states keen to carve out prosperous lives in the western territories and California. A branch line, called the Kansas Pacific, would add to a planned extensive rail network throughout the West, bringing huge economic benefits to the nation, and to this end a few thousand Indians would not be permitted to impede the march of civilisation.

Major General Philip 'Little Phil' Sheridan commanded a new military district incorporating Missouri, Kansas, Indian Territory (now Oklahoma) and New Mexico. Though short in stature, Sheridan had a big personality and was a self-reliant and resourceful officer. Born to poor Irish immigrants in Albany, New York in 1831, Sheridan had worked as a store clerk before attending West Point Military Academy in 1848. He had served in California and Oregon throughout the 1850s before a very distinguished Civil War record had seen him achieve the rank of major general by 1865. His new post-war job was to control the Indians living west of the Missouri River. Sheridan faced two major obstacles to completing this task. Firstly, both the Union Pacific and Kansas Pacific Railroads were being constructed directly through the last remaining buffalo ranges on the southern plains. Secondly, since the conclusion of the Civil War, thousands of new settlers had made the journey west to seek new lives and opportunities, with many settling in middle and western Kansas and eastern Colorado on unceded Indian lands. Between 1865 and 1868 a network of stage stations, homesteads, small towns, surveying parties and railroad construction camps had sprung up all over lands belonging to the Southern Cheyenne, Arapaho, Kiowa and Comanche, all buffalo-hunting peoples. The effect on the seasonal migrations of the buffalo had been devastating, the traditional life of the Indian peoples completely disrupted, and the effective division of the Great Plains into a northern and southern area by the railroads made a permanent reality.

The United States had resorted once more to the treaty as the most cost effective instrument to rid the land of Indians, and an agreement had been reached with some of the chiefs at Medicine Lodge in 1867. The Southern Cheyenne under chiefs Tall Bull and Roman Nose had arrived at the meeting in great style, charging a phalanx of their warriors directly at the confused peace commissioners, discharging guns into the air and screaming and shouting at the tops of their voices before suddenly reining in their horses, bursting into laughter and shaking hands with the stunned Americans. Tall Bull especially was neither defiant nor conciliatory in his remarks to the peace commission, for he knew that Red Cloud was causing the Americans real trouble far to the north and like most plains Indians this encouraged him to speak in a direct manner. Tall Bull, 'a fine, warlike-looking chieftain' according to George Armstrong Custer who was present at the meeting, emphasised that the Cheyenne wanted peace but would give the whites a war if they wanted one. He refused to give up hunting grounds north of the Arkansas River as the Americans demanded, but Senator John B. Henderson of Missouri, the chief negotiator, provided a verbal understanding that the

Cheyenne chiefs could hunt between the Arkansas and the Republican rivers as long as there were buffalo there. The chiefs signed on that understanding. A new reservation was marked out in Indian Territory for the four tribal groups in return for them signing away title to their ancestral lands. Captain Albert Barnitz of the 7th Cavalry wrote that the Indians were 'signing away their rights ... as they have no idea what they are giving up.' If the plan went well, most of these Indians would be peacefully relocated to Indian Territory with the minimum of fuss, and the further development of the southern plains uninterrupted by conflict.

Many of the younger Indian warriors of all four nations were infuriated by the decision their leaders had taken in signing away their birthright, their lands, and their lifestyle. 'Many of the young men were bitterly opposed to what had been done' wrote General Sheridan, 'and claimed that most of the signatures [on the treaty] had been obtained by misrepresentation.' Sheridan was concerned lest civilian incompetence led to war (again) and he travelled to Forts Larned and Dodge to meet with the Indians, most of whom had gathered at these two posts.

At Fort Dodge Sheridan discovered that the young Indian men were in an uproar and ready to fight. The situation required careful handling, so Sheridan met with a large party of chieftains from all four Indian nations in an effort to diffuse the crisis. The chiefs explained that they had been cheated by the civilian bureaucrats and were having a hard time controlling their warriors. They appealed for help from Sheridan, but the General had to send them away because treaty matters were the concern of the Interior and not the War Department. Sheridan knew that the situation would inevitably become worse as he had seen the Indians' anger and frustration with his own eyes, and he understood their plight: '[We] left them without hope of securing better terms, or of even delaying matters longer' wrote Sheridan regarding the Medicine Lodge Treaty. '[The Indians] were more than ever reckless and defiant.'

Among the Indian camps the warriors and chiefs talked and talked, the treaty being denounced from band to band, and dark talk of war spilling from many lips. In middle and western Kansas new settlers were busy constructing houses and marking out property boundaries, secure in the knowledge that their government had dealt with the Indian problem peacefully. In reality, the settlements and homesteads along the Solomon and Saline rivers were defenceless, and the people entirely ignorant of the degree of Indian hostility that was growing stronger and more vocal with each passing day. Sheridan tried to calm the Indians down by ordering the distribution of generous quantities of supplies to the different bands, and sent in three army scouts to act as mediators. The intention was still to have Brigadier General William B. Hazen and his command from Fort Larned peacefully escort the Indians to Oklahoma. But quite suddenly the Indians struck their camps and moved away from the forts, the bands dispersing over the plains as hunting season arrived in July. The Indians went north of the Arkansas River instead of south towards Indian Territory in Oklahoma. Sheridan's overriding concern was the protection of the Union Pacific and Kansas Pacific Railroads, a task that now appeared certain to be tested.

In the Annual Report of the Secretary of War in 1867, John M. Schofield had written of the new railroads: 'When these two great thoroughfares reach the base of the Rocky Mountains, and when the Indian title to roam at will over the country lying between them is extinguished, then the solution of this most complicated question of Indian hostilities will be comparatively easy.' Schofield believed that 'this belt of country will naturally fill up with our own people, who will permanently separate the hostile Indians of the north [the Lakota Sioux and Northern Cheyenne] from those of the south, and allow us to direct our military forces one or the other at pleasure if thereafter they continue their acts of hostility.'[1]

The concept of 'divide and rule' was official American doctrine when dealing with the Plains Indians. Government officials and army officers realised that the key to ridding both regions of wandering Indians was the extermination of the buffalo herds upon which the tribes were dependent. 'I think it would be wise to invite all the sportsmen of England & America there this fall for a Grand Buffalo hunt, and make one grand sweep of them all' wrote General Sherman to Sheridan. 'Until all the Buffalo & consequent the Indians are out from between the [rail]Roads we will have collisions and trouble.'[2] Millions of buffalo still roamed the southern plains, despite the encroaching depredations of white hunters, who shot down thousands every year. The numbers were simply staggering. Around two hundred years ago there were anywhere from thirty to seventy million buffalo in the United States and Canada,[3] forming the basic staple of sustenance, shelter, cultural and religious traditions and practices for many Plains peoples. Throughout the second half of the nineteenth century, white commercial hide hunters, settlers, soldiers and sportsmen all but obliterated every buffalo in the United States. By 1886 there would be only 1,091 buffalo left alive, according to a survey conducted by the

Smithsonian Institution.[4] Scientists then shot forty-four of these remaining animals so they could be stuffed and publicly displayed in museums throughout America.

Along the Solomon River dozens of small settlements and homesteads had sprung up like mushrooms as companies had encouraged whites to purchase cheap land next to the Kansas Pacific. Railroads equalled opportunity, as infrastructure was needed all along their length, stimulating the development of small station towns and stopovers. The Solomon River settlements became the Indians' first targets. No mercy was shown to the white settlers, the Cheyenne remembering the lack of mercy that had been extended to them by Colonel Chivington's soldiers at Sand Creek four years earlier. Men, women and children were butchered and the homesteads burned. The settlers did not grasp the deep-seated enmity the Cheyenne felt towards them, and at the first appearance of war parties the whites were unafraid. 'Unaware of the hostile character of the raiders,' wrote Sheridan, 'the people here received them in the friendliest way, providing food, and even giving them ammunition, little dreaming of what was impending.' The Cheyenne warriors fell upon the homesteaders; their hearts hardened by Sand Creek, with many of the ringleaders having lost close relatives to Chivington's 'Bloody Third.' The kindnesses of the settlers 'were requited with murder and pillage, and worse, for all the women who fell into their hands were subjected to horrors indescribable by words' wrote Sheridan. Thirteen men and two women were killed and five homesteads burned. All the settlers' horses were stolen and two little girls carried off as hostages, never to be seen again.

Sheridan had to meet force with force, and he determined to compel the Indians to go to the reservations defined for them in the Medicine Lodge Treaty. It was a move with the firm backing of the press. Chief Tall Bull was accused of violating the treaty by hunting and raiding north of the Arkansas, including striking at a Kaw village at Council Grove. Major Edward W. Wynkoop was ordered to investigate the murders committed by the Cheyenne on the Saline and Solomon rivers, and his appointment appeared a wise move. Wynkoop had investigated the Sand Creek Massacre and heavily criticised the actions of Chivington and his officers, so was known as fair-minded and a humanitarian.

Wynkoop met with Chief Little Rock at Fort Larned. Both men discussed the atrocities at length, and Major Wynkoop pressed Little Rock to identify and name the warriors responsible for the outrages. The Cheyenne chief named some of the culprits, telling Wynkoop that all of them had lost loved ones at Sand Creek, which perhaps explained the Indians' ferocity against the settlers. Little Rock said that the Cheyennes wanted peace, and he agreed to deliver up the guilty men to the army, but added 'I am but one man, and cannot answer for the entire nation.'

Wynkoop waited at Larned for the return of Little Rock and the guilty warriors, but they never came. The chief had evidently failed in his attempts to coerce the wanted men into giving themselves up, and for that the entire Cheyenne nation would have to pay. Wynkoop wrote to Thomas Murphy, Superintendent of Indian Affairs, telling him that the guilty men would not be delivered as promised, though he added by way of explanation that 'the majority of the Cheyennes feel as Little Rock does in the matter, that they deprecate war and would prevent their people from entering into hostilities by every means in their power, yet they will be powerless to restrain their young men once they fairly enter into it.' In order to avoid the killing of innocents Wynkoop suggested that the wheat should be separated from the chaff: all those Cheyenne who wanted peace should come in and camp around the army forts. They would be protected by troops, with any other Cheyenne refusing to comply being declared hostile and attacked. General Sherman was quick to seize upon this plan. 'compell [sic] their removal south of the Kansas line, and in pursuing to kill if necessary,' he ordered. 'This amounts to war, but I hope only on a small scale.'[5] In Sherman's opinion the blame for any coming conflict lay squarely upon the shoulders of the Cheyenne chiefs who had failed to control their warriors, Sherman failing to understand the nature of tribal society. 'Admitting that some of them have not done acts of murder, rape, etc., still they have not restrained those who have' wrote Sherman, 'nor have they on demand given up the criminals as they agreed to do.' The army high command was deluding itself into believing that the Cheyenne had not been provoked into the attacks. 'No better time could be possible chosen than the present for destroying or humiliating those bands that … have begun a devastating war without one particle of provocation,' wrote Sherman to John Schofield, Secretary of War.

Some members of the press initially recoiled at another war, believing that conflict would only lead to more innocent civilians dying at Indian hands. One newspaper editor wrote sarcastically at the time: 'The war of robbery of Indians may have gone too far. Sand Creek humanity, inspired by the professional ambassador of Jesus Christ, the Master [Chivington], may have done its work too thoroughly.' Other newspapers demanded war, and soon. One editorial screamed: 'Line the Union Pacific road with bayonets!'

Press indecision was soon galvanized behind conflict when the Indians conducted more raids. A wagon train from Mexico was attacked on 28 August at Pawnee Fork by Cheyenne and Arapaho warriors, the settlers killed, scalped and their bodies piled inside the wagons before being set on fire. A second wagon train was also attacked at Cimarron Crossing, and the Union Pacific was attacked between the North Platte and Julesburg. Three white men were killed near Colorado City and a group of settlers at Crows Creek managed to fight off a Cheyenne war party, killing two of their assailants. In response, Governor S.J. Crawford of Kansas raised five companies of volunteer cavalry on 16 September.

The tone of the press changed considerably following the most recent wave of attacks and raids. 'All the mock sympathy for the Plains Indian is not only foolish but wrong,' read one editorial, adding, 'they interpret mercy to mean weakness.' A new slogan for a new Indian war appeared – 'Conquering a Peace.' If the Americans were to continue to attract settlers into the southern plains to develop the economy, they would have to eradicate Indian resistance forever. It would be dirty work for those who had to do it, ran American thinking, but necessary work that would bring with it the dividend of peace and prosperity.

In August Sheridan, as commander of the Department of the Missouri, was asked by acting Governor Frank Hall of Colorado for military assistance. Sheridan ordered Major George Forsyth to raise a company of scouts from the black 9th Cavalry, the famed 'Buffalo Soldiers,' tasked with finding and killing the Cheyenne that were conducting raids. Forsyth hand-picked fifty men and armed them all with Spencer repeating rifles. As executive officer Forsyth appointed decorated Civil War hero Lieutenant Fredrick Beecher of the 3rd Infantry.

Forsyth's unit – christened 'Solomon's Avengers' – left Fort Hays and arrived at Fort Wallace on 5 September without having fired a shot in anger. Five days later the Avengers left Wallace with orders to counter an Indian raid on the Kansas Pacific railhead located near Sheridan, Kansas. Scouts picked up the Indian trail on 11 September, and Forsyth followed the tracks until the 16th, leading the Avengers into Colorado. Although Forsyth knew that the Indian warriors greatly outnumbered his own small command, he pressed on regardless. At dusk on 16 September the Avengers made camp on the south bank of the Arikaree River, close to where it branches off from the Republican. Unbeknown to Forsyth, the large Indian war party, consisting in the main of Cheyenne Dog Soldiers led by Roman Nose, along with some Arapaho and

Sioux, crept close to the camp intent on launching a sudden and devastating dawn assault of their own. The impetuosity of some of Roman Nose's men lost the Indians the element of surprise, Forsyth gunning down a warrior spotted close to the camp in the poor dawn light. Warriors tried to rush the army's horses in an attempt to stampede them, but the soldiers fought them off, although the pack mules were taken. Realising that if his command stayed put it would be annihilated by the hundreds of warriors ranged in the trees along the river, Forsyth ordered the horses saddled, and abandoning their camp the Avengers rode through the shallow river to a sandbank located midstream. Dismounting quickly, they formed skirmish lines.

From all sides throughout the day the Indians bravely launched near suicidal attacks on the sandbank, the warriors wading through the river in an attempt to get at the soldiers. But the concentrated firepower delivered by the Spencer repeating rifles broke up every Indian attack with huge casualties. Indian bullets and arrows also thudded down among the Avengers, killing and wounding men and horses. Soon the river was red with blood, as the bodies of warriors floated past the sandbank or lay motionless in the shallows. On the sandbar Lieutenant Beecher lay dead, along with an army surgeon and two troopers. Another twenty-seven soldiers were wounded, including Forsyth who had a broken leg, a bullet in his thigh and a bleeding head wound after another bullet had grazed his skull. About seventy-five Indian warriors, including Roman Nose, had perished that first day trying to kill the soldiers who had been sent to exterminate them, and dozens more were wounded.

That first night Forsyth managed to infiltrate a handful of his unwounded troopers through the thinned Indian sentinels, and they rode hard for sixty miles to Fort Wallace to fetch help. Between the 20th and 24th the Avengers were besieged upon the sandbank. Their supplies gone, the men resorted to eating spoiled horseflesh and drinking muddy river water. Forsyth was eventually relieved by elements of the 10th Cavalry under Lieutenant-Colonel Carpenter. The fight was soon dubbed the Battle of Beecher Island, in honour of the fallen lieutenant.

Although some Arapaho had taken part in the Beecher Island fight, most of their kinsmen quickly surrendered to General Sheridan at Fort Dodge, keen to avoid conflict. Cheyenne Chief Tall Bull had gathered the shattered Dog Soldiers about him and led them away from Beecher's Island, and they were joined by some Arapaho and Sioux. In the meantime, Governor Hall of Colorado gave his citizens permission to kill any Indian they discovered off a reservation without fear of legal proceedings – effectively a licence to commit murder. This policy was supported by the army high command. 'The more we can kill this year, the less will have to be killed the next war,' wrote General Sherman to his brother, 'for the more I see of these Indians the more convinced I am that they all have to be killed or be maintained as a species of paupers. Their attempts at civilization are simply ridiculous.'[6]

Beecher's Island had demonstrated that a significant force of troops was going to have to be deployed to defeat the Cheyenne and their allies. Throughout the rest of the autumn more Indian raids occurred north of the Arkansas River, with wagon trains and ranches being attacked. Tall Bull led his mixed band in attacks in western Kansas and Nebraska before winter drove them to the Southern Cheyenne reservation villages around Fort Cobb.

Sherman decided upon a winter campaign to defeat the Indians. 'These Indians doubtless expect to relax their war efforts about December,' Sherman wrote, 'when the grass will fail them, but that is the very time we propose to begin in earnest, and I hope that by the time the new grass comes a very small reservation will suffice for what is left.' The *Rocky Mountain News* waxed lyrical about the coming battles, and the reasons for their prosecution:

> We are gradually occupying their country, exterminating their subsistence –
> wild game – and driving them to the wall. Extinction is their hard fate,
> although it would puzzle any one to prove that their existence is any more
> a blessing to themselves or the world than that of any species of wild animal.
> It is our destiny to do it; we could not escape it if we would.

Sherman created two new military districts in preparation for the winter offensive under two army officers to act as agents when the remaining Indians were forced onto reservations. The Sioux would fall under the jurisdiction of Brigadier General William S. Harney, and the Cheyenne, Arapaho, Kiowa and Comanche under Brigadier General William B. Hazen. The winter campaign force would consist of three columns. The main column was Colonel Crawford's 19th Kansas Volunteer Cavalry, eleven companies of the 7th Cavalry under Lieutenant-Colonel George Custer, and five companies of infantry. The main column would work its way down the Canadian River sweeping the Indians before it. The second column was commanded by Colonel A. W. Evans, and Sheridan and his staff would accompany it. The column consisted of six companies of 3rd Cavalry and two infantry companies marching east from Fort Bascom in New Mexico.

Evans would operate west of Crawford's and the first column's line of march, destroying any resisting bands of Indians it encountered, or driving surrendered bands towards old Fort Cobb which had been designated a safe haven for any Indians who chose to give up peacefully. The third column was commanded by Colonel Eugene A. Carr and consisted of seven companies of the 5th Cavalry marching southeast from Fort Lyon. Carr's orders were the same as Evans'. As he advanced he would be joined by Captain W.H. Penrose and five companies of cavalry who were already in the field southeast of Lyon. Once united on the northern Canadian River, Carr and Penrose would operate towards the Antelope Hills and the headwaters of the Red River. Sheridan and Evans would continue southwards with the second column and strike Indian winter camps located along the Washita River.

Before the soldiers were in the field many Indian bands arrived at old Fort Cobb at their own volition to camp for the winter under the protection of the army, desperate to avoid a bloodbath. However, enough bands remained out in the hinterland to convince Sherman and Sheridan of the necessity of the campaign, of striking the Indians when they were most vulnerable in the depths of winter.

Custer's regiment departed Camp Supply early on 23 November 1868 and headed towards the Washita River in Oklahoma. On the 27th Custer's Osage scouts came upon a fresh Indian trail. The 7th Cavalry was driven on through the frozen landscape by its commander, anxious to close with the hostile Cheyenne. After a short rest that night, Custer had his companies remounted and the advance was continued by moonlight. The Osage scouts informed Custer that Indians were nearby and the command halted, only Custer and the scouts moving forward through the trees to climb a small rise overlooking the river. 'Silently the command stretched out its long length as the troopers filed off four abreast,' wrote Custer in *My Life on the Plains*. 'First came two of our Osage scouts on foot … the panther creeping upon its prey could not have advanced more cautiously or quietly than did these friendly Indians as they seemed to glide rather than walk over the snow-clad surface.' The cavalry companies were held back a quarter of a mile, as the horses hooves breaking the frozen crust of snow was audible at long distance and Custer feared being discovered by the Indian village before he could attack. 'Orders were given prohibiting even a word being uttered above a whisper. No one was permitted to strike a match or light a pipe.'

Custer and a scout observed a large pony herd in the moonlight, and heard a dog barking which indicated a village was close by, for war parties never took dogs along with them. A bell tinkled in the silence, attached to one of the Indian ponies, and was further indication of a village close by. 'I turned to retrace my steps when another sound was borne to my ear through the cold, clear atmosphere of the valley,' wrote Custer, 'it was the distant cry of an infant … I could not but regret that in a war such as we were forced to engage in the mode and circumstances of battle would possibly prevent discrimination.' The Battle of the Washita has sometimes been termed a 'massacre', but all the evidence suggests that Custer and his officers were at pains to prevent unnecessary non-combatant casualties, and that their primary target was the warriors. It was, in any event, a quite different fight from that at Sand Creek four years before. Custer's orders before beginning his march to the Washita had read, in part, '… to destroy their [Cheyenne] villages and ponies; to kill or hang [sic] all warriors, and bring back all women and children.'

The companies were dispersed around the presumed site of the village in a loose circle, the men settling down to a freezing night of waiting for the dawn to come, Custer recalling that during 'these long weary hours of the terribly cold and comfortless night each man sat, stood, or lay on the snow by his horse.' As dawn broke the men were roused from their sleeping positions and stiffly mounted their horses. Custer had divided the 7th into four groups. Three companies would charge the village on horseback through some low hills northeast of the camp. Two companies would attack from the south and a further two would move down the shallow river line into the village from the southwest. Finally, Custer and a battalion consisting of companies A, C, D and K would cover the assault from the west, his group including a dismounted section of sharpshooters commanded by Lieutenant William W. Cooke. These groups now began a slow advance towards the village from several directions, out of sight of one another, Captain Albert Barnitz recalling later that 'I could not help thinking that we very much resembled a pack of wolves.' The troopers rode closer and closer to the location of the village, but were met only with silence. It appeared to Custer that he had achieved complete surprise. 'We had approached near enough to the village now to plainly catch a view here and there of the tall white lodges as they stood in irregular order among the trees. From the openings at the top of some of them we could perceive faint columns of smoke ascending.'

A single carbine shot signalled the start of the assault, and Custer turned in his saddle to the mounted band arrayed behind him, ordering them to play the regimental march 'Garryowen'. To the surreal accompaniment of cheerful military music the attack commenced. 'The bugles sounded the charge and the entire command dashed rapidly into the village,' wrote Custer. The Indians were caught napping; but realising at once the dangers of their situation, they quickly overcame their first surprise and in an instant seized their rifles, bows, and arrows, and sprang behind the nearest trees, while some leapt into the stream, nearly waist deep, and using the bank as a rifle-pit began a vigorous and determined defence.

The village belonged to sixty-seven year old Black Kettle, the same Southern Cheyenne chief whose village had been destroyed and his people massacred four years earlier by Colonel Chivington and the 'Bloody Third' at Sand Creek in Colorado.

The fighting was fierce, but within fifteen minutes the troopers had managed to push the warriors out of the village, and continued to fight them throughout the woods and along the river. Casualties were heavy on both sides, and some of the sights witnessed that day were horrific. Custer recalled the fate of a white captive taken by the Cheyenne during an earlier raid.

> One party of troopers came upon a squaw endeavouring to make her escape, leading by the hand a little white boy ... [F]inding herself and prisoner about to be surrounded by the troops and her escape cut off ... She drew from beneath her blanket a huge knife and plunged it quickly into the almost naked body of her captive. The next moment retributive justice reached her in the shape of a well-directed bullet from one of the troopers' carbines.

Some women and children were killed and wounded during the fighting, though a majority remained hiding inside their tepees.

> As soon as we had driven the warriors from the village and the fighting was pushed to the country outside I directed [an] interpreter, to go around to all the lodges and assure the squaws and children remaining in them that they would be unharmed and kindly cared for ... [A]t the same time he [the interpreter] was to assemble them in the large lodges designated for that purpose which were standing near the center of the village. This was quite a delicate mission as it was difficult to convince the squaws and children that they had anything but death to expect at our hands.

Custer did later make the point that those women who were killed mostly had picked up rifles or other weapons, and the soldiers shot them in self-defence.

The Osage scouts, however, were dread enemies of the Cheyenne, and the scouts killed many non-combatant women and children and scalped their corpses in time-honoured fashion afterwards.

Major Joel Elliot, Custer's second-in-command, rode off with eighteen troopers to the east of the village to try to prevent groups of Cheyenne from escaping. In the meantime Custer discovered that he had fifty-three captives, and that large numbers of fresh Indian warriors were moving into positions around the outskirts of the village preparing to attack. A worried Custer had some of his women prisoners questioned, and was shocked to learn that Black Kettle's village was only one of several stretching some ten miles along the Washita, containing perhaps 6,000 Indians in total. Other Southern Cheyenne winter camps were nearby, along with allied Arapaho, Kiowa, Comanche and Apache, and at the sounds of gunfire their warriors had marched towards the intruders determined to kill them. Elliot was soon a casualty, and although Custer did not know of his fate until December, Elliot and his men were wiped out by a large concentration of warriors who scalped, mutilated and dismembered the soldiers' bodies in their fury.

Custer ordered his companies to form a perimeter, and they managed to hold off several probing attacks. To stay put would be to invite a disaster as the Indians heavily outnumbered the 700 or so soldiers and Osage scouts. Custer ordered ponies taken from the Indian herd and given to his captives, the tepees torn down and burned, and the rest of the 800 or so Cheyenne horses shot before beginning a difficult withdrawal. Custer used his Cheyenne captives as a kind of human shield, and the vast numbers of warriors were forced to hold off their attacks on the soldiers for fear of hitting Indian women and children. Custer also left without ascertaining what had happened to Elliot's group, and many in his own regiment later accused Custer of callously abandoning Elliot in order to save his own neck. In reality, there was very little that Custer could have done to assist Elliot, and he had the rest of his men and their safety to consider. One final act undertaken by the troopers, as per their orders, was the summary execution of all Indian warriors who lay wounded and groaning in the bloodstained snow. These men were simply shot before the soldiers pulled out. Eventual casualties were twenty-three members of the 7th Cavalry dead, along with many wounded. Black Kettle and his wife Medicine Woman were both gunned down and killed, along with nine other war chiefs and headmen. One hundred and seventeen Cheyenne warriors were killed in the fighting or executed in the snow, and twenty-five women and children were also killed. Custer had fulfilled his orders and scored a notable victory against the Cheyenne. As the dawn had come up that morning a particularly bright star had been seen in the sky, and from now on Custer was christened 'Son of the Morning Star' by the Cheyenne. They would not forget his attack on Black Kettle's village, and eventually the tables would be turned.

On the reservation around Fort Cobb the Cheyenne were not united. In spring 1869 Chief Tall Bull tried to encourage as many of the young men as possible to join him raiding and hunting north of the Arkansas River, but Chief Little Robe strongly objected to more bloodshed and ordered a furious Tall Bull off the reservation. Tall Bull, at the head of 165 Cheyenne Dog Soldier lodges, rode defiantly out of the reservation, stating he would 'live free or die.' Travelling north through Colorado Territory, Tall Bull's band searched for other Cheyenne groups that had stayed off the reservation throughout the winter in defiance of the army. He made camp at Beaver Creek, but a skirmish with Colonel Carr's troops caused Tall Bull to attack, loot and burn Smoky Hill. He then retreated, with Carr and elements of the 5th Cavalry in hot pursuit into rough and isolated country between the Republican and Platte rivers preparatory to a move north to join up with their northern brethren. Arriving at a place they called White Butte, known to whites as Summit Springs in Colorado, Tall Bull decided to make camp and rest for two days before resuming the trek north. He did not realise, however, that Carr was close behind, and by stopping he gave the soldiers time to close the distance and prepare for an assault.

Little Hawk reined in his horse in alarm and stared incredulously at the blue-clad soldiers erupting from the tree line atop big cavalry horses, a bugle calling loudly in the background. Quickly the twelve-year old Cheyenne boy dragged his horse's head around and kicking wildly with his moccasins he rode swiftly towards Tall Bull's village laid out before him shouting out a warning over and over until his lungs felt fit to burst. Emerging from cover alongside the charging soldiers was a group of fifty Pawnee warriors working as scouts for the army, tough looking young men with Mohican haircuts, Halloween masks of war paint and outfitted in both traditional clothes and odds and ends of blue army uniforms. They charged atop painted Indian ponies, and were led by two white men, the brothers Luther and Frank North. One Pawnee took careful aim at the fleeing Little Hawk's bare back and squeezed off a shot. The rifle cracked out and Little Hawk was thrown from his pony by the force of the impact and died soon afterwards. The scouts later remarked on the courage of that young Indian boy who could so easily have turned tail and run from the village when the soldiers attacked, but they had no qualms about shooting him.

It was 11 July 1869, and the decisive battle for the Southern Cheyenne had just opened. Emerging from cover with the charging troopers was 'The Black-Bearded Cossack,' the nickname of Colonel Eugene Carr, a tough old campaigner. Major Luther North had located Tall Bull's camp that morning, allowing Carr to position his small force of 244 men of the 5th Cavalry on three sides of the village ready for an afternoon attack when most members of the village were slumbering in their tepees after the morning's chores. Reacting to Little Hawk's desperate cries, Cheyenne warriors had tumbled from their lodges and straight into a life-or-death fight. Tall Bull had grabbed a horse and ridden over to the lodge of one of his wives and collected her and her child. Quickly, he had trotted his family over to a narrow and steep ravine and urged them to hide, many warriors also taking up position inside the ravine. Tall Bull then rode his horse to the ravine entrance, dismounted, and drawing a knife, killed the animal before taking position with his rifle. His distinctive white horse had already disappeared from camp after a Dog Soldier named Two Crows had mounted it and ridden off when Carr attacked. The North brothers and their Pawnee mercenaries advanced quickly towards the ravine on horseback, Tall Bull popping up for a second to fire a single shot at them before ducking back into cover. Frank North dismounted and handed the reins of his horse to Luther and told him to ride away, hoping to lure the concealed Indian warrior into revealing his position. The trick worked, and the moment Tall Bull's head appeared above the lip of the ravine Frank triggered off a round that smashed straight into the famous chief's brain, killing him instantly. Amid much screaming Tall Bull's widow, with the child grasped in her arms, implored Frank to spare them, and the scout directed them to pass back to safety before he ordered his Pawnee to finish off the dozen or so warriors concealed in the ravine. A brief but furious battle erupted, but the overwhelming numbers and firepower of the Pawnee tipped the balance and all of the Dog Soldiers were killed, trapped like rats in a barrel.

The cavalrymen charged quickly through the village, shooting down numerous women and children. Singing his death song, Cheyenne Dog Soldier Good Head of Yellow Hair quickly bound a length of rope around his waist that was attached to a stake. He drove the stake into the ground and declared that he would not retreat from where he stood. Private Graham dispatched him with a sabre cut after a brief fight.

Fifteen Cheyenne warriors were dead and about thirty women and children. Another seventeen were captured by the soldiers, while the rest managed to run away. The last great leader of the Southern Cheyenne was dead, and the power of the Dog Soldier fraternities finally broken for all time. The following day, during mopping up operations, another army scout made his reputation as an 'Indian fighter' by shooting Two Crows off Tall Bull's distinctive horse. The name of the scout was William Cody, soon to be known across America as 'Buffalo Bill'.

Notes

1. *Annual Report of the Secretary of War, 1867*, (Washington DC, Government Printing Office, 1868)

2. *Sherman to Sheridan*, 10 May 1868

3. A. Banfield, *The Mammals of Canada*, (Toronto: University of Toronto Press, 1974), 34

4. W. Hornaday, *The Extermination of the American Bison, with a Sketch of its Discovery and Life History*, (1889, reprint: Washington DC: Smithsonian Institution Press, 2002), 6

5. Stanley Hoig, Battle of the Washita: The Sheridan-Custer Indian Campaign of 1867–69, (Lincoln: University of Nebraska Press, 1976), 52

6. *Sherman to John Sherman*, 23 September 1868

6

DEATH IN THE LAVA BEDS

'All you boys what ain't dead had better go on home. We don't want to kill you all in one day!'

Scarface Charley, Modoc leader

Major General Edward Canby realised too late that he was a dead man. Within seconds of the guns being drawn from their hiding places beneath the blankets that the Indians had wrapped around themselves bullets ploughed into the peace commissioners, sending them reeling. Two bullets tore through Canby's skull, spraying blood and brains onto the white canvas walls of the meeting tent. A Modoc warrior bent over the General's prostrated body and quickly drew a razor sharp hunting knife across his throat, severing his windpipe. The meeting, convened on 11 April 1873, was supposed to have been a civilised affair to discover a settlement to constant conflict between the United States and a fierce but small tribe of Indians called the Modoc who inhabited the area around Tule Lake in Oregon Territory. The so-called Lava Bed War would witness a few dozen Indians consistently defeat a hugely superior American force, requiring a massive financial outlay by the United States to bring Modoc resistance to a bloody end.

The Modoc were a people of the Columbia Plateau region, a land of sagebrush covered lava plateaus, wooded mountains, lakes and rivers in the Pacific Northwest home to many different tribal groups. During the salmon run the Modoc fished the well-stocked rivers and they also migrated in small bands to hunt and forage, living in portable tents or earthen dug-out lodges at favourite sites such as Willow Creek on Lower Klamath Lake, the shores of Tule Lake and along Lost River in the present-day states of Oregon and California. The Modoc had first met a white man in the 1820s when a hardy trader working for the British Hudson's Bay Company named Peter Skene Ogden had established a small trading post close to the Klamath tribe who lived north of the Modoc and were their enemies. The entire region was largely ignored by the American government for another twenty years until another hardy pioneer adventurer named Lindsay Applegate led fourteen settlers along a new emigrant trail that he was cutting into Oregon Territory in 1846. Applegate's route was named the South Emigrant Trail, and it was a branch line of the more famous Oregon Trail that was the main route into the rich lands of the Pacific Northwest for thousands of eastern emigrants.

At this time migrants had simply passed through the Great Plains without pausing to settle on their way to Oregon or California, so conflict with the Plains Indians was largely avoided for a further decade. The South Emigrant Trail began near Fort Hall in Idaho and led to the Willamette Valley in Oregon, its purpose being to encourage settlers into western Oregon and to provide a secondary route in case of conflict between the United States and Britain over the status of Oregon Territory, both nations disputing exactly where the border line should be set between America and Canada. Applegate's party were the first white people to enter the strange Lava Beds as they explored eastwards and attempted to pass their wagons around the southern end of Tule Lake. The tortured black volcanic landscape defeated their best efforts, forcing Applegate to seek a route north of the lake. Once the South Emigrant Trail was open the Modoc began to have regular contact with white people, and the contacts soon became violent. It appears that the Modoc viewed the puny whites as a grand opportunity for enriching themselves by raiding the poorly protected wagon trains winding their way through Modoc and Klamath territory. The first raid occurred in 1847, and the Modoc were relatively strong, fielding several hundred warriors led by Old Chief Schonchin. Thorough in the destruction that they wrought, during one raid in September 1852 the Modoc killed sixty-two men, women and children out of sixty-five settlers travelling west, took two young girls captive (and later murdered them), with only one man managing the escape the slaughter and make it to Yreka in California to report the horrific loss of life[1]. Enraged local settlers swore revenge, and one called Jim Crosby organised a group of men who rode out to find the site of the massacre, bury the bodies, and then punish the Modoc. Although Crosby's posse skirmished with the Modoc, they proved to be elusive opponents, and it was not until 1856 that revenge was truly wrought when another settler named Ben Wright, a notorious Indian-hater, led a large party of armed men to Lost River. Wright's group ambushed a Modoc band and slaughtered fifty-two men, women and children in cold blood, equating to roughly ten percent of the entire Modoc nation. Following this, relations with the Modoc were to be permanently fractious, violent and intractable.

For the next twelve years fighting continued on and off and the Modoc had largely remained resistant to American efforts to make peace. However, in 1864 in the midst of the Civil War a council was convened to try to get the Modoc to move onto a big new reservation, and to live alongside other Pacific Northwest tribes such as the Klamath and Snake peoples. As usual, the impetus behind the negotiations was to remove the Indians from valuable land that could be turned over to white settlement. The new agency, called Klamath Reservation, was established by treaty, the Klamath and Snakes renouncing title to their land and moving peacefully onto the agency.

A Modoc leader named Kintpuash, but commonly known as Captain Jack, led the delegation that met with the commission, headed by Alfred B. Meacham, Superintendent of Indian Affairs in Oregon. Both sides deeply mistrusted the other, and the council achieved nothing. When Captain Jack and the other warriors espied soldiers moving up to the council place they panicked, fearing treachery, and immediately fled, leaving their wives and children behind. Meacham decided the matter then and there by ordering the troops to round up the terrified Modoc dependents and load them onto wagons. He issued instructions that they be immediately transported to the new reservation located in the Upper Klamath Valley. One woman, 'Queen' Mary, Captain Jack's sister, was told to go to her brother and persuade the warriors to move peacefully to the reservation without delay. When no soldiers followed Mary to the Modoc camp Captain Jack and his cohorts relaxed a little, and decided to go to the reservation where they would receive supplies, food, shelter and be reunited with their families. They settled at a place appropriately named Modoc Point, and it appeared to Meacham and the Americans that conflict had been avoided and the issue settled.

What the Americans underestimated was the degree of enmity that existed between the Modoc and the other tribes forced to live together on the new reservation. It was a common enough problem all across America. For centuries these tribal peoples had carved out for themselves territories and hunting areas through warfare and competition, and simply shoehorning these disparate peoples onto one patch of land only intensified their mutual dislike and distrust of each other.

The Klamath lost no time in starting to harass the Modoc on the reservation, running off their horses, exchanging shots with Modoc warriors, raiding camps, all undoubtedly designed to force the Modoc to relinquish their section of the reservation to the stronger and more numerous Klamath. The Modoc leaders knew that the harassment would only intensify, so they decided to protect their wives and children by packing up and moving to another part of the reservation. This did no good, as the Klamath followed the Modoc bands and continued to harass them, until Captain Jack and the other leaders lost patience with the whole idea of a reservation and led their people back to the Lost River and their traditional homeland in 1870, now full of white settlers.

American officials eventually woke up to the realisation that the Modoc and the Klamath would not be able to peacefully coexist, and Meacham recommended to the Commissioner of Indian Affairs in Washington DC that Captain Jack's band be given a separate reservation. As the wheels of bureaucracy began slowly to turn in the capital Meacham told Captain Jack to remain at Clear Lake out of harm's way, an instruction the Modoc leader immediately ignored. Parties of Modocs were soon found all over the Lost River region, harassing settlers who were beginning to put down roots on Modoc land. The settlers had no time for the Indians and Meacham's office was soon heavily petitioned, the settlers calling on the government to send the Modoc back to Klamath Reservation post haste. In such a case the sensibilities of local whites took precedence over the fortunes of a few hundred unwanted Indians, so Meacham requested military assistance to solve the crisis.

Meacham telegraphed Major General Edward Canby, commanding the Department of the Columbia, asking him to remove Captain Jack and his followers to Yainax on the reservation. Canby was wary of perhaps triggering another Indian war, and he forwarded Meacham's request to his superior commanding the whole continental Pacific region, Major General John Schofield. Canby recommended that one more peace overture should be made to the Modoc before the troops were sent in. Schofield agreed, and Canby dispatched Major Elmer Otis to attend a conference with Captain Jack at Lost River Gap (now Olene, Oregon) on 3 April 1872. Otis found Captain Jack and the other Modoc leaders to be in an ugly mood, and they flatly refused to return to the Klamath Reservation. The last peaceful avenue having been exhausted, on 12 April the Commissioner wired T.B. Odeneal, Superintendent of Indian Affairs in Oregon, ordering him to move the Modoc onto the reservation and to make sure that the Klamath did not further harass the newcomers as they had done before. Two days later Odeneal sent Ivan Applegate and L.S. Dyer to try to arrange another council with Captain Jack, but they were rebuffed. American patience was exhausted, and as the Modoc continued to provide a real threat to the growing white settlement of the region, the army would have to intervene and restore order. On 6 July Washington gave Odeneal permission to use force to remove the Modoc. Odeneal was a poor choice at such a critical juncture, 'a man who knew almost nothing of the background of the situation and had never met with Jack or the Modocs, was placed in charge of the job of getting Jack to leave Lost River.'[2]

Through the rest of the summer the civil servants dithered, worried about creating a conflict until they could sit on the fence no longer and had to act. On 28 November Major John Green, commanding at Fort Klamath, was asked by Odeneal to provide a force of troops sufficient to deal with Captain Jack's band '... peaceably if you possibly can, forcefully if you must.' Green dispatched Captain James Jackson and forty troopers of the 1st Cavalry to him the following day. Jackson and his company headed for Captain Jack's camp that was located a mile above present-day Stone Bridge, Oregon on Lost River.

When Captain Jack was confronted by the well-armed soldiers he became afraid. His warriors were few in number. An Indian scout translated Jackson's demand that the Modoc lay down their weapons. Captain Jack complied after some bad words were exchanged. When their leader placed his rifle upon the ground the other warriors began to follow suit; that was until a disagreement broke out between one of the grizzled warriors and a young army officer. The warrior, Scarface Charley, began shouting at Lieutenant Frazier A. Boutelle, who was commanding Company B, 1st Cavalry. Each man was soon bellowing at the other in languages the other could not understand, when suddenly both men drew their revolvers and fired. Both missed, but the sounds of gunshots had the Modoc warriors diving for their rifles, and the cavalrymen nervously triggering a ragged volley in their direction. The Modoc immediately began retreating towards the California border while Jackson ordered his men to let them go. One of Jackson's men was dead and seven others were wounded while two Modoc warriors had been slain and three others wounded and carried off the field.

The Modoc retreated as fast as they could towards the extraordinary landscape of the Lava Beds south of Tule Lake, digging in among the black rocks to create what would come to be known as 'The Stronghold.' During the retreat to the Stronghold warrior leader Hooker Jim took a party of his men to a nearby settlement and slaughtered eighteen whites on 29–30 November fuelling calls for the complete eradication of the Modoc by settlers across the region. Captain Jack had already boasted many times in the past that if the Americans warred on his people he would lead them to the Lava Beds and hold the soldiers off from there. The Modoc took advantage of natural features to create their Stronghold, utilising numerous lava ridges, cracks, depressions and caves. Fresh water was available from Tule Lake to the north, and the Modoc herded about one hundred head of cattle into the Stronghold to prevent starvation if they were besieged.

Once in the Lava Beds Captain Jack's band was joined by another small group led by Shacknasty Jim, giving a total Modoc population of just over one hundred women and children and only fifty-three warriors. Against this puny group would be ranged a huge force of soldiers, and it appeared that the campaign to chastise the Modoc would be very short indeed. But the army underestimated the terrain they would have to fight over, the advantages it gave to an entrenched and prepared enemy, and the fighting spirit of the individual Modoc warriors.

The army immediately began transferring units from across the Department of the Columbia to the south end of Tule Lake where two cantonments were speedily established. In the west at Van Brimmer's Ranch the overall commander of the 400-man force organised to defeat the Modoc, Lieutenant-Colonel Frank Wheaton, established his headquarters. The ranch, ten miles from the Stronghold, also contained Major John Green, who exercised command of the forces gathered there, while Captain Reuben Bernard took command of forces at the second cantonment located at Land's Ranch twelve miles to the east.

The forces at Van Brimmer's Ranch under Major Green's command consisted of the 21st Infantry under Major Edwin Mason, two companies of Oregon Militia commanded by John E. Ross, a company of California Volunteers led by Captain John V. Fairchild, and Company F, 1st Cavalry led by Captain David Perry. Artillery support was provided by Second Lieutenant W.H. Miller's two 12-pounder mountain howitzers. In the east at Land's Ranch Captain Bernard commanded a much smaller force consisting of Company B, 1st Cavalry led by Captain James Jackson and Company G under the command of Second Lieutenant John Kyle, supported by a single company of Klamath Scouts led by Dave Hill.[3]

Wheaton planned a converging attack on the Stronghold. Major Green, with the bigger and stronger force in the west, would make the main assault. Captain Bernard, with the eastern group, would move towards the Stronghold and act as a block to prevent any Modoc escaping. Both forces would act in concert and compress the Modoc into a small area south of the Stronghold, pinning them against Tule Lake. The two howitzers would provide fire support for Green's troops, with all members of the assaulting forces attacking on foot.

When the day of the assault dawned on 17 January 1873 a thick fog hung over the Stronghold and the Lava Beds like a death shroud, reducing visibility to only a few dozen yards. Among the black rocks Modoc warriors hunkered down with their rifles, waiting in silence, the fog deadening the sounds of the approaching soldiers. Major Green ordered his troops into skirmish order, placing several yards between each man to cover more ground, the 21st Infantry and the California Volunteers on the left and the Oregon Militia on the right of the line of advance. A detachment of the 21st and Company F, 1st Cavalry were arrayed in a defensive position before the howitzers. Captain Bernard in the east likewise formed his men into a long skirmish line, with Company B, 1st Cavalry and the Klamath Scouts on the left and Company G, 1st Cavalry on the right.[4] Bernard had no way of directly communicating with Green and coordinating his advance with the troops in the west, so three shots fired from Miller's howitzers would be the signal for a general advance on the Stronghold. The guns would then fall silent for fifteen minutes as a humanitarian gesture towards the Modoc, allowing them, if they chose to, to remove their women and children from the battle space.

At the gun line the howitzers were loaded and made ready. Green could see little to his immediate front beyond the long line of blue uniformed soldiers kneeling and waiting. He turned and nodded to Miller who immediately ordered his guns to open fire. The unearthly silence of the foggy morning was suddenly rudely shattered by the ear-splitting reports of the guns as they mouthed their high explosive shells into the impenetrable gloom. Bernard heard the reports and the dull crump of exploding shells somewhere among the Modoc position, and gave the order to advance. In the west Major Green did likewise, and the long line of men began to walk carefully through the difficult terrain, unnerved by not being able to see clearly their objective or their enemy. Among the rocks Modoc warriors bided their time. Miller informed Green that he could not continue to fire his howitzers in support of the attack as he could not see his fall of shot and feared hitting Bernard's men coming up from the east. Green agreed and joined his men who were walking gingerly towards the fog-shrouded objective, their rifles and carbines held at the port, the men ever so slightly bent over so as to minimise the target they presented.

For a mile and a half no Indians were sighted and no firing was heard. Green ordered Company F, 1st Cavalry to begin moving around the extreme right flank of the position in an effort to link up with Bernard's men coming from the east. It was at this point that gunfire broke out as Modoc warriors, observing the army's attempt to surround them, moved forward from their positions and opened a brisk and deadly fire into the exposed company. Casualties soon began to pile up, and the troops tried to press on in the teeth of the enemy fire, shooting as they went, but never once seeing a single Modoc. At 2pm Green's men were halted by a seemingly impassable deep crevasse in the rocks.

Bernard's troops managed to advance to within 500 yards of the Stronghold before the warriors defending that sector opened fire. The terrain in the east was flatter and less rock strewn, so in response to contact being made with the enemy Bernard ordered his men to charge. With a wild yell the troops loped forward about one hundred yards until they came to the crest of a deep gully similar to that which had halted Green's men in the west. The officers judged the gully too deep and too wide to cross and Bernard withdrew his men 150 yards under fire, ordering them to begin constructing crude defensive positions from the sharp volcanic rock that lay all around them. Modoc bullets zipped through the air as they feverishly improvised cover, while other slugs smashed into the rocks throwing razor-like shards in all directions.

Wheaton, with his headquarters group, had followed Green's men as they advanced. Wheaton could see that both of his advancing forces were pinned down and he decided to abandon the attempt to link up Green's and Bernard's men south of the Stronghold. Convening a hasty orders group, Wheaton and Green discussed their next move. Green suggested that the focus of the advance should be shifted to effecting a link-up along the lake shore, north of the Stronghold. Wheaton agreed, and fresh orders were relayed to Bernard by shouting them to him, as both forces were only separated from one another by a few hundred yards. Bernard immediately conferred with his subordinate officers, and within minutes they began ordering their companies to resume the advance. The problem for Bernard was the reluctance of most his soldiers to move from their prepared positions and place themselves once more into the teeth of the enemy's fire. Most simply refused to stand up and faced with this Bernard was forced to hold his position and draw the enemy's fire.

Green's force resumed the advance, moving along the north shore of Tule Lake, all except the Oregon Militia who found themselves stopped by another deep ravine. The California Volunteers, 21st Infantry and Company F, 1st Cavalry, moved behind the Stronghold and made it fifty yards north of the position before the furious Modoc poured down a hail of lead at them that forced the soldiers to hit the dirt. Green remained standing and tried to rally his men to press on with the advance but was wounded and was later awarded the Medal of Honor for his gallantry that day. Company F and half of the 21st Infantry managed to blunder through the Modoc fire and reached Bernard's embattled position, while the rest of Green's force remained pinned down.

Wheaton admitted defeat as darkness fell that evening, and throughout the next day the troops were withdrawn and the assault abandoned. The dead were left where they had fallen, allowing the Modoc to pilfer the corpses for more weapons and ammunition. Overall, the failed assault had cost the army thirty-seven killed and dozens wounded, while not a single Modoc warrior had died. Such was the nature of the terrain and the weather conditions that during the entire battle not a single soldier had even seen a Modoc.

Wheaton was relieved of his command and replaced by Colonel Alvan Gillem, who had previously fought Indians during the Seminole War in Florida. Reinforcements poured in from San Francisco, Nevada and Oregon, while the Oregon Militia and California Volunteers were sent home. The Modoc celebrated a great victory, and the defeat at the First Battle of the Stronghold forced the army to open new peace negotiations with them. Interior Secretary Columbus Delano appointed Alfred Meacham chairman of the new Peace Commission on 25 January 1874. General Canby would accompany the Commission as counsellor. On 19 February the Commission gathered at Fairchild's Ranch, west of the Lava Beds. A messenger was sent to Captain Jack asking him to come to the edge of the Lava Beds and meet John Fairchild and Bob Whittle, two local settlers. Captain Jack agreed to meet the Commission itself if they were accompanied by Judge Elijah Steele of Yreka. Steele had been kind to the Modoc in the past, and Captain Jack invited him to spend a night in the Stronghold during which the future was discussed in great detail. When Steele reported to the Commission the following day the news was not good. In the judge's opinion, Captain Jack intended to assassinate the members of the Commission. Meacham immediately wired this dark news to Delano in Washington DC, but Delano told Meacham to continue with negotiations regardless of the danger to the commissioners.

In April, Colonel Gillem established a camp two and a half miles west of the Stronghold at the edge of the Lava Beds. On 2 April the Commission and Captain Jack met for the first time at a point halfway between the Stronghold and Gillem's Camp. Jack's demands were straightforward and blunt. He wanted a complete pardon for all of the Modoc, the withdrawal of all American troops, and the right to select his own reservation. In reply, the commissioners proposed instead that Captain Jack and his followers go to a reservation selected by the government, and that all Modoc warriors implicated in the slaying of settlers should be handed over to the soldiers to stand trial for murder. Naturally, the meeting broke up without achieving anything.

Among the Modoc, dissention festered. Chief John Schonchin wanted to kill the commissioners, believing that their deaths would make the army go away. Captain Jack wanted peace, but in order not to lose his position of authority he agreed that if further negotiations proved fruitless he would kill the commissioners. On 5 April Captain Jack asked to meet Meacham. Another long meeting was convened at which the Modoc leader demanded the Lava Beds as a reservation. Another stalemate occurred. The only peace offered them was the peace of submission. As each location that the Modocs would accept was rejected by Canby, it became increasingly clear that the only reservation for them would be one they would share with the unfriendly Klamath. And that had no look of peace to the Modocs.'[5]

On 8 April Captain Jack asked to meet the Commission again, but a plot to kill the commissioners was discovered before the meeting and the members remained in Gillem's Camp under army protection. Incredibly, even though it was by now obvious that the Modoc planned an ambush, the religious representative in the group, the Reverend E. Thomas, insisted that they meet one last time to try and broker a peace deal. On the morning of 11 April the Commission, consisting of Canby, Meacham, Thomas and L.S. Dyer went to the meeting tent accompanied by two translators,

Frank and Toby Riddle. They were unarmed and no military escort went with them. In the tent they met with the Modoc leadership, consisting of Captain Jack, John Schonchin, Boston Charley, Black Jim, Bogus Charley, and Hooker Jim. Discussions got under way and they were as animated and heated as before, though on this occasion the commissioners noticed to their alarm that the Modoc were carrying concealed firearms poking out from beneath their blankets. Canby told Captain Jack that unfortunately the Commission could not meet his demands until word had come from Washington. John Schonchin angrily demanded that they should be given Hot Creek for a reservation, while Captain Jack got to his feet and began pacing around. He signalled through the tent flap, and suddenly a pair of Modoc warriors carrying rifles named Brancho and Slolux jumped up from their hiding places and began to run towards the tent. Captain Jack pulled out his revolver, thumbed back the hammer and shot Canby through the head. Thomas fell to the floor mortally wounded, and Meacham was also shot and severely wounded. Dyer and Riddle ran for their lives at the first shots and survived, while Captain Jack and his companions set about finishing off the other commissioners, one cutting Canby's throat. Quick thinking on the part of the two interpreters undoubtedly saved Meacham's life, as they yelled out 'Soldiers are coming!' Captain Jack and his companions ran for the Stronghold, panicked into believing that troops were upon them and Meacham was spared.

The murders of Canby and Thomas spelled the absolute end of any American efforts to make peace with the Modoc. The attack on the Commission was viewed as typical Indian deceit, and the army officers planned another offensive to permanently destroy the Modoc holding out in the Stronghold. On 15 April Colonel Gillem began a general assault. Gillem's troops advanced on the Stronghold from the west while another large force advanced from Hospital Rock under the command of Lieutenant-Colonel Edward Mason, formerly a major commanding 21st Infantry during the first battle. Hard fighting followed throughout the day, the troops forming defensive positions as darkness fell. The offensive was resumed at first light on the 16th. The Modoc fire was accurate and heavy. The breakthrough came in the evening when the troops managed to cut the Modoc off from their fresh water supply at Tule Lake. Gillem spent the night preparing his dispositions for a dawn assault on the 17th, but when the attackers mounted a final charge they discovered that the Stronghold was empty of Modoc warriors. Earlier that morning the Modoc had quietly given up their positions and exited through the rocks, passed silently through the army lines and made their escape. The Second Battle of the Stronghold had cost the army seven killed and thirteen wounded, and once again the canny Modoc had not lost a single warrior in the fighting.

Captain Jack and his followers began moving southeast from the Lava Beds. In an effort to locate the Modocs, Gillem sent out patrols of cavalry and Indian scouts. On learning that the Modocs were in the lava flows south of the Stronghold, he sent a patrol of sixty-eight men drawn from the 12th Infantry and the 4th Artillery towards a place called Sand Butte (now Hardin Butte). The patrol was under the command of Captain Evan Thomas of the 4th Artillery and Lieutenant Thomas Wright of the 12th Infantry; Gillem had instructed them to establish an observation post and evaluate the butte as an artillery position for bombarding the Modocs' suspected hiding place.

The soldiers slowly covered the four miles from Gillem's camp and the patrol arrived at the base of Sand Butte. As the men broke ranks for lunch and a break, a group of twenty-two Modoc under the command of Scarfaced Charley ambushed the command. In forty-five minutes of carnage two thirds of the troops were killed or wounded, including both Thomas and Wright. Most of the survivors were men who fled in panic when the shooting started. Charley ended the carnage by calling down to the men sarcastically, 'All you boys what ain't dead had better go on home. We don't want to kill you all in one day!'

A new operation was begun at once to try to locate and entrap the Modoc in May 1874. With the assassination of Canby command of the Department of the Columbia was given to Brigadier General Jefferson C. Davis, and he immediately assumed field command of the forces arrayed against Captain Jack. US cavalry arrived at a place they named Sore Ass Lake, and finding no water renamed it Dry Lake. They were tired and their horses needed attention after riding hard to try to locate the fleeing Modoc, so they made camp and rested, not realising that Captain Jack and his companions were much closer than they realised.

At dawn on the 10 May a small group of Modoc warriors crept silently up to the slumbering cavalry encampment. They levelled their rifles towards the sleeping men and opened up a fusillade of shots that sent the soldiers reeling from their blankets and searching wildly for boots, carbines and gun belts. Confusion reined for a few moments until experienced officers and NCOs restored order among the troopers and began to react to the threat.

Two groups of Modoc was visible; the small group of warriors attacking the camp, and a larger group visible atop some bluffs that overlooked the soldiers camp. With the cavalry were the mounted Warm Springs Indian Scouts, who were detailed to cut around the firing warriors and outflank them. In the meantime the cavalry mounted up and charged to the foot of the bluffs ready to thunder up to the crest and defeat the Modoc. However, many soldiers hesitated as rifle bullets cracked through the trees around them, and it appeared as though indecision was spreading through the ranks. This was quickly arrested when 1st Sergeant Thomas Kelley bellowed out in his best parade ground voice 'God damn it, lets charge!' With a crazed yell the troopers and their mounts crashed up the bluffs as the Indians retreated as fast as they could down the reverse slopes, routed. The retreating Modoc were harried for four miles until the cavalry gave up, exhausted and desperately needing water.

The consequences of the Battle of Dry Lake were enormous for the Modoc. A single warrior, Ellen's Man, had been killed during the fighting, but Hooker Jim, Bogus Charley and Scarface Charley collectively blamed Captain Jack for his death and broke away from the band with their followers. Towards the end of May Bogus Charley and Hooker Jim surrendered to Davis's forces on the promise of immunity from prosecution for the murders of the peace commissioners and white settlers. In return for immunity both leaders agreed to help the army track down and capture Captain Jack and his followers. On 4 June Captain Jack was cornered and captured and the Modoc War was over. Retribution followed swiftly.

Davis made immediate preparations to execute the leaders of Captain Jack's band but was prevented from doing so by an order from the War Department. Washington wanted the Indians given a fair trial before they were killed, and not shot out of hand by soldiers. The Modoc were made prisoners of war and transported to Fort Klamath. Shortly after their arrival Captain Jack, John Schonchin, Black Jim, Boston Charley, Brancho and Slolux were charged with the murders of Canby and Thomas and placed on trial for their lives. On 8 July all six were found guilty and sentenced to death. The trial papers were sent to President Ulysses S. Grant at the White House, and Grant upheld the death sentence for Captain Jack, John Schonchin, Black Jim and Boston Charley. Brancho and Slolux had their death sentences commuted to life imprisonment and they were sent to Alcatraz. On 3 October the condemned men were hanged at Fort Klamath. President Grant ordered that the remaining members of Captain Jack's band, numbering thirty-nine men, sixty-four women and sixty children be treated as military prisoners of war. They were transported to the dreaded Indian Territory and forced to live on the Quaw Paw Reservation. They were forbidden to leave for thirty-six years, until finally in 1909 the American government relaxed its rules and allowed some to move to Oregon and live on the Klamath Reservation.

It has been estimated that if the United States had granted Captain Jack's original request for a separate reservation away from their tormentors, the Klamath, the total cost would have been $20,000. The Modoc War, created because of American bureaucratic intransigence and a lack of understanding of intertribal enmity, eventually cost the United States over $4,000,000 and the lives of eighty-three soldiers, civilians and Indian scouts.

Notes

1. *Named Campaigns — Indian Wars*, United States Army Center for Military History, accessed 18 December 2007
2. Keith A. Murray, The Modocs and their War, (Norman: University of Oklahoma Press, 1967)
3. Annual Report of the Commissioner of Indian Affairs 1873, (Washington DC, Government Printing Office, 1874)
4. Ibid.
5. Albert Britt, Great Indian Chiefs: A Study of Indian Leaders in the Two Hundred Year Struggle to Stop the White Advance, (Ayer Company Publishers (Facsimile), 1969)

7

SON OF THE MORNING STAR

'Let us bury our dead and flee from this rotting atmosphere.'
Captain Walter Clifford, 7th Infantry
The Little Bighorn, 27 June 1876

Lieutenant-Colonel George Armstrong Custer was lying where he fell, naked except for his socks and the instep from one of his boots. The sun beat down on his sun-blackened corpse as he had lain like spoiled meat upon the dry, coarse grass of the Little Bighorn valley until the relief column had found him. Known as 'Son of the Morning Star' to the Cheyenne since he had sacked Black Kettle's village on the Washita River in 1868 and *Pahuska* to the Lakota Sioux, the warriors of both nations had taken their time with the 'Boy General' during the great battle beside the river in June 1876.

Custer was the most famous military officer of his generation and adored by the public. Born in Ohio in 1839 to a local blacksmith of Hessian German descent, Custer had graduated almost bottom of his class at West Point not through lack of intelligence but disinterest in academia. A man of action, Custer's meteoric rise from junior subaltern to brigadier general at the age of only twenty-three during the Civil War was astonishing, but based on his abilities as the finest cavalry commander in the Union Army. He finished the war a major general of volunteers. Custer had reverted to his substantive rank of captain in 1866 and been promoted to lieutenant-colonel in 1867 on assuming command of the 7th Cavalry. Hungry to get his general's stars back through military victories, Custer had been an aggressive Frontier commander keen to get to grips with the Indians.

Now that career was over. The thirty-six year old Custer had been killed by gunfire during the closing stages of his 'Last Stand', a bullet smashing through his brain after entering near his left ear. Another had struck him in the left breast, beneath the heart, after first passing through his raised right forearm as he was in the act of firing his Webley revolver. Death had been instantaneous. After death the Indians had stripped him, cut off one of his fingers, and Cheyenne women had jammed sewing awls into his ears so that he might hear better the Cheyenne warnings not to make war upon them again. A warrior had jammed the shaft of an arrow up Custer's penis, and another had slashed his left thigh to the bone. Numerous arrows protruded from his body. Around the famous Custer were 210 of his officers and men. Custer's Last Stand entered legend and Custer with it, becoming the poster boy of the campaign to avenge the 'massacre' on the banks of the Little Bighorn. The Lakota Sioux and their Northern Cheyenne allies would be made to feel the wrath of a nation horrified by the catastrophe that had befallen their favourite son in the centennial year of the Republic.

Less than two years earlier Custer had been tasked with precipitating the end of Sioux dominance over their territory. Red Cloud had achieved what he thought was eternal peace from American interference in Lakota lands when he had won his war in 1868 and forced the army to abandon their forts along the Bozeman Trail. However, the United States was determined to return once they had pacified the southern plains, and return they did in force.

In 1874 the Black Hills Expedition had trooped unchallenged and unnoticed into the spiritual homeland of the Lakota peoples, and returned crying 'Gold from the grass roots down!' It had been known since 1859 that gold deposits existed in the Hills, but Custer's 1874 expedition confirmed that the deposits were worthy of further investigation, Custer calling them 'very important and of promising richness.' Within a few short weeks 15,000 miners were digging up the Black Hills, all searching for the yellow metal the Indians said drove the white man mad. The Sioux responded by asking the Americans to remove the miners who were in violation the 1868 Fort Laramie Treaty negotiated by Red Cloud. Instead, the Americans offered to buy the Black Hills from the Sioux.

By autumn 1875, a crisis point had been reached. The Indians would not sell the Hills, and the gold prospectors would not voluntarily depart from them. President Grant had no intention of committing electoral suicide by standing by the terms of the Fort Laramie Treaty and removing the white interlopers from Sioux land. On 3 November, at a meeting at the White House, Grant, under the advice of Interior Secretary Zachariah Chandler,

Secretary of War William W. Belknap and Commissioner of Indian Affairs Edward P. Smith, decided to force those Sioux in the 'Unceded Lands' onto the reservations and to give unofficial approval to white exploitation of the Black Hills. The Unceded Lands were the vast land holdings to the west of the Great Sioux Reservation which the Indians had been permitted to continue to hunt over and camp upon in the 1868 treaty. In response, Sioux war parties raided the Gallatin River Valley and the upper Yellowstone River in Montana Territory, also in violation of the Treaty. The government's swift response to this opportunity was to issue an ultimatum to all Sioux still off the reservations to report to their agencies for counting no later than 31 January 1876. The Sioux were in their winter camps and largely unable to trek to the reservations, and many bands never even heard about the ridiculous order until after the ultimatum had expired.

On 18 January the Indian Bureau embargoed the movement of guns and ammunition to the Lakota Sioux for hunting purposes, creating further tension. Over 3,000 Sioux remained off their reservations in the Unceded Lands, and these so-called 'Winter Roamers' were shortly joined by thousands more Lakota and Northern Cheyenne who abandoned their agencies, fed up with food shortages and a degrading existence. Sitting Bull increasingly became one of the main draws encouraging Lakota to leave the reservations, his absolute refusal to sell his land and go quietly into history gaining widespread respect among Indians and widespread hatred among whites. 'If the Great Spirit desired me to be a white man he would have made me so in the first place,' said Sitting Bull. 'It is not necessary for eagles to be crows.' Crazy Horse was equally emphatic, stating 'One does not sell the earth upon which the people walk.'

On 1 February the problem of compelling the recalcitrant and unruly Indians into going to their reservations was handed to the War Department. Major General Philip H. Sheridan, commander of the Military Division of the Missouri, was placed in charge of operations and he began marshalling the small number of units under his command for a spring campaign. Sheridan instructed his subordinate commanders to 'strike the unfriendlies' hard.

The plan was deceptively simple. Three columns of troops and Indian scouts, numbering in total about 2,400 soldiers, would converge on the hostiles' homeland, . The Indians would be forced to fight a series of engagements on the army's terms and would be defeated and captured or killed. The three column commanders were Brigadier General George Crook, Brigadier General Alfred Terry, and Colonel John Gibbon.

Lieutenant-Colonel Custer and the 7th Cavalry formed the largest contingent of Terry's column. Known as the Powder River Expedition or the Centennial Campaign, few in the east believed that the Sioux and their allies would be able to withstand such a concentrated assault by a modern, well-armed military force. The generals did, however, face some very big challenges. The country they were invading with a relatively small number of men was enormous, as big as western Europe. No proper communications system existed which meant that commanders in the field could not coordinate the movements of the three columns once they were on the march. Supply issues would also plague the expedition, especially so since their Indian adversaries were extremely mobile and wary of engaging the army in a conventional battle forcing the army columns into long, weary pursuits. The Sioux and Cheyenne would also prove capable of fielding a very large number of warriors who were prepared to fiercely resist, numbering in excess of 2,000 men.

Terry was a wealthy lawyer, a bachelor who sported heavy chin whiskers and a mild and sensitive character who was on his first field campaign. Terry's column would ride east from Fort Abraham Lincoln in present-day North Dakota. The second column, which would march east from Fort Ellis, Montana, was commanded by John Gibbon, the testy and conservative colonel of the 7th Infantry known as 'Old Poppycock' after his liberal use of the expression. The third column would march north from Fort Fetterman in Wyoming Territory under George Crook. Crook was considered one of the more able officers out west, but he was plagued by eccentricity and often erratic thinking. Crook marched out on 1 March and straight into the teeth of a blizzard. Sixteen days of riding through sub-zero temperatures had severely eroded his men's morale, but on 17 March a screening force of half-frozen cavalrymen numbering ten companies stumbled across a large Northern Cheyenne and Oglala Sioux village near the Powder River in Montana.

The village consisted of 105 lodges quietly nestled in the snow-blanketed countryside, and contained prominent Cheyenne Chief Two Moons. Commanding the attack force was Colonel Joseph J. Reynolds, 3rd Cavalry. Reynolds, although only fifty-four years old, was in his own words 'an old man'. He rode wearing a truss because of a rupture and suffered from a problem with his testicles making it uncomfortable for him to sit in the saddle. He wore dentures that also caused him discomfort. The last place he should have been was leading troops through an arctic wilderness of snow and ice. Reynolds organised his strike force into three two-company squadrons.

Captain Anson Mills led companies E and M from the 3rd Cavalry; Captain Henry E. Noyes companies I and K from the 2nd Cavalry; and Captain Alexander Moore Company E, 2nd Cavalry and Company F, 3rd Cavalry. The three captains pushed their men forward through the deep snow, the wind blowing hard in their faces. They halted at 2.30am and sat shivering and cursing on their horses while scouts tried to locate the village again in the dark.

The village was eventually pinpointed in between high ground in a forested area on a bend in the river. Reynolds ordered Noyes' squadron to assault the village from the south, one company under Lieutenant Egan storming the village while the other company would run off the Indian pony herd. Moore's squadron was ordered to dismount and take up covering positions on bluffs overlooking the village from the west. They would provide fire support to Noyes. Mills' squadron was told merely to assist Moore on the bluffs.

The attack went in at 3.30am. 'Women screamed,' recalled Cheyenne warrior Wooden Leg, 'children cried for their mothers. Old people tottered and hobbled away to get out of the reach of the bullets singing among the lodges.'[1] Journalist Robert Stahorn, riding with the troops, wrote: 'With the savages swarming out of their tepees and scattering almost under our feet, we fired right and left at their retreating forms.'[2] According to Stahorn's report, the army happily shot fleeing men, women and children in the back.

Moore's squadron never made it into position atop the bluffs, and instead a force of enraged Sioux and Cheyenne warriors opened a brisk fire from the hills. Noyes managed to run off the Indian pony herd, but then incredibly stopped for a coffee break, dismounting his company. The companies entered the village late, and in small numbers. When the Indians realised that only a few dozen soldiers were inside the village they rallied and returned to fight. 'The Indians, seeing the paucity of our numbers,' recalled Second Lieutenant John G. Bourke, 'regained confidence and rushed forward to cut us off.'[3] Volley fire kept the warriors at a distance.

Reynolds panicked in the face of unexpectedly determined resistance, and he ordered the village burned and his companies to withdraw while under sporadic Indian rifle fire. Many of Reynolds subordinates thought he had lost his nerve. 'We practically abandoned the victory to the savages,' wrote a disgusted Bourke afterwards. Much of the Indian property was overlooked in the sudden withdrawal, and dead soldiers (and perhaps a few wounded) were abandoned on the field. The Indians also managed to recapture most of their ponies. Reynolds led his column away from the Powder River to rejoin Crook's main force, and the harsh weather conditions caused further casualties among his men including sixty-six troopers who required treatment for frostbite. Crook and Sheridan were furious with Reynolds for his 'shamefully disgraceful' actions, and the Colonel and his subordinates were deemed militarily incompetent.

The Indian survivors of Reynold's botched attack trudged for three days through deep snow to find sanctuary with Crazy Horse's Oglala band. 'After a few days the two bands together went northward' said Cheyenne Kate Big Head, 'and found the Hunkpapa Sioux, where Sitting Bull was the chief.'[4] The bands decided to stay together throughout the spring and summer hunting season, largely as a protection against the soldiers known to be hunting for them. In the meantime Crook aborted his march due to a lack of supplies coupled with the brutal weather conditions and returned to Fort Fetterman.

Gibbon's column trooped out of Fort Ellis on 30 March and began heading east. Gibbon's was the smallest of the three columns, consisting of four companies of the 2nd Cavalry and five companies of the 7th Infantry totalling 450 men. In addition, Gibbon had two Gatling machine guns and a Napoleon gun (a light artillery piece) and twenty-five Indian scouts and attached civilians. General Terry's departure was delayed by the weather and a lack of forage for the column's horses and eventually he left Fort Lincoln on 17 May, followed by Crook again on 29 May. Terry's column consisted of twelve companies of Custer's 7th Cavalry and three and a half companies of the 6th and 17th Infantry Regiments totalling 925 soldiers. Three Gatling machine guns, forty Arikara scouts and 200 civilians pushed the strength of the column up to 1,140 men. Finally, Crook had been given an opportunity to improve on his first failed expedition against the Sioux and Cheyenne, and would take out the strongest column of all numbering 1,350 men. Fifteen companies from the 2nd and 3rd Cavalry, five companies of mounted infantry and 260 Crow and Shoshone scouts constituted Crook's potent force.

By early May the hard winter was a memory, and the plains had come alive once again, turning green as fresh spring grass covered thousands of square miles of rolling prairie. The Indians had struck their winter camps and the bands had begun to move west towards Rosebud Creek in Montana. This placed the hostile Indians on a collision course with an unsuspecting Crook, who on the morning of 17 June had halted his weary column astride the upper Rosebud. Around 1,000 warriors led by Crazy Horse and a dozen other Sioux chiefs opened fire on Crook's men at 8.30am. The firing was very heavy from both sides, but few casualties were caused. Five companies of the 3rd Cavalry under Lieutenant-Colonel William B. Royall were cut off from the rest of Crook's command by the Indians' buffalo hunting tactics and narrowly avoided being destroyed. Crook decided that to take Indian pressure off his column he should strike at the Sioux village that he believed was located on the Rosebud's nearby Dead Canyon. Crook's intelligence was faulty, for the warriors had ridden fifteen miles from Sitting Bull's village. Captain Anson Mills was dispatched at 10.30am with three 3rd Cavalry companies into Dead Canyon, followed by Captain Henry Noyes and five 2nd Cavalry companies as support. The two officers discovered no village, and Crook realised that he would be unable to support them if they attacked the main Indian camp as he had wounded who could not be moved. At 12.30pm Crook ordered Mills and Noyes to abandon their search.

Finally, at 2.30pm, after six hours of continuous fighting, the Sioux broke off contact with Crook and faded away. The column's ammunition supply had been seriously eroded, Crook's men having fired off over 25,000 rounds, but managing to kill only thirty-six Sioux warriors. Crook's own casualties amounted to ten dead and twelve wounded. Crook claimed a victory, but Sheridan considered the Rosebud a 'victory ... barren of results.' Another officer wrote that the column had 'little pride on our achievement.' The Sioux also believed that they had been victorious, and it emboldened them considerably. Crook was forced once again to quit the field and return to base for supplies. Importantly, due to the primitive communications available at the time, neither Gibbon or Terry were aware of Crook's reverse at the Rosebud, and both officers continued to advance towards where they believed Sitting Bull's camp to be.

On 21 June Custer, acting as a forward screen for Terry, linked up with Gibbon's column on the Yellowstone River. Terry's column joined with Gibbon's and continued to advance as a single unit with the 7th Cavalry in the vanguard. Terry's Arikara scouts informed him that the Sioux and their allies were now camped somewhere in the valley of the Little Bighorn River, a tributary of the Bighorn. Terry immediately ordered Gibbon to march up the Yellowstone and block the Bighorn at its mouth. Meanwhile, Custer and the 7th Cavalry, as Terry's most mobile unit, were to hurry up the Rosebud, and if they could locate the hostile Indians they were to attack them from the south and drive them like buffalo towards Gibbon to destroy. Terry, not knowing what lay ahead of him, gave Custer vague orders that Custer would exploit to his own benefit when the time came. They read, in part:

> It is, of course, impossible to give you any definite instructions in regard to this move [up the Rosebud], and were it not impossible to do so the Department Commander [Terry] places too much confidence in your zeal, energy and ability to wish to impose upon you precise orders which might hamper your action when nearly in contact with the enemy.[5]

As Custer mounted his regiment and prepared to leave the main column Gibbon called out to him, 'Now Custer, don't be greedy, but wait for us.' Custer turned in his saddle and shouted back, 'No, I will not.'

The orders Terry had given to Custer allowed the 'Boy General' a great degree of latitude in their interpretation, and Custer intended to exploit Terry's confidence in him the moment an opportunity for restoring his battered prestige appeared. Before the campaign Custer had testified before a Congressional committee in Washington DC concerning corruption in the Interior Department and his damning evidence had led him to run afoul of President Grant. It was only through Custer's powerful military friends that his career had been saved and he was given command of the 7th. Now in the field, Custer was afraid that the Indians might move camp again and disappear before he had a chance to attack them.

Custer lived up to his nickname in the 7th of 'Hard Ass' as he pushed his column along under a merciless summer sun that burned and parched the troopers and exhausted their horses. Twelve miles on the first day was followed by thirty-three on the second and twenty-eight on the third, eventually bringing Custer to a fresh and broad Indian trail heading off towards the Little Bighorn River. The trail was fresh because about 3,000 Indians had recently passed over it heading for Sitting Bull's huge encampment. They were angry at the continued white invasion of the sacred Black Hills and had abandoned their agencies to seek out the hostiles.

On the evening of 24 June Sitting Bull had made his way up to a ridge from where he could see the massive village laid out along the river and the Bighorn Valley beyond. He had made offerings to the Great Spirit and prayed for the protection of his people. The next day Custer's Crow scouts finally had the village in sight from a distant hilltop known as The Lookout. Custer joined them, but even with the aid of binoculars he could not see any Indians or tepees. The Crow warned him that there were enough

Indians down in the valley to fight for several days, but Custer laughed off the warning, saying, 'I guess we'll get through them in one day.' Custer was more concerned that the hostiles may have spotted the approach of his regiment and would scatter, robbing him of his victory, so impatiently he gave the order to attack immediately.

There has been much subsequent criticism of Custer regarding the tactics he employed before and during the battle. Custer, in fact, fell back on his previous Civil War experience and deployed his regiment in a textbook pivot-manoeuvring force-reserve formation. He had successfully used this tactic against Indians at the Battle of the Washita in 1868. Second-in-command Major Marcus A. Reno with three companies was ordered to advance up the Little Bighorn valley and attack the village from the east, providing Custer's pivot. Reno would hold the enemy in place by gunfire and movement so that the warriors would batter against his battalion while Custer, with five companies, would swing northwest across the top of the village before sweeping south into the Indian encampment, providing the manoeuvring force. Custer would launch a determined attack against the enemy's flank and rear. The Indians would then be crushed between Custer and Reno and defeated. Captain William Benteen with three companies was ordered to sweep the badlands to the south of the river for any Indians, providing Custer with flank protection and the reserve, which is held until it can be deployed as the situation demands. Captain Thomas McDougall with one company would protect the slow-moving pack train as it closed up to the battle, and was a further addition to the reserve. The plan was simple, but the only problem that Custer faced was a lack of any field intelligence before he committed his troops to battle. No scouting had been conducted, and so he had no idea of how many Indian warriors his men would be facing or the extent of the village. It was perhaps typical of the disdain Custer and other officers had for Indian fighting abilities that a thorough reconnaissance was not attempted. No-one suspected that the 7th Cavalry was going to be facing the largest concentration of warriors ever seen on the plains.

The Indian village was truly enormous, containing upwards of 1,000 tepees and about 7,000 men, women and children, including perhaps 2,000 warriors. The camp had been established fifteen miles from the mouth of the Little Bighorn River on level grass-covered flats above the surrounding prairie. It was tucked in behind bluffs that rose 300 feet above the river. A drop in the valley floor meant that the village was only visible at the last moment from a south-easterly approach, the direction from which

Reno's battalion was riding. Closest to Reno's point of assault were 260 lodges of Hunkpapa Sioux under the leadership of chiefs Gall, Crow King, Two Moons and Sitting Bull, who was also the de facto leader of the Sioux inside the whole village. Camped with the Hunkpapa were twenty-five lodges of Yanktonnai and Santee Sioux from the east.

The next section of the village contained 240 lodges of Oglala Sioux under chiefs Big Road, He Dog and Crazy Horse. Next door stood 150 Minneconjou Sioux tepees under the leadership of chiefs Lame Deer, Hump (or High-Backbone) and Fast Bull, and then 110 lodges of Sans Arc Sioux under Spotted Eagle and Fast Bear. Next, a combined circle of Blackfoot Sioux, Brule and Two Kettle tepees completed the Lakota section of the camp. At the northern head of the camp stood 120 lodges of Northern Cheyenne under several prominent chieftains including Dirty Moccasins, Old Bear, Crazy Head, Lame White Man, Old Man Coyote and Last Bull. Kill Eagle, a Sioux warrior, said there were so many people in the camp that 'the Indians there [were] as thick as maggots on a carcass.'

Reno took the lead with his three companies in extended order as they advanced towards the eastern end of the village. Reno rode with a small headquarters staff including his assistant adjutant-general Lieutenant Benny Hodgson and itinerary officer Second Lieutenant George 'Nick' Wallace. Company A was commanded by Captain James 'Mitchie' Moylan, Company G by Lieutenant Donald McIntosh and Company M by the experienced officer and crack shot Captain Thomas 'Tucker' French, who had been promoted from the ranks many years earlier. Custer's battalion turned north and crossed the river and eventually disappeared out of sight on high ground.

Reno ordered his battalion to attack the village, and with bugles sounding, the three companies charged across the low-lying open ground, the Indians slow to react to the sudden and unexpected appearance of soldiers. The Indians, in fact, were caught completely by surprise, Chief Low Dog later recalling: 'I did not believe it. I thought it was a false alarm. I did not think it possible that any white men would attack us, so strong as we were.' The village was slumbering after a huge scalp dance the previous night to celebrate their victory at the Rosebud three days before. South of the village on bench land the Indians' 20,000 ponies grazed contentedly, while people slept or bathed in the river. Women and a few warriors were out digging turnips when Reno's charging troopers were first spotted. Chief Red Horse of the Minneconjou recalled: 'Suddenly one of the women attracted my attention to a cloud of dust rising a short distance from the camp.' Cheyenne chief Two Moons was surprised when 'Sioux horsemen came rushing into camp shouting "Soldiers come! Plenty white soldiers!"'.[6] 'It was somewhere past the middle of the afternoon and all of us were having a good time,' recalled Cheyenne Kate Big Head. 'We found our women friends bathing in the river and joined them. Other groups ... were playing in the water ... Two Sioux boys came running toward us. They were shouting, "Soldiers are coming!" We heard shooting. We hid in the brush.'[7]

Reno's battalion got to within 500 yards of the nearest lodge circles when hundreds of mounted and dismounted warriors began pouring out of the village and laying down a withering fire that halted the charge. Second Lieutenant Charles A. Varnum, Custer's supervisor of scouts who was attached to Reno's battalion, was shocked. 'We observed a number of Indian tepees, and as we worked out toward the left, we could see yet more ... there were certainly more Indians than I ever saw together before.' Reno ordered his men to dismount and form skirmish lines. Buglers blew calls and sergeants bellowed out the order 'Dismount and prepare to fight on foot!' One in five soldiers was detailed as a horse-holder, and the cavalry mounts were taken back out of range of the fighting.

Reno's decision to halt his battalion before he reached the village gave the Indians precious time to grab their weapons and run and fetch their horses from the huge pony herds. Many of the 7th Cavalry troopers were raw recruits, and equally raw riders. When Reno suddenly halted his charge at the village, several soldiers continued on into the tepee circles on uncontrollable mounts. Private George Smith of Company M was dragged from his horse and killed in the village. Private Roman Rutten was more fortunate, galloping through part of the village before managing to regain control of his horse and ride safely back to his company. Private John Meier's horse followed Rutten's, and Meier came through the village wildly firing his revolver at the circling Indians, in the process killing Hunkpapa Sioux Chief Gall's entire family. Meier then regained control of his mount and rode to safety. Another private, Henry Turley, was not so lucky, and he was dragged off his horse and butchered by the infuriated Indians.

Reno's three companies deployed into skirmish order at 3.15pm, which meant there was about five yards between each trooper on the line, and opened up a continuous and heavy fire against the hundreds of warriors beginning to emerge from a ravine in front of the village. Reno had ninety-three men fighting on the line, with a further thirty-one acting as horse-holders in the rear. Shortly afterwards, dozens of mounted warriors began to infiltrate around Reno's left flank. Gunfire rippled along the skirmish line, as the commands of officers and shouts of NCOs mingled in the smoky air with the screams and taunts of the Indians, who were still emerging in large and seemingly limitless numbers from the ravine. In the village, the many different chiefs were trying to organise a response to Reno's attack, Minneconjou Chief Red Horse recalled that:

> We came out of the council lodge and talked in all directions. The Sioux mount their horses, take guns, and go fight the soldiers. Women and children mount horses and go, meaning to get out of the way.

Reno managed to advance his companies about 100 yards, but could not go further as he began to worry seriously about his exposed flanks. The Indian fire was getting heavier, Private William Slaper of Company M recalling: 'I remember that I ducked my head and tried to dodge bullets which I could hear whizzing through the air.' Lieutenant Varnum recalled the Indian warriors' tactics as they came through the billowing gun smoke and dust haze to engage the skirmish line: 'As a rule, the Indians fired from their ponies; they were just scampering around us and pumping those Winchester rifles into us as fast as they could.' Captain French ordered 1st Sergeant John Ryan to take ten men off the skirmish line and form a mini-skirmish position in thick woods located fifty yards to the east. Ryan returned shortly afterwards reporting the woods clear of Indians, so French had the battalion's horses moved there, freeing up more men for the gun line. Reno thus far had given a good account of himself, walking coolly about the rear of the skirmish line, encouraging his men and firing his revolver at the Indians. French and Lieutenant Hodgson did the same, calling on the men to keep calm, mark their targets before they fired and keep down, as the Indians were returning a considerable fire themselves. However, the men soon began to run short of ammunition as they blasted away, frantically working the breeches on their single-shot Model 1873 .45–50 calibre Springfield carbines, and men were forced to come off the line and run to retrieve shells from reserve ammunition packs located inside their saddle bags.

Reno was informed that the Sioux were infiltrating the woods northeast of the skirmish line by swimming the river. Hodgson took command of the line while Reno went to investigate with Lieutenant McIntosh and a platoon from Company G. In the meantime Captain Moylan ordered Varnum to move the battalion's horses from the woods, fearing that the Indians were about to circle around and attack from the rear. While Reno was in the woods, word was sent that the skirmish line was in danger of being flanked. He gave orders for the three companies to begin a slow and steady withdrawal, and to keep up their fire as they did so. Companies A and G fell back while Company M gave them covering fire. But this movement was not as orderly a withdrawal as Reno attempted to portray it at his 1879 Court of Inquiry. Soldier Wolf, a Northern Cheyenne warrior said that:

> the troops retreated and the Indians all rushed in among them. They were all mixed up. The soldiers seemed to be drunk; they could not shoot at all. The soldiers retreated to the timber and fought behind cover.[8]

The pressure of the situation was beginning to show, for Reno was seen taking swigs from a whisky bottle. During the movement to the woods several men were hit by the heavy Indian fire, Sergeant Miles O'Hara of Company M being struck in the chest by a bullet which knocked him over. He raised himself into a seated position and yelled to his comrades 'For God's sake, don't leave me.' But in their haste and panic O'Hara's cries were ignored and he was killed by the Indians. German-born 1st Sergeant William Heyn of Company C had his left kneecap blown off by a bullet, but was dragged into cover by his men. Another German sergeant, Charles White of Company M, had his elbow smashed but made it into the woods under his own steam.

A second skirmish line was formed at the edge of the woods, close to the meandering river. Reno, becoming increasingly agitated at the rapidly unravelling situation, continued to pull heavily on his whisky bottle while his men kept up a rapid fire against the advancing mass of warriors before them. Private Thomas O'Neill of Company G later wrote 'at this time the fighting was terrific, the Indians charging up very close. They would deliver their fire, wheel their ponies and scamper to the rear to reload.'

As Custer moved along the opposite bank of the river a forward reconnaissance was conducted by Custer himself, his Crow scouts and several officers confirming the position of the village before he committed his battalion to the attack. According to Crow scout White-Man-Runs-Him, when Custer spotted the size of the village he 'looked whiter than ever'. The scouts began to sing their death songs, and Custer released them shortly afterwards. Reno's fight in the river bottoms could be heard by Custer and his battalion, and it was a reassuring sound for it meant that the pivot part of the battle plan was working. Private Peter Thompson of Company C, a Scotsman, recalled: 'we came in sight of the Indian village and it was truly an imposing sight to anyone who had not seen anything like it before … the white canvas [buffalo hides] gleaming in the sunlight.' Custer was pleased, believing that he had achieved a measure of surprise against the Indians. Although Custer may have been startled by the size of the Indian camp, he had committed himself to action and there was to be no turning away. Reno, after all, was heavily already engaged and he expected Custer's support. Trumpeter John Martin, shortly to be dispatched by Custer to Captain Benteen, later wrote:

> There were no bucks to be seen, all we could see was some squaws and children playing and a few dogs and ponies. The General seemed both surprised and glad, and said the Indians must be in their tents asleep.

Rejoining his battalion, Custer shouted: 'Hurrah boys! We've got them! We'll finish them up and then go home to our station.' Custer then gave orders that a runner, Private Martin, was to ride to Benteen and order the captain to hurry along his battalion and bring the reserve ammunition.

Martin, carrying the message from Custer, mounted atop a wounded and bleeding horse found Benteen's battalion some time later, having been shot at by Indian warriors on his ride east. He handed Lieutenant William Cooke's hastily scribbled note to Benteen, the message reading 'Benteen – Come on. Big village, be quick. Bring packs. P.S. Bring pacs [sic].' It made little sense to Benteen as how could he 'Be quick' and manage to bring along the reserve ammunition which was packed on mules slow poking for miles back on the trail under Captain McDougall. Along for the experience as a civilian observer was Custer's younger brother Boston, who was attached to the Pack Train. When Benteen questioned Martin about Custer's situation he could get little from the newly-arrived immigrant whose command of English could at best be described as tenuous. Benteen later wrote that Martin, whose real name was Giovanni Martini, was 'a thick headed, dull witted Italian, just about as much cut out for a cavalrymen as he was for a King …'[9] Benteen decided to move his battalion back onto the 7th Cavalry's trail already used by Custer and Reno, a move that would ultimately save Reno but doom Custer.

Back in the woods, Captain French appeared and asked Reno what they were going to do. 1st Sergeant Ryan, who was close by, shouted above the gunfire: 'There is nothing to do but mount your men and cut your way out. Another fifteen minutes and there won't be a man left.'[10] The two officers stared at Ryan, whose outburst verged on insubordination, but they said nothing in reply. Reno then asked for French's opinion, and his opinion was the same as Ryan's – get away while they still could. Reno, heeding French's advice, ordered him to mount his men and to 'follow me.' Reno's indecision and low morale was affecting the other officers, and several were also observed swigging from whisky bottles while they waited for orders. Reno told all three companies to fetch their horses, mount up and retreat northeast to some high ground that he had seen on the opposite side of the woods across the river.

The Oglala Sioux Crazy Horse arrived at the woods with his many followers, and he determined to immediately press the soldiers on the skirmish line. The Oglalas moved in close and fired into the woods, wounding two troopers as the companies began to mount up. Reno was mounted, and trying to communicate with Custer's chief scout, Bloody Knife, who was sitting on his horse a few yards away, when an Oglala bullet tore into the Ree Indian's head spraying blood and brains all over Reno's face and tunic. Bloody Knife toppled backwards off his horse, Reno gagging and wild-eyed. Suddenly, the Major yelled out the order to mount, then the order to dismount, and then mount, his nerve gone. He spurred his horse in the direction of the river and screamed out to his confused men: 'Any of you men who wish to make your escape, follow me!' Someone else added 'Every man for himself,' and the withdrawal to the river disintegrated into a ragged retreat without any covering fire or movement by companies. Men simply grabbed the nearest horse and charged off. Some officers never heard Reno's withdrawal order and tried to prevent the skirmish line from evaporating, while some officers and men could not find horses and were faced with either running after their mounted comrades or going to ground like rabbits in the dense vegetation. 1st Sergeant Ryan recalled: 'Private George Lorentz of my company ... was shot, the bullet striking him in the back of his neck and coming out of his mouth.' Lorentz, along with many other troopers, pitched off their horses as Indian bullets laced the trees. 'I could hear nothing but the continual roar of Indian rifles and the sharp resonant bang-bang of cavalry carbines,' recalled Private Slaper, 'mingled with the whoops of the savages and the shouts of my comrades.' Once the companies exited the woods they face a wide stretch of open ground before they reached the river, and if they managed to ford the shallow river, a riverbank of slippery clay that rose eight to ten feet. Indian warriors pressed into the woods, and also onto open ground behind the woods, and the soldiers were forced to run a deadly gauntlet of rifle and arrow fire in their belaboured efforts to reach safety.

Lieutenant Varnum desperately tried to restore some order to the retreat, yelling out to the men: 'For God's sake, men, don't run! There is a good many officers and men killed and wounded and we have to go back and get them.' Reno whirled around in his saddle on hearing this and bellowed: 'I am in command here, sir!' Varnum was disgusted by the mess Reno's hasty decision had made of the three companies, which up to the point when Reno had ordered them to vacate the woods had been holding their own against the Indians. 'I have no idea how the order to charge or fall back was communicated to the troops,' wrote Varnum. 'All I heard was some men yelling that they were "going to charge," or something like that.'[11] Varnum's interjection made no difference to the disordered and wild retreat to the river, into which men and horses plunged, a trail of corpses stretching away behind them from the woods. 'As we emerged from the thicket the war whoop burst forth from a thousand throats' wrote Private Thomas O'Neill, adding that 'It was a race for life.' The Indians were all around, firing into the packed ranks of panic-stricken troopers bunched up at the river and becoming increasingly bold in their attacks, some warriors physically wrestling soldiers off their saddles before dispatching them horribly with various bladed weapons. O'Neill recalled the carnage before the river:

> It was hand-to-hand conflict, both Indians and troopers striving to pull each other from their horses, after emptying their weapons, and both succeeding in a great many instances. I saw six or seven of our men in the act of falling from their horses after being shot. One poor fellow close to me was shot in the body, and as he was falling to the ground, was shot again through the head. I heard the shots as they struck him.[12]

American Horse, an Oglala warrior, recalled that 'it was like chasing buffalo, a grand chase.' Company M trooper Private James Darcy only just made it, later writing:

> One big Sioux rode alongside of me as we went along full gallop, and tried to pull me from the saddle. He had been shot in the shoulder, and every jerk he made at me the blood gushed from the wound and stained my shirt and trousers. He was a determined devil and hung on to me until we almost reached the river.[13]

A mad scramble ensued on the opposite bank of the river, as the soldiers attempted to spur their horses up the steep and slippery bank while bullets thudded into the soft clay and arrows zipped past their ears. The fighting was at very close quarters, as the milling horses and constant gunfire had created a thick pall of dust and smoke that settled over the ford limiting visibility to about fifty feet in any one direction.

Company M was the last unit to leave the woods, and the last to reach the ford, by now thick with screaming, painted warriors. Private William O. Taylor, Company A, was confronted by a scene of complete horror at the river as men and horses plunged into the deep water. Taylor 'saw a struggling mass of men and horses from whom little streams of blood was coloring the water near them.' Lieutenant Hodgson was felled in the river, shot through the legs. Hodgson, wild-eyed and soaked, screamed out: 'For God's sake, don't abandon me!' but many soldiers rode past him. Trumpeter Charles Fischer, a German-born trooper in Hodgson's company, rode past the distraught officer and kicked out a loose stirrup. Grabbing the stirrup with one hand, Fischer's horse dragged the crippled Hodgson part of the way across the river before Hodgson lost his grip and Fischer rode on. Private Morris, after emptying his revolver at a group of warriors attempting to bar his entry to the river, plunged his horse into the water and came upon Hodgson, who was yelling 'Don't abandon me! I'm shot in both legs' to every passing trooper. Morris gave the officer a stirrup, and Hodgson clung on with both hands and was dragged to the river bank. As Morris's horse began to climb to safety, an Indian bullet struck Hodgson in the temple, killing him instantly, his body rolling back down to the water's edge. Nearby, Company M Privates Henry Turley and William Rye lay wounded and bleeding among the many corpses of their comrades. Both men were abandoned. An Indian warrior came upon Turley, picked up the trooper's hunting knife, and inserted it in Turley's right eye all the way to the hilt. Englishman Private Henry Gordon lay face down in the mud, his neck gashed open by a heavy Indian bullet, slowly bleeding to death.

Once clear of the murderous ford Reno appears to have realised his mistake in permitting such a disordered retreat, and he attempted to organise some covering fire for the dozens of men still fighting their way through the masses of Indian warriors. Shortly afterwards, Reno led the remains of his battalion 700 yards from the river to some high bluffs. Captain Benteen and his battalion now approached from along Custer's trail, and discovered the remains of Reno's command standing about on the bluffs. The officers and men were soaked, splattered with mud and clay, and their expressions were shocked and disbelieving. Many were wounded, and some, including Lieutenant Varnum, were openly sobbing. Reno sat atop his horse, his face still splattered with Bloody Knife's brains, hopelessly firing his revolver at some Indians in the far distance. When he spotted Benteen, Reno hurried over. 'For God's sake, Benteen, halt your command and help me!' exclaimed Reno in an unsteady voice, 'I've lost half of my men!'[14] 'Where's Custer?' replied Benteen, but no one knew for certain. Benteen decided to reinforce Reno on the bluffs before moving out to assist Custer, who was presumably some way down river attacking the Indian village from the rear.

The men from Benteen's battalion watched helplessly as more of Reno's troopers tried to ford the river and reach safety, many being shot down and killed. It was 4.15pm, an hour since Reno had halted his charge on the village and formed his first skirmish line. Thirty-seven of his officers and men were now dead and another fourteen were wounded. Twenty-two men were unaccounted for, most still hiding in the woods across the river while Indian warriors tried to hunt them down. These officers and men would eventually manage to rejoin Reno's command atop the bluffs later that day after most of the warriors suddenly left to deal with a new threat to their village downriver.

Custer, with 210 officers and men, had moved down Medicine Tail Coulee after he had dispatched Trumpeter Martin to Benteen with orders to bring his battalion forward. Custer emerged from the coulee at a ford over two and a half miles from Reno's position and prepared to attack the village. Custer's battalion, as the manoeuvring force the strongest unit on the field that day, consisted of Company C under Second Lieutenant Henry M. Harrington, Company E (known as the Gray Horse Troop for its grey and white mounts) under Lieutenant Algernon 'Fresh' Smith, Company F under Captain George Yates, Company I under Irish-born Captain Myles Keogh, and Company L under Lieutenant Jimmi Calhoun, Custer's brother-in-law. Custer's small headquarters section included his brother Captain Tom Custer, who acted as aide-de-camp, Lieutenant Cooke as adjutant, and Lieutenant George E. Lord as assistant surgeon. Always interested in publicity, Custer was accompanied by a newspaper reporter named Mark Kellog as well.

Company E led the battalion's advance down the coulee, and on reaching the ford were confronted by a small party of Indian warriors on the opposite bank near the Sans Arc camp who opened fire. This initial firing alerted the huge village, spread out for thousands of yards along the meandering river bank, that more soldiers were attacking the village from the north, and large numbers of warriors began to organise themselves and prepared to cross the river at several points close to Custer, while hundreds more abandoned the fight against Reno and rode to join them. Thirty-three year old Lieutenant Smith was struck by a bullet at the ford and unhorsed. His men fished him from the river and carried him to the rear so that Dr Lord could attend to his wound. Inexplicably, Custer then ordered that his battalion turn away from the ford, perhaps intending to repeat his plan of eight years earlier at the Washita where he had managed to capture the Indian non-combatants, preventing further attacks on his men by the warriors. Thousands of women and children had already begun to flee from the sounds of fighting up Squaw Creek to the west, so perhaps Custer intended to move further along the riverbank, having underestimated the size of the Indian encampment, ford the river and round up the non-combatants. Bugles sounded, and Custer led companies F and C in a sharp exit right from Medicine Tail Coulee and into Deep Coulee. Company E waited until the other two companies had passed and then followed. Companies I and L did not have time to get clear of Medicine Tail Coulee before hundreds of warriors started to appear before them.

Custer and F, C and E companies emerged from Deep Coulee and began to strike out for high ground across open country. Company E, now under the command of twenty-two year old greenhorn Second Lieutenant Jack Sturgis, was soon fighting a rearguard action as the Indians quickly followed the troopers. As this manoeuvre occurred, Custer's battalion became permanently split into two formations unable to support each other. Companies I and L – under firebrand Irishman Captain Keogh – never managed to get closer than a quarter of a mile to Custer, as Custer and companies F, C, and E moved to high ground. Keogh did try, dismounting his men and forming skirmish lines that laid down three heavy volleys that drove many of the warriors to ground, and was heard distinctly by Reno's shattered command three miles to the east. Keogh's firing took some of the pressure off Custer's three companies, allowing them to retreat to higher ground, to a place now called Custer Ridge. C and F dismounted and formed skirmish lines around the summit, and Company E followed along and also dismounted quickly some way from the summit, forming the south skirmish line.

Hundreds of warriors were still moving towards Custer's men, firing as they came, so Custer ordered Lieutenant Harrington to take a platoon of Company C back down the hill to reinforce Sturgis and Company E.

This movement was unexpected by the Indians, and momentarily relieved the pressure on the skirmish line.

Minneconjou Sioux Chief Hump rallied hundreds of warriors and rushed the south skirmish line, warriors shooting, stabbing and clubbing their way into the position. Company C was outflanked and rolled back, with only a few men surviving to flee to Custer Ridge. About twenty grabbed their horses and rode southwest for a short distance before being killed. Lieutenant Harrington, according to Indian witnesses, escaped the carnage atop a sorrel-hued horse and rode off pursued by many warriors. After a time this officer reined in his horse, dragged out his revolver and blew his own brains out. Some historians believe that Harrington was among several soldiers taken by the Indians and burned alive in the village later that evening during victory celebrations, though this has always been denied by the Sioux and Cheyenne.

The survivors of Company C desperately tried to get clear of the battlefield or flee to Custer's intact position up the hill. Thirty-five year old Irish-born Sergeant Jeremiah Finley, a veteran of the Washita in 1868, rode frantically towards a place now called Calhoun Ridge, firing his revolver. Accompanied by 1st Sergeants Edwin Bobo and August Finckle, the three NCOs did not get far. Finley and his horse were killed, and the goateed Finley was later found decapitated and shot full of arrows. Around his body were twenty spent cartridge casings, indicating that he had fought hard before being overwhelmed.

Private John Brightfield was shot twice in the chest and took another bullet through his forearm when Company C was overrun. Unable to rise, Brightfield was beaten to death by screaming warriors. Private Nathan Short did manage to ride off the battlefield. Short rode all the way to the junction of the Rosebud and Yellowstone rivers before he was killed by Indians. His skeleton, intact inside a tattered uniform, and the skeleton of his horse, were discovered many weeks after the battle.

Company E, firing desperately, was driven en masse into a nearby ravine. Trapped in the natural cul-de-sac, the Indians lined the ravine walls and poured fire down onto the tangled mass of men and horses, killing them all. Crazy Horse and his Oglalas now arrived on the field fresh from routing Reno. The great warrior rallied his men with an impassioned war cry and told them simply: 'Today is a good day to fight. Today is a good day to die. Cowards to the rear! Brave hearts follow me!'[15] Crazy Horse's target was Captain Keogh's stranded and embattled squadron consisting of companies I and L, his Oglala warriors coming en masse out of the gunsmoke and dust to strike in a frenzied wave between the two army formations. The squadron was split, with Keogh and Company I continuing to try to reach Custer, while Calhoun's company was quickly cut off and surrounded.

The Calhoun fight was commented on by several of the Indians present as a 'good fight'. Oglala warrior Red Hawk said: 'at this place the soldiers stood in line and made a very good fight.'[16] Calhoun's semi-circular defensive position was heavily engaged by the Indians who moved around on foot, using the undulating terrain as cover from the soldiers' guns. Northern Cheyenne warrior Wooden Leg recalled that 'The warriors all dismounted before they began to fight, leaving their ponies in gullies, safe against the firing.' The warriors crept closer and closer to Calhoun's extended company, blazing away with repeater rifles and old muzzle loaders. 'Fighting at long range continued for about an hour and half' recalled Wooden Leg, 'during which time the warriors crept steadily closer to the soldiers, who could not see them though they could see the soldiers all the time.'[17] The Indians targeted the army horse-holders, Hunkpapa Chief Gall later saying: 'We tried to kill the holders, and then by waving blankets and shouting we scared the horses down the coulee.'[18] Calhoun's little command managed to repel several probing Indian attacks, but the number of warriors grew by the minute, as did their overwhelming firepower. The fight was not one-sided, with the troopers managing to inflict some casualties on the elusive Indians, as Wooden Leg later recalled:

> I saw one Sioux walking slowly toward the gulch, going away from where were the soldiers. He wobbled dizzily as he moved along. He fell down, got up, fell down again, got up again. As he passed near to where I was, I saw that his whole lower jaw was shot away. The sight of him made me sick. I had to vomit.

Sitting Bull later recalled that Calhoun and his company could not match the rate of firepower of the Indians, saying 'They could not fire fast enough'[19] and subsequent analysis of the battlefield has demonstrated that many of the Indians were armed with Winchester or Henry repeating rifles. The troopers were using single-shot Springfield carbines. A man could loose off perhaps twenty-five shots from a repeating rifle in a minute, but operating a Springfield carbine he would be lucky to squeeze off ten rounds in the same time. Subjected to a withering crossfire, and with no cover, Calhoun's company was shot to pieces.

Sensing the moment of victory a mass of Indian warriors, some mounted but most on foot, burst from cover and charged over Calhoun Hill and the remnants of Company L. Crazy Horse rode through the soldiers, several times nearly being hit by bullets, and he counted coup on at least one trooper before Company L was exterminated. Thirty-year-old Calhoun made his last stand a quarter of a mile from his brother-in-law, Custer watching the terrible events unfolding in the valley before him through borrowed field glasses. Calhoun had once written to Custer: 'If the time comes, you shall not find me wanting.'[20] He and his company were true to those words, and the Indians later remarked that the soldiers fought hard before being killed. Calhoun and his second-in-command, twenty-two-year-old Second Lieutenant John Crittenden who was on loan to the 7th from the 20th Infantry, fell dead at the rear of their men.

The mass of warriors came off Calhoun Hill and onto Captain Keogh's position. Company I was annihilated shortly afterwards as Keogh continued to try to fight his way through to Custer. Thirty-seven mounted men confronted hundreds of Sioux and Cheyenne warriors led by chiefs Crazy Horse, Two Moons, Gall and Crow King. There should have been sixty-seven effectives in Company I, and as in all of Custer's companies there was a shortage of junior leaders. Keogh was lacking two officers, two sergeants and three corporals, vital to maintaining the cohesion and discipline of the fighting company, and in transmitting orders. Foolish Elk, a warrior who was in the thick of the fighting, later recalled: 'The men on horses did not stop to fight ... the men on foot ... were shooting as they passed along ... The Indians were so numerous that the soldiers ... knew they had to die.' No warning of the impending attack was transmitted to Keogh from Calhoun, and Calhoun's company was not visible to Keogh's men as the Irishman held his troopers on dead ground between Custer and Calhoun Hill. In a replay of the destruction of Company C just minutes before, Company I troopers scattered and were soon killed. Northern Cheyenne warrior Little Hawk recalled: 'The soldiers ran and went along the straight ridge [Custer Ridge] where they chased them like buffalo and as long as they had their backs toward Indians the Indians rode right in among them.'[21] Captain French, commander of Company M with Reno's battalion, later remarked that 'To turn one's back on Indians is throwing life away.' Foolish Elk said that those Company I troopers who had lost their horses tried to retreat on foot, firing their revolvers as they ran, 'defending themselves as best they could.'[22] Keogh, who was mounted atop his black charger 'Comanche', died in a tight headquarters group cut down by a ragged Indian volley at the end. Keogh was hit three times, and his wounded horse was later recovered from the field by the relief force and nursed tenderly back to health by the regiment. Comanche became the 7th Cavalry's honoured mascot, and lived on until 1891 but was never ridden again.[23] Company I mascot Joe Bush, a bulldog, also survived the final few smoke and dust filled minutes of carnage and was likewise rescued by the relief two days later, still standing sentinel among the mutilated remains of his former masters.

Custer saw all of this in breaks between the swirling clouds of dust and gunsmoke that blanketed the battlefield, and he knew that he would be next. The Indians were rapidly crossing the quarter of a mile of ground between the prostrated bodies of Keogh's squadron and would arrive in overwhelming numbers. There was no sign of Benteen and his three companies, but at this stage even the timely arrival of the regiment's senior captain probably would have only added to the number who would die. The Indians were so numerous and well-armed that the outcome was a foregone conclusion unless Custer could get clear of the battlefield with his remaining company and link up with the rest of the regiment to the east. Of the 210 men Custer had led west along Medicine Tail Coulee, only about forty-five remained alive, most forming Company F (thirty-five strong), his last intact unit under the command of thirty-three-year-old Captain George Yates. Second-in-command was twenty-two-year-old Second Lieutenant William Reily, formerly of the black 10th Cavalry, whose troopers were known derisively as 'Buffalo Soldiers' by the Indians. The rest were Custer's small headquarters group that included his brother Tom, his brother Boston who had earlier ridden up from the Pack Train without orders and a few stragglers who had made it to the hill after the destruction of the companies in the valley and on Calhoun Ridge.

Custer ordered his remaining men to mount up with the intention of riding off the battlefield to the west. This move was foiled by the sudden appearance of forty or fifty Cheyenne warriors who were late joining the battle from a hunting expedition, and they immediately opened fire. Yates turned his Company F away and tried to retreat to the lower slopes of Custer Hill but lost some of his men in this manoeuvre. Hundreds of Sioux and Cheyenne warriors now closed the distance from their victories in the valley, and they crept slowly closer and closer, taking their time sniping at the troopers spread about the hill in defensive postures. Northern Cheyenne Chief Two Moons said:

The smoke was like a great cloud – swirling like water round a stone. We
shoot, we ride fast, we shoot again. Soldiers drop, and horses fall on them.
Soldiers in line drop …[24]

There was no rush yet. Custer had some of the remaining horses led to
the summit of the hill and shot to provide improvised breastworks. Behind
the carcasses he placed seven of his best marksmen, and the fire from these
soldiers inhibited any immediate Indian charge to overwhelm the defences.
The rest of Custer's men settled themselves onto the slopes of the hill and
opened sporadic fire on the advancing Indians. Thirty-nine cavalry horses
were shot in the head by troopers desperate for some cover from the blizzard
of Indian lead sweeping the hillside. In the breeze the Indians could discern
Custer's headquarters group bunched around the regimental colours, and
Captain Yates by the Company F guidon. Oglala warrior American Horse
recalled that 'There were so many Sioux and Cheyennes that the whole
country seemed to be alive with them, closing on the troops and shooting.'[25] When warriors came too close to the hill Lieutenant Cooke led
a charge down the slopes which repulsed them for a while. Two Moons
later wrote: 'The shooting was quick … Some of the soldiers were down
on their knees, some standing … We circled all around them …'[26] By this
method Custer's final defences were slowly weakened until the Indians
launched a final rush on the hill's summit, Two Moons recalling how 'We
charged through them with our ponies. When we had done this … the
fight was over.'[27] Minneconjou warrior Red Horse remembered those last
terrible minutes of carnage atop the hill: 'These soldiers became foolish,
many throwing away their guns and raising their hands saying, 'Sioux, pity
us – take us prisoners.' The Sioux did not take a single soldier prisoner, but
killed all of them; none were left alive for even a few minutes.'[28] However,
Custer's final stand garnered some praise from warriors who were in at the
kill, tending to dispute Red Horse's claim that some of the soldiers tried
to surrender. Soldier Wolf, a Northern Cheyenne, said: 'Reno's men were
frightened and acted as if they were drunk – as I think they were. Custer's
men fought well and bravely.'

The fighting was hand-to-hand at the end, as Oglala warrior Horned
Horse, who fought alongside Crazy Horse, later recalled how 'the smoke
and dust was so great that foe could not be distinguished from friend.' In
such a situation, the Indian warriors were at a physical disadvantage. Most
lacked upper body strength or developed muscles, disdaining physical labour

as women's work, whereas the white soldiers were generally bigger and stronger. In some cases it took three or four Sioux or Cheyenne warriors to wrestle a crazed white trooper to the ground and kill him.

Custer died with his headquarters staff around him, including his orderly, Flag Sergeant John Vickory, Danish Corporal William Teeman, and Chief Trumpeter Henry Voss. Death had been instantaneous. Tom Custer went down fighting, blasting away with a brace of revolvers until felled by a bullet in his left side and another in the arm. Yates was down, and Reily lay unconscious behind a dead cavalry horse. The remaining troopers that were still alive tried to flee the slaughter atop the hill, but all were quickly killed by the Indians. Sergeant Major William Sharrow was ridden down by warriors about half a mile from Custer Hill, firing and reloading his revolver as he ran. Adjutant Cooke's orderly, Private Boss Tweed, mounted his horse at the end and rode fifty yards before he was shot from his saddle. The horse survived, Tweed did not. As he lay stunned on the ground warriors killed him with axes, and then shot an arrow into each of his eyes.

The fighting ended about 5.30pm. Thousands of Indian men, women and children swarmed over the battlefield, collecting weapons, stripping clothing from the dead, killing the wounded and mutilating the soldiers' bodies. The Cheyenne remembered Sand Creek and the Sioux remembered the Washita. No-one was spared. When Lieutenant Reily regained consciousness behind the dead horse he found an Indian warrior standing over him. Wrenching the revolver from Reily's hand, the warrior shot the young officer point blank in the face. Tom Custer was on his hands and knees, blood pouring from his mouth as he watched warriors moving over the dead of Company F. Alongside him lay four dazed and wounded troopers. The Indians attacked them with clubs, axes and tomahawks. Tom Custer's throat was cut, his stomach slashed open so that his guts fell out onto the grass, his ears were skinned and his face caved in. Over fifty arrows were shot into his corpse, and he was scalped. George Custer, found dead in a seated position against other bodies, received similar treatment. The true details of the mutilation of Custer and his men were suppressed for decades after the battle by the American military, and a story was invented for Custer's wife Libbie that told of her husband's body being left intact by the Indians as a mark of respect. The truth was the Cheyenne and Sioux vented decades of wrath and fury against the lily-white corpses of the American soldiers that lay stripped and naked across the dry hillsides. These men had come to attack and kill Indians without warning, and had paid the price for their leader's vainglorious arrogance. Custer was dead, but in death he would find everlasting fame, and his death would be avenged by a United States strong and determined enough not to permit the Plains Indians the freedom they craved.

Although the hated 'Son of the Morning Star' was dead, the Battle of the Little Bighorn still had one act left to play. Major Reno and the remains of the 7th Cavalry were still alive, but trapped by the number of wounded troopers they had to care for, preventing them from exiting the battlefield. The sounds of heavy firing from over four miles away down the valley had been plainly audible to Reno and Benteen's men atop the bluffs. Reno did not move his command forward immediately, even though he knew that Custer must have been heavily engaged with the Indians. Many of his subordinate officers were perplexed by Reno's inaction, Lieutenant Edward Godfrey, commanding Company K, remarking: 'The command ought to do something or Custer will be after Reno with a big stick.'[29] One officer, Captain Thomas Weir, commanding Company D, decided to take matters into his own hands and act, with or without Reno's permission. After a heated exchange with Reno – during which Reno refused to grant Weir permission to take his company towards the sound of the guns – Weir rode off with his orderly anyway. Company D second-in-command, Second Lieutenant Winfield S. Edgerly, believing that his commander had obtained permission, followed on with the rest of the men at 5pm. Disobedience began to spread like a canker through the battalion, and at 5.25pm Captain Benteen, without orders, led companies H, K and M out towards Weir, Benteen ignoring several 'recall' signals blown by Reno's trumpeter.

After riding out for about a mile, Weir halted his company on a ridge that today bears his name and was joined by Benteen's squadron. Several officers and men claimed to have observed the last minutes of Custer's Last Stand through field glasses from a distance of around three miles, though this is disputed. What they clearly observed within a short time was hundreds of Indian warriors leaving the scene of the Custer fight and moving rapidly towards them at Weir Point. The Sioux and Cheyenne evidently intended to finish the job they had begun earlier that afternoon when they had routed Reno's battalion in the river bottoms, and the destruction of Custer's battalion freed up the warriors to do so. 'As soon as we had killed all the different soldiers [Custer's battalion]' said Minneconjou Red Horse, 'all went back to kill the soldiers on the hill.' A mass of warriors began moving off the Custer battlefield; 'the Sioux took the guns and cartridges off the dead soldiers.' continued Red Horse, 'and went to the hill on which the soldiers were, surrounded and fought them with the guns and cartridges of the dead soldiers.'[30]

As the Indians began to press Weir and Benteen's companies, another disorderly retreat occurred that resulted in a few more casualties. Complete disaster was only averted by the bravery of Lieutenant Edward Godfrey, who dismounted Company K and fired a volley at the advancing Indian warriors, giving the other three companies time to beat a hasty retreat towards Reno's position on the bluffs. Godfrey was alone among the officers in being able to control his men's panic and terror when confronted by hordes of powder-blackened and blood-stained warriors surging across the open ground towards them. His method was simple – he threatened to shoot any man who refused to obey his orders. His actions give some indication of the poor morale and training of the troopers, who would often break and run when faced with a determined Indian assault. Godfrey dismounted his company several times during the retreat to the bluffs to fire volleys, the effect being to slow down the Indian advance and buy time for the companies piling onto two parallel ridges on the bluffs.

By 6pm all the companies were trying to dig in on the ridges under increasingly accurate and heavy Indian rifle fire. The pack animals and horses were placed in the centre of the defensive position and between them a rudimentary aid station established where Dr Porter worked feverishly attempting to patch up the dozens of wounded whose numbers grew as the hours wore on. The Indians occupied several adjacent ridges, and their shooting was deadly accurate, as Private William Slaper of Company M discovered: 'While laying face down on the ground a bullet tore off the heel of my boot as effectively as though it had been sawed off!'

The troopers lay in their company positions hardly daring to move or raise their heads to fire, sheltering behind a few packing cases or piles of stones, or hunkered down in shallow rifle pits scraped out of the bone dry earth. 'After lying there a few minutes' recalled Lieutenant Godfrey, 'I was horrified to find myself wondering if a small sagebrush, about as thick as my finger, would turn a bullet.' Varnum narrowly avoided being struck in the head, the bullet 'throwing up so much dirt in my eyes that I could scarcely see for an hour or more.'

Water was soon gone, and the men were to be tortured by thirst over the next two days, driving some to make heroic and often one-way trips to the river under a withering Indian fire to fill canteens and cooking kettles. Fifteen men would receive the Medal of Honor for securing water for the wounded, including Englishman Private James Pym of Company B and Scotsman Private Peter Thompson of Company C, who was wounded.

The Indians were cautious when it came to launching an assault on white soldiers who were dug in and ready for them. 'The soldiers on the hill dug up the ground' recalled Red Horse, 'and the soldiers and the Sioux fought at long range, sometimes the Sioux charging close up.' 'There was no full-fledged charge' wrote Private Charles Windolph of Company H, 'but little groups of Indians would creep up as close as they could get, and from behind bushes or little knolls open fire.'[31] One man won himself no honours over the coming hours atop the ridges. Reno was mentally shattered by the retreat from the river bottoms, and found solace in a whisky bottle. Often very drunk, actual field command unofficially passed to Benteen, who did a fine job of trying to hold the men together under the most difficult and trying of circumstances. On the night of 25 June the white soldiers atop the ridges listened in horror to the sounds of celebration coming from the Indian village, where drums beat hour upon hour and huge bonfires lit up the valley. It was a 'scene of demoniacal celebration and frantic revel'[32] according to one observer. The relief force would later discover the charred heads of several white men hanging from lodge poles in the remains of the village, fuelling rumours that some cavalrymen had been taken alive and tortured to death by the Indians that night. Two days of sniper fire killed another eighteen men from Reno's and Benteen's battalions, and wounded forty-six.

The men atop the ridges watched the vast assemblage of Indians, horses and travois leaving the valley the following day, thousands of people with perhaps 20,000 horses, trailing away from the scene of their greatest victory over the soldiers since Captain Fetterman and his men had been slain in 1866. The Indians left when word reached them from their scouts of the approach of another large contingent of soldiers from the east – Brigadier General Alfred Terry and the rest of the column.

Terry and Colonel John Gibbon linked up with Reno on the morning of 27 June. 'Where was Custer?' was the question on everyone's lips. Terry's weary men, after relieving Reno, entered the remains of the Indian camp to ominous sights. 'We came across a dead cavalry horse which had been cut open' recalled a horrified Private Nathan Coon of the 7th Infantry, 'and a dead naked soldier was forced head foremost into the horse's belly.' The camp rubbish pile revealed more disturbing clues to Custer's fate. A soldier held up a pair of bloodied men's drawers, calling out for his commander when he spotted the words 'Sturgis – 7th Cavalry' neatly printed on the back. Another trooper dug into the pile of abandoned Indian rubbish and pulled out an officer's buckskin shirt, soon identified as belonging to Lieutenant James Porter, Company I. Bullet holes front and back and blood stains indicated Porter had been wearing the blouse when he was struck.

Terry ordered platoon-sized patrols dispatched into the surrounding hills in an effort to locate Custer's battalion. It wasn't long before a young officer appeared before Terry's headquarters group, ashen-faced and trembling. 'I have a very sad report to make' stated the officer to his general. 'I have counted one hundred and ninety-seven dead bodies lying in the hills.' A murmur rippled through the assembled staff, Terry asking: 'White men?' The young officer dropped his gaze to the floor, and replied 'Yes, white men.' A look of horror passed over Terry and his officers, mingled with a dread sense of disbelief. Terry, Gibbon and their column, along with Reno, Benteen, and the remnants of the 7th Cavalry, rode up to Custer Hill and were confronted by the remains of the Indians' great victory. Strewn about across the slopes and in the valleys lay bloated corpses dense with legions of fat flies; bodies in all manner of postures, most naked and heavily mutilated after death. Horses lay everywhere, and the stench was appalling. 'His crotch had been split up with an axe' ran the report on the remains of Private Thomas 'Boss' Tweed, Lieutenant Cooke's orderly, whose body was identified about fifty feet from Custer's, 'and one of his legs thrown up around his shoulder. He was shot with arrows in both eyes.' Private Edwin F. Pickard of Company F, whose blown horse had saved him from following Custer to his death, was distraught at the sights that he found around Custer Hill, recalling that 'it made me sick to see my fellow troopers of F Troop lying on the hillside, dismembered, with stakes driven through their chests, with their heads crushed in, and many of them with their arms and legs chopped off.'

The mutilations visited upon Custer and his dead troopers were nothing new to the Indian wars. Many Indian peoples deliberately desecrated the dead in order to protect themselves in the afterlife. For example, scalping was performed with such alacrity by Plains Indians because they believed that a person's hair held his power. Remove the hair and you take away his power to harm you when you meet again in the afterlife. Similarly, chopping the arms, legs or head off a dead soldier was an act of spiritual self-protection. The mutilation certainly went further than spiritual belief at the aftermath of the Little Bighorn, for many years of rage and sorrow were also transferred onto the bodies of their hated 'Bluecoat' enemies. Such odious mutilations were not limited to the Indians, as the Sand Creek Massacre had shown the world ten years before.

The Terry-Gibbon column was paralysed at the scene of Custer's defeat. The men pitched camp, and would in due course begin the unpleasant business of burying corpses that had lain out in the hot sun for days. 7th Infantry Captain Walter Clifford wrote about the miserable task in his diary.

> Our camp is surrounded with ghastly remains of the recent butchery. The days are scorching hot and still, and the air is thick with the stench of the festering bodies ... The repulsive-looking green flies that have been feasting on the swollen bodies of the dead are attracted to the campfires by the smell of cooking meat ...[33]

The 7th Cavalry had been decimated, losing 272 men killed, scores wounded, and 344 army horses killed or captured by the Indians. Sioux and Cheyenne casualties have never been satisfactorily established. The relief force found a few dead warriors dressed in funeral garb where the village had stood, and the Indians themselves later recalled that many dead and wounded warriors were carried away by their families, and that men were still dying of their wounds months after the fight. Indian casualties were probably nowhere near as heavy as those inflicted on the army as the Indians had generally fought using the terrain as cover, while the soldiers had fought out in the open. Surveys of available sources average out the total number of Indian deaths at between thirty and forty.

The Custer family was devastated. George Custer was dead, as were his brothers Tom and youngest brother Boston, who had ridden forward from the pack train and was killed on Custer Hill, along with Custer's teenaged nephew Harry 'Autie' Reed who had accompanied his uncles as a civilian on the campaign and Custer's brother-in-law James Calhoun.

Reno's and Benteen's wounded, numbering sixty in total, were hauled the fifteen miles to the Bighorn River on litters and mule travois, before being loaded aboard a stern-wheel river steamer named the *Far West*. In only fifty-four hours the skipper of the *Far West*, Captain Grant Marsh, navigated his vessel 710 miles along the Yellowstone and Missouri rivers to Bismarck in Dakota Territory. Only one trooper died during the journey east.

News of the disaster reached the east on 4 July, during celebrations marking one hundred years of independence. The *Helena Herald* headline ran: 'A Terrible Fight – General Custer and his Nephew killed – The Seventh

Cavalry cut to pieces – The White Number Killed 315.' Official confirma-
tion was released by the army the next day in a wire from Bismarck that
read:'General Custer attacked the Indians June 25, and he, with every officer
and man in five companies, were killed.' The death of Custer and his boys
at the hands of the savage 'Red Man' had a similar impact on the public
as later historical events like Pearl Harbor in 1941 and the September 11
attacks in 2001. Disbelief and horror soon turned into anger and calls for
revenge. As for the decimated 7th Cavalry, they would stay in the field until
26 September, their task still not completed.

Notes

1. Jerome A. Green (Ed), *Lakota and Cheyenne: Indian Views of the Great Sioux War 1876–7*, (Norman: University of Oklahoma Press, 1994), 6

2. Thomas Goodrich, *Scalp Dance: Indian Warfare on the High Plains 1865–79*, (London: Stackpole Books, 1997), 219

3. Ibid: 220

4. Jerome A. Green (Ed), *Lakota and Cheyenne: Indian Views of the Great Sioux War 1876–7*, (Norman: University of Oklahoma Press, 1994), 14

5. Dale T. Schoenberger, *The End of Custer: The Death of an American Military Legend*, (Surrey, British Columbia: Hancock House: 1995), 26

6. W.A. Graham, *The Custer Myth*, (Stackpole Books: 2000), 102

7. Geoffrey C. Ward, *The West: An Illustrated History*, (New York: Little, Brown And Company, 1996), 300

8. Jerome A. Green (Ed), *Lakota and Cheyenne: Indian Views of the Great Sioux War 1876–7*, (Norman: University of Oklahoma Press, 1994), 51

9. Dale T. Schoenberger, *The End of Custer: The Death of an American Military Legend*, (Surrey, British Columbia: Hancock House: 1995), 104

10. Ibid: 107

11. E.A. Brininstool, *Troopers With Custer*, (Omaha: University of Nebraska Press, 1989), 108

12. Robert J. Kershaw, *Red Sabbath: The Battle of Little Bighorn*, (Hersham, Surrey: Ian Allan Publishing, 2005), 125

13 Kenneth Hammer, *Men With Custer: Biographies of the 7th Cavalry, June 25 1876*, (Custer Battlefield Historical Museum Association, 1995), 82

14. Dale T. Schoenberger, *The End of Custer: The Death of an American Military Legend*, (Surrey, British Columbia: Hancock House: 1995), 133

15. Ibid: 194

16. Gregory F. Michno, *Lakota Noon: The Indian Narrative of Custer's Defeat*, (Mountain Press Co., 1999), 175

17. W.A. Graham, *The Custer Myth*, (Stackpole Books: 2000), 105

18. Gregory F. Michno, *Lakota Noon: The Indian Narrative of Custer's Defeat*, (Mountain Press Co., 1999), 177

19. W.A. Graham, *The Custer Myth*, (Stackpole Books: 2000), 72

20. Dale T. Schoenberger, *The End of Custer: The Death of an American Military Legend*, (Surrey, British Columbia: Hancock House: 1995), 198

21. Jerome A. Green (Ed), *Lakota and Cheyenne: Indian Views of the Great Sioux War 1876–7*, (Norman: University of Oklahoma Press, 1994), 62

22. Robert J. Kershaw, *Red Sabbath: The Battle of Little Bighorn*, (Hersham, Surrey: Ian Allan Publishing, 2005), 159

23. Captain Keogh's horse 'Comanche' is today preserved and displayed at the L.L. Dyche Museum at the University of Kansas, Lawrence.

24. W.A. Graham, *The Custer Myth*, (Stackpole Books: 2000), 103

25. Jerome A. Green (Ed), *Lakota and Cheyenne: Indian Views of the Great Sioux War 1876–7*, (Norman: University of Oklahoma Press, 1994), 50

26. Dale T. Schoenberger, *The End of Custer: The Death of an American Military Legend*, (Surrey, British Columbia: Hancock House: 1995), 205–206

27. Ibid: 206

28. W.A. Graham, *The Custer Myth*, (Stackpole Books: 2000), 37

29. Dale T. Schoenberger, *The End of Custer: The Death of an American Military Legend*, (Surrey, British Columbia: Hancock House: 1995), 216

30. W.A. Graham, *The Custer Myth*, (Stackpole Books: 2000), 62

31. Charles Windolph, *I Fought With Custer: The Story of Sgt Windolph, Last Survivor of the Battle of the Little Bighorn as told to Frazier and Robert Hunt*, (Bison Books, 1987), 101

32. Dale T. Schoenberger, *The End of Custer: The Death of an American Military Legend*, (Surrey, British Columbia: Hancock House: 1995), 229

33. Francis B. Taunton, *A Scene of Sickening, Ghastly Horror: The Custer Battlefield – 27–28 June 1876*, (London: Johnson-Taunton Military Press, 1983), 88

1. Colonel Kit Carson, the ruthless frontiersman recruited by the US Army to defeat the mighty Navajos in the American Southwest, 1863–64. Library of Congress, LC-DIG-cwpbh-00 514.

2. Cheyenne peace delegates photographed at the White House in Washington, DC. The United States made over 300 treaties with American Indians, and broke every one of them. Library of Congress, LC-USZ62-11880.

3. Chief Red Cloud (left) shaking
hands with Chief American Horse.
Red Cloud was the only Indian leader
to win a war against the US Army,
buying his Lakota Sioux followers a
few more years of peace in the Fort
Laramie Treaty of 1868. American
Horse was a close ally of Sitting Bull,
and fought at the Battle of the Little
Bighorn in 1876. Library of Congress,
LC-USZ62-11568.

4. Major General Edward Canby,
the only US Army general killed
during the Indian Wars when he was
assassinated during peace negotiations
with the Modoc tribe in Oregon
Territory, 1873. Library of Congress,
LC-B8172-6574.

5. Lieutenant General 'Little Phil' Sheridan, distinguished Civil War leader and later commander of the troops sent to pacify the Sioux and Cheyenne during the 1876–77 war. Library of Congress, LC–USZ62–131934.

6. Brigadier General Alfred Terry, Custer's superior during the 1876 invasion of Lakota Sioux territory. Library of Congress, LC–BH83–142.

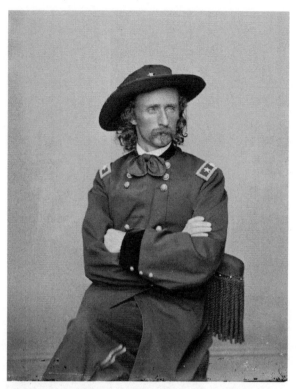

7. Lieutenant Colonel George Armstrong Custer, 7th Cavalry, photographed when a Major General of Volunteers during the American Civil War. His death at the Battle of the Little Bighorn in Montana Territory in 1876 was one of the defining moments of the American West. Library of Congress, LC-BH831-1314.

8. Sitting Bull, spiritual leader of the combined Lakota Sioux tribes during the war for the Northern Plains, photographed after his return from exile in Canada in the 1880s. Glenbow Museum, NA-4452-4.

9. Rain-in-the-Face, a Hunkpapa Sioux leader who fought Custer at the Little Bighorn, photographed at Fort Keogh in 1880. Glenbow Museum, NA-207-19.

10. Comanche – a 7th Cavalry horse that survived the Custer Massacre in 1876 to become almost a national treasure until his death in 1891. Library of Congress, LC-USZ62-11937.

11. Chief Joseph, leader of the Nez Perce tribe during their epic trek across the Pacific Northwest in 1877. Photographed in defeat in 1901. Glenbow Museum, NA-1461-28.

12. One-armed Brigadier General Oliver Otis Howard (pictured here as a major general during the Civil War), who commanded the American forces in pursuit of Chief Joseph and the Nez Perce in 1877. He was nicknamed 'General Two-day Behind' by the Nez Perce for his failure to catch them as they headed for Canada. Library of Congress, LC-B8172-3719.

13. Geronimo (right), leader of the Chiricahua Apache, his son and two braves on the occasion of his final surrender to American forces, Tombstone, Arizona, 1886. Glenbow Museum, NA-2190-1.

14. Major General George Crook, an officer who warred against both the Sioux and the Apache. Library of Congress, LC-BH826-30695.

15. Survivors of Chief Bigfoot's band of Minneconjou Sioux massacred by American troops at Wounded Knee, December 1890. Library of Congress, LC-USZ62-22971.

16. Brigadier General Nelson A. 'Bearcoat' Miles (second left), one of the US Army's most successful Indian fighters and later defender of Indian rights after Wounded Knee. Photographed 'Viewing hostile Indian camp' at Pine Ridge Reservation, 1891. Library of Congress, LC-USZ62-11786.

8

LONG KNIVES ON THE MARCH

'Who slew Custer? The celebrated peace policy of General Grant, which feeds, clothes, and takes care of their noncombatant force while men are killing our troops ... [and] the Indian Bureau, with its thriving agents and favorites as Indian traders, and its mock humanity and pretence as piety – *that* is what killed Custer.'

New York Herald, June 1876

The Sioux and Cheyenne camp on the Little Bighorn was too large to stay together for very long, and soon after the victory over Custer the various bands began to move off in different directions, searching for fresh hunting grounds, fresh grazing for their ponies, and scouting out winter quarters. Some bands withdrew towards the south-east and the Bighorn Mountains, while Sitting Bull and the Hunkpapa bands travelled north-east towards the borderlands with Canada.

Long Dog's band went north-west, while Crazy Horse's Oglala followers headed for the sacred heart of the Sioux nation, east to the Black Hills. Before they broke up the great camp on the Little Bighorn, the many chieftains had met many times to discuss what had occurred and what was to come. Collective Indian opinion seemed to be that the defeat of Custer and his men would destroy the resolve of the Americans to continue to wage war against the northern plains peoples. The army would give up its attacks in the same way it had conceded defeat to Red Cloud in 1868. The Sioux and Cheyenne would be left in peace.

The reality, of course, was entirely different. Custer's defeat had inflamed public opinion against the 'hostile' Indians of the west, and the government and the army began to set in motion plans to bring about a final solution to the Indian problem on the northern plains. This time, the gloves would truly be off. When Gibbon's men and Reno's survivors saw what the enraged Indians had done to the bodies of Custer and his men they conveniently termed it a 'massacre' and spoke of the 'savage barbarity' of the Indian. Few cared that Custer had come to attack a peaceful Sioux and Cheyenne village, where he would have killed women and children as well as warriors. The sun-blackened corpses on the Little Bighorn were not a testament to one officer's folly in placing himself and his forces in a position where they were defeated, but evidence instead of a people who must be controlled, a race of devils led by a cunning and feared despot named Sitting Bull. The Indian victory over Custer very effectively galvanised the United States into ridding the plains of this unwanted, misunderstood and alien culture called the Sioux. Sitting Bull became the focus of that campaign, effectively America's 'most wanted man.' He was a demonised figure lurking in the subconscious of every American, and few understood the fight from his point of view.

Sitting Bull was but one of many Indian leaders who were passionate believers in the legitimacy of their own culture over their own territory, of the independence of that culture from America, and jointly aggrieved by the lies and deceits of the American government towards them. American success or failure in defeating Sitting Bull and the Teton Sioux would have important ramifications for its relationships with other Indian peoples. Snuffing out prominent leaders would make resistance less likely among other tribes, as the United States demonstrated omnipotence over its native peoples.

All of these events were watched with barely disguised disgust and disbelief by the authorities north of the border in the British Dominion of Canada. In contrast to the Americans, the Canadians had tried to handle their own 'Indian problem' with kid gloves, and had so far avoided serious bloodshed in removing Indian peoples to what it termed 'reserves.' The Canadians, and the British Foreign Office in London, thought that American Indian policy was unwise and inflammatory, and they watched with disquiet as the fallout from that policy approached the Canadian border.

Many Lakota Sioux began to look to the north as the situation in America rapidly deteriorated for them. The Americans had realised that, by removing the buffalo, the Indians would not survive for long. Starvation would bring them to their knees, making them obedient to American will. Canada began to look like a place of refuge for some of the Sioux and their leaders, as their territorial integrity was violated as army columns criss-crossed the plains searching for villages to destroy and Indians to fight throughout the winter of 1876–77. For the Americans, the post-Custer campaign was not the definitive sweep of the plains that it was designed to be, and the Indians would prove once again to be elusive and skilled opponents.

The Battle of the Little Bighorn was to claim several more casualties over the coming years, especially among the surviving officers. The experience had been so traumatic, and the scale of the disaster so complete, that some officers' careers were destroyed by the political fallout. Custer became enshrined as a national hero, alongside those who had perished with him, whereas Reno and many of the other officers who had survived were castigated for not having saved Custer or for their behaviour atop Reno Hill during the siege. Captain Thomas B. Weir, who had commanded Company D, and who had deliberately disobeyed Reno's orders not to advance his men in Custer's direction once Benteen had come up, was so ridden with guilt that he drank himself to death before the end of 1876. He was only thirty-eight years old. Similarly, Captain 'Tucker' French, whose cool marksmanship while in command of Company M on Reno's first skirmish line in the river bottoms earned him widespread praise, also succumbed to the bottle. Within thirty months of the battle French had been dismissed from the army for alcoholism and eventually died in 1882 aged just thirty-nine. The greatest suspicion was placed on Reno, whose conduct in the field led many to call for his court-martial for cowardice. In 1879 Reno was exonerated at a court of inquiry, but not exactly excused for his behaviour in the river bottoms and atop Reno Hill. With his career effectively over, Reno also drank heavily and was dismissed from the army in 1880. He died from cancer in obscurity in 1889. Custer's widow Libbie worked tirelessly to further the memory of her husband, her work effectively protecting his image as a great military hero until the second half of the twentieth century, when historians began to re-evaluate the 'Boy General' and his actions. They had plenty of material to work with: the last white survivor of the battle, Lieutenant Varnum, died in 1936.[1]

The death of the press darling Custer, though he was not to be missed by many of the officers and men who had served alongside him, nonetheless provided the Americans with a great opportunity. A grand military campaign would be unleashed across the plains, determined once and for all to bring the Sioux and their allies to heel. Illegally ignoring the restrictions imposed by the 1868 Fort Laramie Treaty, the American government tore up the document and decided to use blunt force to solve the problem. Custer's death and the grisly stories circulating concerning the mutilation of his men by the Indians contributed to a hardening of white opinion towards any negotiations with the Sioux or other native peoples. By simply ignoring the reasons why Custer ended up naked and mutilated under the harsh Montana sun, the final elimination of the last barrier to complete white settlement of the West was to be a national crusade punishing and meting out 'justice' to those who had dared to resist Washington's will.

Perhaps the greatest service George Custer ever performed for his nation was in being killed in such a manner as to sufficiently inflame citizens, soldiers and politicians alike that the urge to finally dispossess the Sioux and Cheyenne became irresistible.

Major General Philip Sheridan dispatched within days of receiving word of the debacle on the Little Bighorn every available unit within the Division of the Missouri to reinforce Brigadier Generals Alfred Terry and George Crook. Reinforcements amounted to eighteen companies of cavalry and ten of mounted infantry. The depleted 7th Cavalry was restored to full strength by the addition of 500 partially trained recruits.

By the late autumn of 1876 Sheridan had assembled a formidable force of 3,743 officers and men to deploy in two columns against the dispersed Lakota Sioux, Northern Cheyenne and Arapaho. 'I have stripped every post from the line of Manitoba to Texas,' cabled Sheridan to General-in-Chief William T. Sherman, adding, 'We still want more mounted men.'[2] The problem was the fact that the Indian clans and bands that had defeated Custer and Reno in June were now dispersed over thousands of square miles of terrain, and winter was just around the corner. Because Terry and Gibbon had idled at the site of Custer's Last Stand for almost a month, all the Indian trails leading off from the former village were now cold.

The army column, named the Yellowstone River Expedition by Sheridan, meandered dejectedly northeast along the Tongue River Valley, following old Indian trails. By the time the column halted at the Powder River it was in a bad way. Heavy rainstorms had dissolved whatever fighting spirit existed among the troops, especially among the new recruits brought in to shore up the devastated 7th Cavalry. The trails were mud baths, and the expedition's supplies became exhausted. Crook's and Terry's columns spent a fruitless summer trying to locate the hostiles, but the Indians proved to be highly mobile and extremely elusive opponents. As the campaign dragged on into autumn logistical problems began to undermine the expedition. Crook's column actually began to run out of supplies, necessitating a desperate search for food before winter set in. Crook's column consisted of five companies of the 2nd Cavalry, ten companies from the 3rd and ten companies from the 5th, reinforced with three companies each from the 4th and 9th Infantry and four companies of the 14th Infantry. Captain Anson Mills and 150 men from the 3rd Cavalry were detached from the column in early September with orders to locate mining settlements in the Black Hills and get supplies to the main column. The men were in such desperate straits that Crook had already put the entire expedition onto half-rations, with many of the units resorting to eating horses to try to keep up their strength.

Captain Mills' companies rode through hills known as the Slim Buttes close to the present day town of Reva, South Dakota on the evening of 8 September. His scouts suddenly and unexpectedly came upon a small Indian village tucked into a fold of ground. The camp, consisting of thirty-seven lodges and a small herd of ponies, was a band of Minneconjou Sioux under Chief American Horse, who had taken part in the Battle of the Little Bighorn. Mills decided to launch an attack on the village the next morning, in the meantime deploying his troops to surround the camp until he was ready to unleash his assault. The Sioux remained unaware of Mills' presence until, to the familiar sounds of blaring bugles and shouted commands, the hated 'Long Knives' were suddenly upon them once again.

The soldiers shot down any of the few dozen warriors inside the village who tried to resist their assault, including American Horse, who was mortally wounded. Most of the Sioux grabbed their children and babies and fled from into the open countryside, while a dying American Horse took shelter in a nearby cave with fifteen women and children. When the soldiers came to take his surrender, American Horse refused the offer of treatment by an army surgeon and died, along with two wounded women and a young child. One young boy was found alive inside one of the tepees in the village, miraculously having slept through Mills' attack. Those Minneconjou Sioux who escaped being taken prisoner fanned out into the countryside seeking nearby Sans Arc, Oglala, Brule Sioux and Northern Cheyenne villages. Crazy Horse was soon informed of the attack, the Minneconjou telling him that their village had been assaulted by about 100 white soldiers. Crazy Horse sallied forth at once with an impressive force of between 600 and 800 enraged warriors, ready once again to beat the arrogant *wasichus* as they had three months before. Unbeknown to Crazy Horse and the other Sioux war chiefs, Crook had effected a junction with Mills at Slim Buttes, his soldiers now greatly outnumbering the fast approaching Sioux, who were devouring the ten miles to American

Horse's camp in a great feathered and war-painted pony column, many wearing an assortment of hats or jackets taken from Custer's dead alongside their traditional buckskins, blankets and war bonnets.

On arrival at American Horse's camp the Indians observed that the village was still standing, and was crawling with 'Bluecoats.' Undeterred by the odds now stacked at least two-to-one against them, the Sioux settled themselves onto nearby bluffs and opened vigorous rifle fire that surprised Crook and his men. The hills were alive with puffs of smoke, as bullets whined into the camp and clipped branches off trees. Crook immediately ordered a defensive perimeter established to protect his horses and pack mules, and then he ordered the Indian village burned. Soon the tepees had burned through to reveal smouldering lodge-poles, a great cloud of black smoke rising into the sky over the village. The Sioux on the bluffs watched as four companies of infantry formed into skirmish order and began to advance steadily up the hillside towards them, while cavalrymen on foot followed closely behind. For forty-five minutes the fighting was intense, as soldiers and Sioux banged away at each other from behind rocks and trees until the army pressure drove most of the Sioux off the hills.

Before the village had been burned the tepees had been thoroughly searched, and a large supply of dried meat that the Sioux had placed in storage for the coming winter was distributed to the famished soldiers. The searches also turned up many items that had been taken from the Custer battlefield, and which confirmed for most of the officers and men of Crook's command the righteousness of their actions in attacking and destroying American Horse's village. The guidon (small flag) of Company I, 7th Cavalry was found, along with a pair of bloodstained leather gloves that had belonged to the commander, Captain Miles Keogh. Army Springfield carbines and ammunition were also recovered from the camp before it was torched.

On 10 September Crook mounted up his men, and under sporadic Sioux attack the weary column plodded towards the Black Hills, still hoping to find some of the mining communities that had sprung up across the Sioux heartland. Five days later Crook's force ran into a supply column and was saved from starvation. The Battle of Slim Buttes cost the army two soldiers and a civilian scout killed. Sioux losses were about ten men, women and children shot and killed.

The government was not dissuaded by the poor performance of its army in the field during the late summer of 1876, and immediately set about enacting legislation designed to end the 'Sioux problem' for all time. The Sioux Appropriation Act came into force in violation of the 1868 Treaty, and the reservation Sioux lost forever both their remaining Unceded Lands and the sacred Black Hills. Both were signed away by various minor chiefs virtually at the point of a gun.

Sheridan realised that in order to prevent further outbreaks among the agency Sioux strong measures were required. The army was dispatched to the reservations and proceeded to confiscate all the ponies and firearms they could locate. The Sioux could no longer reinforce the 'hostiles' under Sitting Bull and Crazy Horse, or cooperate with the renegade Northern Cheyenne under Dull Knife, as Sheridan intended. The time had also come for Sheridan to deal with the hostile Sioux resisting all overtures to turn themselves in to the American authorities and return to their reservations. A winter campaign was instituted to decide finally the issue and compel their surrender – or their utter destruction.

On 14 November Crook took the field once again at the head of a 2,000-strong force tasked with subduing the Northern Cheyenne. Colonel Ranald S. Mackenzie, 4th Cavalry, commanded a detachment from the main column that consisted of six companies of his own regiment reinforced by one company of the 2nd Cavalry, two of the 3rd and two from the 5th Cavalry, totalling about 1,100 men. Mackenzie was further reinforced by a detachment of Pawnee warriors working as scouts for the army, whose job was to locate the hostiles. The Pawnee were traditional enemies of the Cheyenne. November on the northern plains was the time when Native peoples were settling down into sheltered winter camps along quiet creeks where there was plenty of timber for fuel. The Indians would have been busy gathering in food supplies for the harsh months to come when movement became almost impossible and food could be short.

The army approached the camp, which had been located by the Pawnee on 24 November. The village stretched along Bates Creek near the north fork of the Powder River in Wyoming Territory. The bands of Dull Knife and Little Wolf occupied 173 buffalo-hide tepees nestling in thin, snow-blanketed woods. The camp was lively and noisy, and, as darkness fell, a big celebration soon filled the surrounding countryside with the rhythmic thump of drums and chanting and singing. Big bonfires were lit, and as the Cheyenne warriors danced their bodies cast eerie shadows through the dark woods in which the soldiers had quietly concealed themselves. Mackenzie decided to delay his assault until dawn the next day, better to catch the

Indians off guard, as most would be sleeping off the previous night's exertions. The army would issue no warning to the slumbering village, and if women and children were killed along with warriors, so be it. Mackenzie's plan also called for the capture and destruction of the village, the intention being to force the Cheyenne survivors to surrender or perish in the frozen countryside bereft of shelter. The tepees and camp equipment would be burned and the Cheyenne ponies captured. Destitution would be visited upon Dull Knife and his followers.

As dawn light began to filter into a leaden sky overcast with snow, Mackenzie unleashed his troopers in a charge against the village, bugles shattering the calm of the creek bed. Ragged gunfire rippled along the ranks of charging troopers as they closed the distance to the nearest tepees. Warriors piled from them clutching their rifles and bandoliers, while terrified women and children fled in the opposite direction, away from the danger. In their haste to escape the soldiers, blankets and buffalo robes were left in the tepees with terrible consequences for the non-combatants. The warriors soon engaged the Pawnee scouts and soldiers in vicious hand-to-hand fighting. Outnumbered and outgunned, the soldiers pushed the warriors back through the village, until after a hard fight the Cheyenne men disengaged and withdrew in the same direction as their women and children.

Twenty-five Cheyenne lay dead inside the village, alongside Lieutenant J.A. McKinney and five enlisted men. Twenty-six soldiers were wounded, and within a short time the cavalry companies had managed to capture dozens of fleeing Indians. The soldiers, under orders, looted the village and then fired the tepees, reducing the village to a scene of devastation within minutes. 'From the hilltops we Cheyennes saw our lodges and everything in them burned,' recalled Iron Teeth, a Cheyenne woman. The Cheyenne ponies were rounded up and taken by the soldiers and Pawnee. For those Cheyenne who had fled into the surrounding countryside a new ordeal was beginning, as Mackenzie had so designed. Short of warm clothing and lacking shelter, many froze to death. 'Those were terrible days,' said Cheyenne warrior Beaver Heart, 'The nights were alive with the cries of men tortured with wounds and women and children dying of cold.' The Cheyenne survivors of the attack were left to fend for themselves, Crook being satisfied that those whom MacKenzie had failed to kill would be finished off by lack of shelter from the elements and starvation, or they would surrender and come in to the agencies.

Large groups, including Dull Knife and Little Wolf and their followers, surrendered to the soldiers to avoid further suffering. Only a few hardy souls managed to walk for eleven days through the snow all the way to Crazy Horse and his Oglala village to find shelter among the Sioux. During the march extreme measures were taken to keep people alive, Beaver Heart recalling: 'Children were warmed back to life by stuffing them into the stomachs of butchered horses.'[3]

Colonel Nelson A. Miles, known as 'Bear's Coat' to the Indians, had taken to the field on 5 November with fifteen officers and 434 enlisted men of the 5th Infantry and ten scouts. His job was to clear the hostiles out of the Yellowstone and Missouri River valleys. Miles' men were specially equipped with buffalo overcoats and hats, and the force would trek north with the intention of trapping the remaining Sioux between his advancing army and the Canadian border. Driving the Sioux across the border was also an option if the Indians refused to fight him, and the Lakota hostiles would then become another nation's problem.

While Crook and Mackenzie were dealing with the Northern Cheyenne on the Powder River, Colonel Miles had constructed a temporary base of operations at the mouth of the Tongue River. The 5th Infantry launched a series of patrols in force into the area between the Yellowstone and the Missouri rivers, leaving the remaining resisting Sioux no place to hide – except Canada. In large bands under their own chiefs thousands of Sioux, at a walking pace with all of their earthly possessions tied to horses or travois, slowly wound their way north through the Montana landscape, looking for a line of stone heaps that would signify their salvation and their freedom. The stone cairns, called the 'Medicine Line' by the Indians, marked the international border between the United States and British Canada.

Miles had effectively defeated the Sioux by December 1876, and Mackenzie had done the same to the Northern Cheyenne, driving Dull Knife's survivors through wintry conditions to Crazy Horse's band camped in the Tongue River valley. Crazy Horse soon became concerned for his own people as well as the Cheyenne refugees that he had taken in. The winter would be particularly difficult this year as game was fast disappearing and the army would continue to campaign through the snow and ice. Crazy Horse was concerned about the strain on their remaining food stores by having to feed Dull Knife's people, who quite literally had lost everything. He therefore decided that the time had come to make a peace with the soldier chiefs, and he sent out a small delegation to talk to Miles. Unfortunately, the delegation was ambushed and killed by a party of Crow Indians acting as scouts for the army. Crazy Horse and the other Sioux chieftains were furious and decided to continue raids against the soldiers in the hopes of drawing Miles into the field, where he could be defeated.

Miles did indeed come out to fight, moving his forces onto high ground in the Wolf Mountains in the Tongue River country in early January 1877. The weather was cold and overcast, with a light snow falling, on the morning of 8 January when Miles' piquets reported the approach of a large group of Indian warriors. Miles had with him companies A, C, D, E and K, and detachments of companies B and H of his own regiment, the 5th Infantry, supported by companies E and F of the 22nd Infantry. In total, including Indian scouts, Miles deployed 436 men against Crazy Horse and Two Moons, who had around 500 warriors in the field.

At 7am Crazy Horse and Two Moons, splitting their forces between them and approaching Miles' position from different directions, began a series of attacks on the army's perimeter:

> Lakota and Northern Cheyenne warriors charged K Company's lines. Steadying his men, the lieutenant [Carter] withheld the order to fire until the warriors were well within rifle range. Brief, heavy skirmishing ensued until the Indians were repulsed by the three companies stationed along the river and a few well-placed artillery rounds … Falling back into the hills, the warriors regrouped and charged again, this time probing the far eastern side of K Company's front line.[4]

Attempts to flank Miles' lines proved to be futile, as Miles handled his men flexibly and they managed to beat off every Indian assault:

> Throughout the early hours of the battle, the warriors repeated this action in an attempt to collapse Carter's line and force him to retreat across the river. Each advance, however, was met with rapid exchanges of rifle fire accentuated by the roar of artillery, which eventually forced the warriors to retreat to the shelter of the hills.[5]

It began to snow heavily during the fighting and, as the weather conditions deteriorated, Crazy Horse and his men withdrew. Casualties were three soldiers killed and eight wounded, and three Sioux warriors confirmed dead and an unknown number wounded. Tactically the Battle of the Wolf Mountains was a draw. But strategically it was a victory for the army.

Within weeks of the battle, the bonds that had held the non-agency bands together began to dissolve. In late January the first of many messengers sent out from Cantonment Tongue River and Camp Robinson in Nebraska arrived at the Lakota and Northern Cheyenne camp near the headwaters of the Bighorn River. These messengers bore promises of good treatment from the military, which was now trying to convince these bands to surrender before campaigning renewed in the spring.[6]

Crazy Horse was unable to hold his coalition together and he was wise enough to realise that continued resistance was no longer an option. In February the tribal councils met but could not agree on whether to continue the war against the Americans or surrender. Many of the band chieftains took their people into Miles' post at Camp Robinson or to the Great Sioux Reservation and surrendered in return for shelter and rations. By May 1877 only Crazy Horse and his own band remained free, but on the 6th he too led his people in to Camp Robinson in Nebraska and placed himself at the mercy of his enemies. He was met by Lieutenant William Philo Clark, who was Crook's representative at the post and chief of Indian scouts, and the two men shook hands. One of Crazy Horse's most prominent warriors stepped forward and placed his own war bonnet on Clark's head and gave the officer his long feathered pipe.

The last free Sioux in the United States had been captured. Only a few hundred under the leadership of Sitting Bull, Black Moon and a few dozen senior chiefs remained at liberty just across the border in Canada. There they lived at peace, but under the watchful eyes of 'the Great Mother's Redcoat Pony Soldiers' as the Sioux called the Northwest Mounted Police. Soon Sitting Bull's camps in Manitoba would attract thousands from the Sioux reservations. One event that helped to depopulate the reservations was the demise of Crazy Horse. The great warrior had resigned himself to reservation life, but rumours persisted that he was preparing to escape and join the other hostiles in Canada. On 5 September the army moved to arrest Crazy Horse, and while he was resisting confinement in the guardhouse at Camp Robinson a soldier bayoneted the Indian leader. Crazy Horse died of his wound shortly after.

Notes

1. Dale T. Schoenberger, *The End of Custer: The Death of an American Military Legend*, (Surrey, B.C.: Hancock House, 1995), 257.

2. Francis B. Taunton (ed.), *Army Failures Against the Sioux in 1876: An Examination*, (English Westerners' Society, 1987), 20–21.

3. Robert J. Kershaw, *Red Sabbath: The Battle of Little Bighorn*, (Hersham, Surrey: Ian Allan Publishing, 2005), 196.

4. Jeffrey V. Pearson, 'Nelson A. Miles, Crazy Horse , and the Battle of Wolf Mountains,' *Montana: The Magazine of Western History*, 51 (Winter 2001), 54.

5. Ibid., 55.

6. Ibid., 66.

9

'FIGHT NO MORE FOREVER'

'Some one has said, history repeats itself ... If our Government cannot keep its plighted faith, even with the Indian, if it has no sense of honor left the civilised nations of the globe will not be slow to find out, and when they do, there is reason to fear a chapter in our history remains to be written which mankind shall tremble to read.'

Major H. Clay Wood, Assistant Adjutant-General
Department of the Columbia, 1876

Lewis and Clark and the Corps of Discovery were the first white people the Nez Perce ever encountered in their wild and rugged lands in the Pacific Northwest, when the two army captains struggled out of the Bitterroot Mountains more dead than alive in September 1805. Lewis and Clark passed through the Nez Perce villages again on the journey back from the far west in May 1806. Both explorers agreed that the Nez Perce were the noblest of the 'noble savages' they had encountered and they had 'shown much greater acts of hospitality than we have witnessed from any nation or tribe since we have passed the Rocky Mountains.'[1] To the Americans, as explorers and settlers began to move into Oregon Territory during the early 1830s, the Nez Perce were agreeable and peaceful. They were 'an honorable exception to the general Indian character,' wrote the Commissioner of Indian Affairs in 1843, 'being more noble, industrious, sensible, and better disposed towards the whites.'[2] The Nez Perce had accepted a Christian mission in 1836, and the whites expected that these part-time buffalo hunters, root-gatherers, horse-breeders and salmon fishermen might yet become farmers without too much trouble. The problem for the Nez Perce was, in common with most of the other Indians discussed in this book (except those inhabiting the arid regions of the southwest), their land.

By the early 1840s the U.S. Government was casting a proprietory eye on the Nez Perce domain. Elijah White, Sub-Agent for Indian Affairs west of the Rockies, wrote:

> The arable land in this upper country is confined almost entirely to the small streams, although further observation may prove that many of extensive rolling prairies are capable of producing wheat. But the rich growth of buffalo grass upon it will ever furnish an inexhaustible supply for innumerable herds of cattle and sheep. I know of no country in the world so well adapted to the herding system.[3]

White's estimation of the potential of the river valleys on Nez Perce territory for white use was tempered by his own desire not to see any harm done to the tribe themselves, and, ever the optimist, he wrote: 'I am happy to feel assured that the United States Government have no other thought than to regard the rights and want of the Indian tribes in this country.'[4] Captain Benjamin Alvord, 4th Infantry, sent up-country to look the land over and inspect the Indians, was disappointed to discover that the sole agency actually attempting to 'civilise' the Nez Perce were missionaries, a husband and wife team name Spalding, and that the government 'has done nothing for any of these Indians. They have received no schools, ploughs, blacksmiths or vaccination.'[5]

In 1855 the Nez Perce political leadership signed a treaty that allowed complete American ownership of all of their lands. It was the brainchild of Governor Isaac Stevens of Washington Territory, who strove to end the inter-tribal warfare throughout the region that was seen as an impediment to white settlement. His solution was physically to separate the various tribal peoples of the region by placing them on separate reservations. No longer would the Nez Perce war with the Cayuse, or the Wallawalla with the Umatilla, or the Yakima with the Palouse. The effect was to open up vast areas of the Columbia Basin to white settlement.

The Nez Perce would go to a separate reservation in their old country, consisting of eight million acres, including the Wallowa and Imnaha Valleys, vital for grazing their huge herds of Appaloosa spotted horses, and for harvesting the camas root which was an important part of their diet. The Nez Perce complied to this move to prevent bloodshed with the Americans, but not all the Nez Perce agreed with the sale: many of the younger warriors and a few firebrand chieftains forming a strong anti-treaty party. They were right to be wary of American promises, for the 1855 treaty soon appeared to be as legally water-tight as a sieve. Written into its promises were caveats permitting the Americans to build roads through the reservation, fell timber and to enter and settle any lands not actually occupied and cultivated by the Indians. Most Nez Perce still lived a semi-nomadic, hunter-gatherer lifestyle, so hardly any of the millions of acres was 'under cultivation,' and whites had their pick of tribal lands.

All around them, between 1855 and 1858, other Pacific Northwest tribes rose against the injustices perpetrated against them by the Americans, but the Nez Perce did nothing. They sat and watched, sold horses to the army (for which they were never fully compensated) and argued among themselves over what to do. The leaders of the peace faction, chiefs Old Joseph and Lawyer, counselled non-violence and accommodation with the whites, and their arguments won through. Although the treaty was worthless, the reservation was not inundated with white settlers for the moment, and even when small gold deposits were discovered by prospectors in 1860 at the western end of the Lolo Trail, the terrain, climate and Nez Perce sentinels kept most whites away. 'Richer diggings than that would be necessary to start a stampede across 150 miles of snow-swept plateau with winter at hand and the dreaded Nez Perce gauntlet to be run.'[6] Miners were not interested in the valuable Nez Perce grazing lands, so they could afford to be ignored.

So accommodating were the Nez Perce leaders to the needs of the gold miners that, in 1861, they granted them permission to construct a landing stage for steamers and a supply depot on a plot of land between the Snake and Clearwater rivers. The whites went much further, and months of hammering and sawing illegally produced the town of Lewiston. Settlers started marking out allotments and gardens, erecting fences, and boozing themselves silly in several dubious taverns and saloons that mushroomed on the back of the mining trade. Gut-rot liquor found its way to the local tribes and soon intoxication led to fights, social breakdown and murders among the Nez Perce.

The chieftains demanded that the Americans honour one of the terms of the 1855 treaty, namely to provide troops to disperse unwanted whites, but the Americans countered with the offer of another treaty further to reduce the Nez Perce domain. Deep divisions now opened up among the various leaders of bands of Nez Perce, some of whom had profited from close cooperation with the whites, and others who stood to lose their lands should the new treaty be signed. Chief Lawyer wanted once again to accept the treaty; chiefs Old Joseph and Big Thunder wanted the Americans to send troops to expel the unwanted whites; and Chief Eagle-from-the-Light wanted to wage war on the whites and kill as many as he and his warriors could lay their hands on. Disagreement was so great that in 1863 the Nez Perce leaders dissolved a united tribal system that had been in operation since 1842, reverting to a loose alliance of bands, with chieftains exercising authority only over their immediate followers. Big Thunder and Eagle-from-the-Light withdrew their bands from the treaty negotiations and left to hunt and fish. All believed that the Americans would have to make separate treaties with the different bands, but in this they were deceived, for the Americans made the treaty with Lawyer alone and reduced the Nez Perce reservation by three quarters without consulting anyone else.

The peacemaker, Old Joseph, dumbfounded by the Americans' arrogance, symbolically burned his Bible and a copy of the 1863 treaty, and declared to his followers that he would have nothing more to do with the whites. Old Joseph had been the first Nez Perce baptised by the Spaldings in 1836. His loss to the white cause was a mistake the Americans would come to regret deeply over the next decade. His son and heir as leader of the Wallowa Band, Chief Joseph, later said of this period:

> Our fathers gave us many laws, which they had learned from their fathers. These laws were good. They told us to treat all people as they treated us.[7]

The Americans treated the Nez Perce badly, and in return Chief Joseph would follow his father's laws and eventually be driven to war with the whites.

Chief Lawyer soon discovered that he and his band had also been cheated by the Americans. The monies promised in the treaty were not forthcoming, as corrupt agents stole from the Indians and diverted some of the supplies due for the reservation. In 1866 an investigation was launched by Congress, which was growing concerned that many Nez Perce chiefs had become vociferously anti-white. The report said:

> For the last three or fours years the reservation has been overrun with white people, not only those in search of gold, but by others who have made locations there for agricultural purposes, and who have erected buildings, enclosed lands, and exercised all the rights of ownership over it.[8]

A new agent, John Monteith, was sent to the agency at Lapwai. Some of the bands that lived around Lapwai had begun farming and sending their children to schools run by Presbyterians. The problem was the anti-treaty bands. They remained on their lands, hunting and fishing and ignoring the whites. Hunting parties from these bands conducted six-month long buffalo-hunting expeditions to Montana, where they regularly fought with the Lakota Sioux. They resisted the spread of Christianity, and turned instead to the Dreamer Cult, a forerunner of the more famous Ghost Dance religion, promising Indian cultural renewal and the disappearance of the whites. The Dreamers attracted hundreds of angry and disillusioned Nez Perce, and it promoted the warrior culture and independence. The Americans viewed the Dreamer Cult as a dangerous conspiracy against their authority. Still the whites increased in numbers, encroaching onto the remaining reservation lands with their stock, always with their eyes firmly on the beautiful grazing lands still under Indian control.

The Nez Perce realised that the government cared little about their rights, and 'would not enforce any treaty regulations that would injure the white settlers.'[9] Even worse, although the Nez Perce could claim to have never killed a white man, they were prey to all the brutality and casual violence of white Frontier society. Between 1860 and 1877 around thirty Nez Perce were murdered by whites.[10] 'Whites guilty of horse and cattle stealing, fence burning, rape, assault, fraud, and various other crimes were in little danger as long as their accusers were Indians.' Most cases never made it to court, but 'when they did the defendants easily won their freedom because Indians were not allowed to testify against a white man.'[11]

Old Joseph died when relations with the whites were at their worst in 1871. He was succeeded as leader of the largest Nez Perce band, the Wallowa, who numbered around 250 people, by his son Rolling-Thunder-from-the-Mountains, known to history as Chief Joseph. Old Joseph had told his son never to sell the Wallowa Valley, but with Old Joseph barely cold in his grave white settlers broke into the Wallowa and claimed more land. Chief Joseph protested, and for once someone listened. John Monteith, the new agent at Lapwai, complained on Joseph's behalf to the Indian Bureau and, in an extraordinary outcome which no-one had expected, President Grant set aside the entire Wallowa Valley country in an 1873 executive order, ordering it to be given to the Nez Perce as a protected reservation.[12] Grant's decision outraged Governor L.F. Grover and the citizens of Oregon, who argued vociferously that this new reservation was an obstacle to the development of their territory, and the Wallowa band should be removed to the reservation at Lapwai, as agreed in 1863. Grover wrote directly to the Interior Secretary, Columbus Delano, pouring scorn on Joseph's people. 'This small band wish the possession of the large section of Oregon simply for room to gratify a wild, roaming disposition,' wrote Grover, 'and not for a home … If the Government shall admit that one subchief, out of more than fifty joined in council, can, by refusing his signature or by absenting himself, defeat the operation of a treaty, the policy of making treaties would be valueless, and but few treaties would be binding.'[13] Grant buckled under pressure from Oregonians, and, fearing censure at the polls, he penned another executive order in 1875 reversing his earlier decision and opening the Wallowa Valley to unrestricted white settlement and exploitation. What could be so freely given could also be swiftly taken back – after all, the Nez Perce could not vote, and were not even American citizens.

The army watched developments with growing unease, for it was usually civilian corruption and incompetence that drove the Indians onto the war-path, leaving the small and overstretched post-Civil War army to deal with the result. Brigadier General Oliver Howard, an elderly, one-armed Civil War veteran, anti-slavery campaigner, and local military commander for the region, assigned Captain Stephen Whipple, 1st Cavalry, to investigate the matter further. Whipple's findings convinced Howard that the President was wrong, calling it 'a great mistake to take from Joseph and his band … that valley.'[14] Howard firmly believed that Grant was wrong, and it could lead to trouble. Whipple had done little to dissuade Howard from his belief in a coming conflict, writing of the Nez Perce and Joseph's band in particular:

> They are proud-spirited, self-supporting, and intelligent … Experience shows that the two races [Indian and white] may not dwell together in a friendly way, especially on the borders, nor can an exception be looked for here.

Of their impending removal to Lapwai Whipple wrote:

> They may go without physical resistance, but it is by no means certain they will do so … They all realise that after they go to Lapwai reservation, or one similar, they will be obliged to give up their horses, which constitute their main wealth, and that as a community they will cease to exist.[15]

Joseph and the Wallowa band, as well as the other anti-treaty bands, had a great deal to lose.

By 1876 three chieftains had come to prominence as anti-treaty leaders, and because of the Dreamer Cult they were attracting considerable numbers of younger warriors away from the chiefs at Lapwai still cooperating with the Americans. Chief Looking Glass was a great warrior whose band was located off the reservation above Kooskia, on the Middle Fork of the Clearwater River. The prominent leader and shaman White Bird, also a respected warrior, lived on White Bird Creek. Finally, the fearless and experienced Chief Toohoolhoolzote led a small band that occupied the country between the Salmon and Snake rivers. Below these three older leaders were four fast-rising firebrands, chiefs Joseph and his brother Ollikut of the Wallowa band, and chiefs Hahtalekin and Hushhushcute of the Palouse band.

Joseph came to be immortalised as the leader of Nez Perce resistance, but he was no such thing. He was influential, and his opinions were carefully considered, but he was not really a warrior any longer, and his later fame mainly stemmed from the fact of his being leader of the largest band. There was no single leader of the Nez Perce, but rather a loose confederation of hunting bands, each following its own set of chiefs.

The Wallowa band had much to lose. Joseph and his clan controlled a territory of a million acres, twice as large as Lapwai Reservation, containing just 55 men and 195 women and children. The band had about 4,000 horses, or 15 head of stock per man, woman and child, so they were very wealthy, in addition to a stock of gold and American currency. They were well armed, with plenty of ammunition, and their tepees and camp equipment was of the finest quality and workmanship.

Secretary Delano decided to send a commission to the Nez Perce in 1876 with authority to try to resolve the impasse. Headed by Howard, the five-member commission met with Joseph at Lapwai. Howard soon realised that Joseph was no ignorant savage to be bullied or bribed, but an intelligent and charismatic leader 'in the full vigour of his manhood.' Howard described Joseph as 'six feet tall, straight, well-formed, and muscular; his forehead is broad, his perceptive faculties large, his head well formed, his voice musical and sympathetic, and his expression usually calm and sedate, when animated marked and magnetic.'[16] Howard made clear that the government wished to absorb the Wallowa Valley into the ceded territories, and for Joseph and his people to move onto the Lapwai Reservation. Joseph's reply to each of the commissioner's requests was an emphatic 'no'. In return for giving up one million acres, the band would receive 5,000 acres of reservation farmland. It was a ludicrous proposition, but Howard knew that he had some iron in his glove, commenting:

If the Indians hesitate to come to the reservation, government directs that soldiers be used to bring them in hither. Joseph and Ollikut know that we are friendly to them, and if they comply there will be no trouble.'[17]

At a second council on 4 May 1877 Joseph was joined by part of White Bird's band, and by Toohoolhoolzote, described by Howard as '… a large, thick-necked, ugly, obstinate savage of the worst type.'[18] Toohoolhoolzote told Howard that he had no right to compare him and other Indians to small children, and that the American government did not have the right to think for the Nez Perce.

While Howard and the other commissioners argued with the Indians, over three heated meetings, Howard made secret preparations for war. Whipple took a company of cavalry across the Wallowa to the confluence of the Snake and Grande Ronde rivers. Captain Trimble moved a company to the white settlement at Lewiston, and two companies departed from Vancouver to a camp at Wallulu.

At the third council on 7 May Toohoolhoolzote again spoke, claiming that it was wrong to separate the Indians from their lands, lands that were theirs by inheritance, and he demanded that Howard and Monteith tell the truth regarding their intentions. 'The law is, you must come to the reservation,' replied Monteith, 'The law is made in Washington; we don't make it.'[19] Toohoolhoolzote told the commissioners: 'Part of the Indians gave up their land; I never did. The earth is my body, and I never gave up the earth … What person pretended to divide the land and put me on it?' Howard replied that he did, and he was acting in the name of the Great Father, the President. 'My orders are plain, and will be executed,' said Howard. 'I hoped the Indians had good sense enough to make me their friend and not their enemy.'[20] Howard threatened to have Toohoolhoolzote arrested and sent to Indian Territory. Howard's resolve to use force to move the remaining Nez Perce to Lapwai seemed to take the fight out of the leaders. 'After this the Indians talked in a different spirit; readily agreeing to go with us the next day, first to inspect the valley of the Lapwai, and afterward other portions of the reservation where small farms could be set apart for the Indians' cultivation.'[21] On 15 May, at a final council, the anti-treaty bands were instructed to report to particular reservations, and given between thirty and thirty-five days to complete the resettlement. White Bird's band would go to Kamiah, Joseph's and Hasotin's to Lapwai and Sweetwater, and Hushhushcute's to the Clearwater.

When Joseph arrived home in the Wallowa many of the lesser chieftains and warriors were angry that he had sold out against the wishes of his late father. Joseph argued forcefully and eloquently that a war with the Americans would only end in their complete destruction, telling them: 'it is better to live in peace than to begin a war and lie dead.'[22] Even though many in his band branded their leader a coward, Ollikut, the band war chief, stood by his brother, and the council was eventually persuaded to sanction the move to Lapwai. Joseph later said of his momentous decision:

> I knew I had never sold my country and that I had no land in Lapwai; but I did not want bloodshed. I did not want my people killed. I did not want anybody killed … I said in my heart that, rather than have war, I would give up my country. I would give up my father's grave. I would give up everything rather than have the blood of white men upon the hands of my people.[23]

The haste of the move meant that the Wallowa band had to leave behind many head of cattle, as there was insufficient time to gather them in, much to the delight of arriving white settlers. They eventually camped two miles from the reservation, and, with ten days remaining before they would have to report, they tried to enjoy the last of their freedom. All five bands gathered together, representing some 600 Nez Perce, and the collected chieftains debated the events of the past and their uncertain future long into the night.

The warriors were restless, and many were only held in check by their respect for certain chiefs. One warrior named Wal-lait-its could contain himself no longer. His father had been mortally wounded by white men months before, and his dying wish was that his son should avenge his death. A group of warriors had paraded through the tepee village one day, and Wal-laits-its had been rebuked by an older man after he failed to control his horse. 'See what you do,' shouted the man. 'Playing brave you ride over my woman's hardwork food. If you so brave, why you not go kill the white man who killed you father?'[24] Shamed and humiliated, the younger man decided to act, and with two companions, Red Moccasin Tops and Swan Necklace, the trio rode out of the village seeking revenge. Unable to find the man responsible for Wal-lait-its' father's murder, they instead rode to the cabin of another white man known to be cruel to Indians, and killed him. Continuing on, they killed four more settlers and wounded a fifth, before riding back into the Nez Perce camp declaring what they had done, and tried to organise the other warriors into a larger raiding party. Joseph and Ollikut returned to the camp from a trip to the Salmon River just as twenty warriors rode proudly out of the camp, but their words did not deter the young men, and as they were from a different band from Joseph and his brother the two chiefs had no authority over them.

The second raid was a disaster, giving the Americans the excuse they needed for war. After seizing and consuming a large quantity of whiskey from a settler's home, the warriors went on a drunken rampage, killing fifteen white men, raping several women and looting many homesteads. The rest of the Nez Perce camp was 'shocked at the many killings. Family after family hastily struck their tipis and moved away, anxious to avoid being classed with the guilty.'[25] Most of the Wallowa band sought shelter with Looking Glass on the Clearwater River. White Bird and Toohoolhoolzote moved their bands to White Bird Creek. On 15 June 1877 Howard dispatched Captain David Perry and two companies of the 1st Cavalry, reinforced with eleven civilian volunteers, to White Bird Canyon.

The soldiers rode out in companies and deployed before the large Indian camp on White Bird Creek. Indian leaders rode out to meet them, one carrying a large white flag. As Perry and his headquarters group approached the Indians a shot boomed out from behind him – a civilian volunteer had fired at the Nez Perce peacemakers. Immediately, a Nez Perce warrior raised an old muzzle-loading musket and fired, Perry's trumpeter falling dead from his saddle. Confusion reigned as Perry's officers ordered their men into action, and Indian warriors came forward to defend the camp. Perry's remaining 119 men outnumbered and outgunned the 65 Nez Perce warriors, many of whom were only armed with bows. But it was the warriors who quickly established the upper hand, cutting the companies into sections, Perry losing the civilians on his flank when they fled the field. In a confused fight, amid cries, rippling carbine and musket fire and thick gunsmoke, the Nez Perce managed to corner a group of nineteen soldiers against a rock wall and killed them all. 'It was just like two bulldogs meeting,' recalled Nez Perce warrior Yellow Wolf:

> Those soldiers did not hold their position ten minutes. Some soldiers … were quickly on the run. Then the entire enemy force gave way.[26]

Men fell everywhere, many inexperienced young volunteers who had never heard a shot fired in anger. For the warriors it was different – they were experienced fighters who had won their honours in countless battles with other tribes throughout the region and down on the plains against the mighty Sioux. The warriors fought hard to allow the older men and women to pack up the camp, gather the horses and begin to move off into the hinterland. Perry's command was routed, and as the Indian warriors slowly withdrew Perry was unable to give chase. Yellow Wolf recalled, 'We did no scalping. We did not hurt the dead. Only let them lie.'[27] Thirty-four soldiers were dead, and another four were wounded, demonstrating the cool-headed and deadly accurate Nez Perce fire. Indian casualties were astonishingly light – only two warriors wounded. As the Indians withdrew they picked up sixty-three army carbines from the dead or abandoned by panic-stricken soldiers, and large amounts of ammunition from loose cavalry horses whose saddle-bags contained the troopers' reserve ammunition packs.

Howard and his superiors were stunned by the enormity of the military reverse at White Bird Canyon. The fight should have been a foregone conclusion, the army fielding more men and better weapons. Howard was shocked, 'fearing that the uprising would spread to the treaty Nez Perces as well as other Northwest tribes ...'[28] The only way to prevent this was to contain the Nez Perce by pouring troops into the region.

Howard took the field at the head of a small army numbering 227 regulars and 20 volunteers, to pursue and attack the Nez Perce camp that by now had moved from White Bird Canyon towards White Bird Creek. Howard also ordered Colonel John Gibbon, who had relieved Major Reno and the shattered 7th Cavalry at the Little Bighorn with a mixed force of 200 regular troops and civilian volunteers, to move on the Nez Perce. Another deployment was Captain Whipple and two companies of cavalry, ordered to arrest Looking Glass, who was camped with his band on the Nez Perce reservation. Howard's decision to go after Looking Glass was heavily influenced by local settler gossip that suggested that the chief was going to join the 'revolt.' In the meantime, the Nez Perce at White Bird Creek had received some welcome reinforcements in the shape of another band, including two fine warriors named Rainbow and Five Wounds, who were returning from a buffalo-hunting expedition to the plains.

On 1 July, Whipple's command, which included a section of Gatling machine guns, was spotted approaching Looking Glass' camp between the forks of the Clearwater River. Warriors turned out of their tepees, unsure of the soldiers' intentions. Suddenly, a group of civilian volunteers spurred their horses towards the village, firing rifles and pistols as they charged, yelling and cursing. Whipple had no alternative other than to order his bugler to sound the charge and support these hotheads. The Indians fled, leaving behind most of their camp equipment, several being felled by carbine bullets, and Looking Glass waved his arms in the air trying to surrender to the soldiers. Forty Nez Perce warriors managed to get most of the people out of harm's way, and while the soldiers were busy looting the abandoned village Looking Glass led them towards the main hostile camp at White Bird Creek. Looking Glass was furious, and could not believe that the Americans had attacked. 'My horses, lodges and everything I had was taken away from me by the soldiers we had done so much for,' said Looking Glass. 'Now, my people, as long as I live, I will never make peace with the treacherous Americans. I did everything I knew to preserve their friendship and be friends.'[29] Whipple had sent word shortly afterwards through Indian scouts that the attack on Looking Glass had been a mistake, as indeed it was, but Looking Glass was in no mood to believe him. 'It is a lie,' he declared in council. 'He [Whipple] is a dog and I have been treated worse than a dog by him. I am ready for war.'[30]

Ten days after the attack on Looking Glass, Howard's scouts located the main hostile camp on the Clearwater River, where it had moved after the returning buffalo hunters, and Looking Glass and his people had joined up with it. Howard's army had been reinforced, and now numbered 400 soldiers, 180 scouts, teamsters and packers, and was accompanied by a pair of Gatling machine guns and a howitzer. The gloves were off as far as Howard was concerned, and he planned to launch a surprise attack on the large village that was tucked into a bend of the river. Disregarding non-combatant casualties, Howard intended to hit the village with the latest in nineteenth-century military technology.

Howard's troops dismounted, fanned out by companies into woods close to the village and lay in wait, weapons locked and loaded. The two Gatling guns were rolled forward on their carriages and set up, along with the howitzer, shells being broken out of the limber and primed. Howard scanned the peaceful village through field glasses and gave the order to fire. A great cacophony of noise erupted as gunners cranked the Gatling's handles, feeding long brass magazines of bullets into the breech, and the multi-barrel arrangement spitting hundreds of rounds towards the standing tepees. Accuracy was difficult, but the heavy machine-gun bullets filled the air, kicking up lines of dirt and blowing holes through the thin-skinned tepees.

The bellowing of the Gatling guns went on and on. Suddenly, with a sharp report, the howitzer reared back on its carriage and a high-explosive shell crashed into the village, kicking up a cloud of dirt, debris and flying shrapnel. The village had erupted like an ant's nest at the first shots, warriors rushing out to defend their women and children, while older chiefs oversaw the effort to pack up the camp and gather the hundreds of horses nearby. Suddenly, the Gatling guns and howitzer fell silent and bugle calls rent the air as Howard's troopers charged towards the village, intent on overrunning it. Chief Toohoolhoolzote had gathered twenty-four warriors to him moments before the main attack opened, and they had taken up good defensive positions before the camp. Soon, the deadly accurate fire of Toohoolhoolzote and his companions stopped the charge in its tracks, officers ordering their men to hit the dirt and find cover.

More warriors began to make their presence felt on Howard's flanks and rear, until, with dawning horror, the general realised that his command was surrounded and under siege. Joseph was sometimes on the firing line, but mostly in the village, getting people and animals away from danger. His brother, Ollikut, led the Wallowa band's warriors against the soldiers, fighting hard all day. Five bands were present, and each followed its own leaders. All day long accurate sniper fire from the Nez Perce kept the troops pinned down, and the Indians were too close to the army lines for Howard to be able to use his Gatling guns or artillery safely. Hand-to-hand fighting erupted here and there along the perimeter as excited warriors occasionally dashed forward to kill soldiers with their traditional edged weapons or count coup. Howard's command was immobile for hours, giving the rest of the Nez Perce camp time to get away with most of their property and possessions. After a time the Nez Perce fire slackened as the warriors melted away to join their fleeing camp, until they were all gone. Howard was in no position to follow them. Thirteen of his men were dead and twenty-three were wounded. The Nez Perce had once again come off much better, losing four killed and six wounded.

When the Nez Perce camped again a council of chiefs was held to debate what to do. Toohoolhoolzote, White Bird and Looking Glass proposed that the entire camp should cross the mountains and join their Crow allies on the Montana plains. Looking Glass told them that the war would be over if they went to the plains, far away from 'One-Arm' Howard, who would not follow them. They would be able to hunt in peace with their friends, little realising that the Crow were working as scouts for the army. Joseph objected to this plan, for it meant the final abandonment of their lands. His speech was impassioned and eloquent:

What are we fighting for? Is it our lives? No. It is for this fair land where the bones of our fathers are buried. I do not want to take my women among strangers. I do not want to die in a strange land. Some of you tried to say

once, that I was afraid of the whites. Stay here with me now and you will
have plenty of fighting. We will put our women behind us in these mountains
and die on our own land fighting for them. I would rather do that than run I
know not where.[31]

Joseph was defeated in a vote, and the Nez Perce committed themselves to
crossing the wild Bitterroot Mountains by way of the difficult Lolo Trail.

Howard, in the meantime, was being lambasted by his superiors for having
lost the hostiles. Reluctantly, he gathered together his little army and, through
intelligence from his scouts, he began to follow the Nez Perce onto the
Lolo Trail. He telegraphed ahead to Missoula, Montana, instructing Captain
Charles C. Rawn, 7th Infantry, and a platoon of thirty-five men to move to
the end of the Lolo Trail and block the Indians' progress. Taking along 200
civilian volunteers to stiffen his ranks, Rawn constructed a small log fort at
the eastern end of the trail and dug in to await the arrival of the Nez Perce.

On 25 July the Nez Perce column came struggling down out of the mountains, a vanguard of warriors soon discovering the strange little wooden fort
incongruously blocking their path. The Nez Perce had been nine days on
the trail, trekking through fearsome country, their horses dragging travois
loaded with packed tepees, camp equipment and personal possessions, some
Indians riding, others walking. Women trekked with babies strapped to
backboards, old people managed as best they could, and everywhere, to the
front, rear and flanks, warriors covered the withdrawal armed with captured
army carbines and pistols.

Joseph, Looking Glass and White Bird rode forward to the fort, with its
Stars and Stripes flag fluttering in the wind, and indicated that they wished
to parley. Rawn listened to what the Indians had to say through an interpreter. The chiefs told Rawn that they were on their way to the Crow,
and they would pass peacefully down the Bitterroot Valley without harm-
ing any white settlers if Rawn would permit them to pass freely. The civilian
volunteers had no stomach for a fight with the Nez Perce, whose reputation
had already preceded them, and they strongly suggested to Rawn that he
agree to the Indian proposal. Rawn could only count on his thirty-five
regulars - hardly enough to stop over 200 Nez Perce warriors if he refused
them safe passage. He let them go, and thereafter Rawn's little post in the
wilderness was dubbed 'Fort Fizzle' in the press.

Some days before, Howard had ordered Colonel Gibbon to intercept
the fleeing hostiles. During the time the Nez Perce were on the Lolo Trail

Gibbon had been busy moving his command, numbering 163 regulars and 35 volunteers, by forced march from his base at Fort Shaw in Montana to intercept the Nez Perce as soon as they came into range. When the Nez Perce had crossed the Continental Divide they had slowed their pace considerably, believing that, as they had left Howard's military jurisdiction, they no longer had anything to fear from the army. They made camp in the Big Hole Valley and rested. General-in-Chief William Sherman ordered Howard to continue to pursue the hostile Nez Perce until they were captured or 'driven beyond the boundaries of the United States,'[32] a tactic already used against those Lakota Sioux followers of Sitting Bull in the winter of 1876–77.

Gibbon was not a man burdened with a conscience. His idea of a successful engagement with the Indians was eerily similar to Sand Creek. He did not care one iota whether Indian women and children were gunned down alongside warriors. Gibbon was one of a select few senior officers involved in the Nez Perce War who was promotion-hungry, and on the Frontier army promotion was often measured in decades. His eyes were firmly set on a brigadier general's star, and killing Indians, lots of Indians, was a sure-fire method of attracting attention in Washington. Custer had tried the same approach on the Little Bighorn thirteen months before.

With surprise on his side, largely because, having felt secure outside of Howard's jurisdiction, the Nez Perce had posted no guards, Gibbon's troops silently crept towards the sleeping camp at first light on 9 August. Their silent approach was blown when they ran into a solitary horse-herder, who was immediately shot dead. As the shot stirred the Nez Perce from their slumbers, the soldiers spread out in skirmish lines, took aim at the ninety tepees before them, and poured sustained volley fire into the village before their officers ordered the charge. Gibbon had caught the Nez Perce completely unawares, and the carnage was horrible. 'Women were shot without hesitation,' wrote Lieutenant Charles Wood, on Howard's staff, 'children were gunned down.' Once inside the village the soldiers went on a killing frenzy, murdering everyone they encountered, recalled Wood, and 'even babies had their heads crushed with a kick or a clubbed rifle.'[33] Yellow Wolf, a Nez Perce warrior, remembered years later the pitiful sights in the village:

> Wounded children screaming with pain. Women and men crying, wailing for their scattered dead! The air was heavy with sorrow I would not want to hear, I would not want to see, again.[34]

Unlike at Sand Creek in 1864, where the Cheyenne had been forced out of their village and into the hinterland, at Big Hole the Nez Perce managed to organise a few warriors who fell on the troops. The lieutenant commanding Gibbon's left flank was killed, and his men became disorganised without a leader in the face of a fierce counter-attack. Gibbon was soon forced onto the defensive, as more and more Nez Perce warriors began to surround his men, accurate sniper fire once more causing the troops to go to ground. Joseph was prominent in getting the village packed up and moving.

The soldiers began to run out of ammunition and water before the Nez Perce started to evaporate into the mist like wraiths, and then the vanguard of Howard's weary column appeared to relieve Gibbon from a situation that too closely resembled the Little Bighorn for comfort. There would be no general's star for Gibbon on this day, not with thirty-three of his men dead, and thirty-eight (including himself) wounded. In the Nez Perce column there was great sorrow and sadness. Twelve warriors, including Rainbow, Five Wounds and Wal-lait-its, had been killed, along with seventy-seven women, children and elderly non-combatants. The dead they left behind were exhumed by Bannock Indian scouts accompanying Howard and ritually scalped and mutilated before Howard ordered them re-buried.

The Battle of Big Hole had a profound effect on the Nez Perce attitude towards the whites. The killing of so many women and children hardened their hearts, and made them determined not to surrender to the army. Howard became the most despised person in the Nez Perce world, for they held him ultimately responsible for the crimes committed by his soldiers, and from now on all whites were fair game as far as the Indians were concerned. As they retreated from the Big Hole they shot down messengers and scouts, ransacked white ranches and stole cattle and horses, attacked stage stations, camping parties and gold prospectors.

The Nez Perce trekked on, entering Yellowstone National Park, which had been established as a sanitised version of the American West (minus dangerous wildlife and Indians) in 1872. Howard and his forces were a day behind, but the Nez Perce hurried on, aware of his presence and unable to rest properly, because if they stopped the army would catch up and attack them again. Howard detached Lieutenant George Bacon and a small cavalry force and instructed him to ride hard across country to reach Targhee Pass before the Indians and cut them off. It was Fort Fizzle all over again.

In the meantime, although they knew nothing of Bacon's mission, the chiefs nonetheless realised that they had to somehow slow Howard down.

A group of warriors, some led by Ollikut, backtracked towards Howard's column while their relatives continued on, and raided Howard's horse and mule herd on the night of 20 August at Camas Meadows. The Nez Perce managed to run off the army's mules, vital for carrying the column's supplies, and Howard was halted for several days while officers were sent out to purchase new mules from local settlements. For the first time the pressure was taken off the main Nez Perce column.

Howard, meanwhile, sent out messages to all local army commanders, asking them to join in the effort to stop the Nez Perce. Brigadier General Alfred Terry was contacted, and asked 'that if the hostiles should reach the park [Yellowstone] and cross into the Big Horn country, on the passes of the Stinkingwater, Colonel Miles should be ordered to attack them.'[35] Howard referred to Colonel Nelson A. Miles, one of the army's ablest and most aggressive officers, stationed with his 5th Infantry along the Canadian border to contain incursions from Sitting Bull and the 5,000 Lakota Sioux refugees camped inside the British Dominion. The Nez Perce fugitives entered Yellowstone National Park, as Howard had predicted, injuring some tourists and narrowly missing running into General Sherman, who was holidaying in the park, and moved across north-western Wyoming, swinging northwards. Lieutenant Bacon waited at Targhee Pass, but when no Indians materialised he backtracked to Howard, narrowly missing them. Colonel Samuel Sturgis and the reinforced 7th Cavalry were directed to leave the Crow Agency for the Clark River Valley, another army unit being drawn into the effort to stop the Nez Perce.

The Nez Perce chieftains had decided to emulate their old enemy, the Sioux, and head for Canada to seek British protection, abandoning America entirely. They quickened their pace, trying to cover the miles that separated them from freedom and safety across the 'Medicine Line.' Sturgis was the first to attempt to prevent such a move, moving his men to Hart Mountain in the upper Yellowstone Valley, where he expected to block the Nez Perce path. Joseph was aware of Sturgis' deployment, and he sent a party of warriors around the soldiers during the night. The next morning these warriors stirred up a huge cloud of dust, and when Sturgis and his officers saw this, they thought that the hostiles had managed to creep past during the night. Sturgis ordered the 7th Cavalry to pursue, abandoning his blocking position at the mouth of the pass, allowing the main body of Nez Perce to pass through unscathed.

On 13 September Sturgis and his men caught up with the Nez Perce rearguard at Canyon Creek and fierce fighting broke out. The warriors turned and took cover in gullies and behind rocks, opening fire down the canyon as the cavalrymen tried to advance. The main Indian column hurried away from danger, leaving some of the warriors to slow the army down once again. A long running battle was fought along the canyon floor until darkness fell and Sturgis, short on ammunition and food, halted. Three of his men were dead, and another eleven were wounded. In return, the soldiers had only managed to wound three of the warriors that faced them.

A message was sent to Miles at Fort Keogh:

Joseph and his band have eluded Sturgis and he is now continuing his retreat toward British Columbia, and we believe aiming at refuge with Sitting Bull. He is travelling with women and children and wounded at a rate of about twenty-five miles a day; but he regulated his gait by ours. Will lessen our speed to about twelve miles a day and he will slow down. Please at once take a diagonal line to head him off with all forces at your command.[36]

Sherman had dispatched Lieutenant-Colonel Charles Gilbert in late August to assume field command of Howard's forces, as the commanding general had lost his faith in 'General Two-day Behind,' as the Nez Perce now mockingly called Howard, believing that he lacked sufficient drive and determination to defeat the Indians. Gilbert, however, failed to locate Howard in the rugged terrain, so Howard kept his command. Sherman's communications barely concealed his disgust for his subordinate's lack of zeal, one telegram reading: 'That force of yours should pursue the Nez Perces to the death, lead where they may ... If you are tired, give the command to some young energetic officer.'[37]

As soon as Howard slowed the rate of his march to twelve miles a day the Nez Perce conformed, utterly exhausted and in desperate need of rest and the chance to camp, hunt and gather food. They moved north across Montana, eventually arriving at the foot of the Bear Paw Mountains. They made camp and rested as they were now only thirty miles from the Canadian border, and only a day or two of marching would see them under Mountie protection. Little did they realise that Miles was rapidly closing on them as he force-marched his men to intercept them before they crossed the border.

Miles also wanted a general's star, and figured that if he was the man to capture Joseph and the Nez Perce, it would be his. His wife's two influential uncles, General-in-Chief Sherman and Senator John Sherman, would aid him in this endeavour. Importantly, for his plan to work Miles had to capture the fugitives *before* Howard arrived on the scene, as Howard outranked him and could take all of the glory. Miles' forces numbered 600 men, drawn from the mounted 5th Infantry, with attached companies from the 2nd and 7th Cavalry. He also had with him a large body of Cheyenne and Sioux warriors recruited off the reservations, who were looking for horses to capture and scalps to lift.

On the morning of the last day of September the Indian camp had arisen early and the pack animals were almost ready to leave when a large body of mounted soldiers and Indians were spotted rapidly approaching. They were about four miles away and closing. Panicked women and children hastily packed up what they could, as the warriors once again took up covering positions before the village. Miles, overly excited at finally setting eyes on his prize, and also realising how close they were to the Canadian border, had sounded the charge too early and alerted the Indians. White Bird quickly moved a party of warriors forward, and, firing from cover, they pole-axed Miles' 7th Cavalry troopers in the centre, killing two officers and twenty-two men, and wounding another forty-two. It was not an inspiring beginning for Miles. The Indians suffered as well, several notable leaders falling dead in their effort to defend the village, including Ollikut, Lean Elk and Toohoolhoolzote.

The 7th Cavalry survivors took shelter in gullies and behind rocks and returned the Indians' fire. A squadron of the 2nd Cavalry, along with the Cheyenne and Sioux scouts, veered to the left of the village and dashed into the Nez Perce horse herd on the west side of the village. The 7th Cavalry companies were barely holding their own until the 5th Infantry came up to support them. Companies got around the sides of the village and pushed the Nez Perce rear, and with most of their horses and pack animals being driven off by the Cheyenne and Sioux they were going nowhere. 'Unhappily, but prudently, Miles decided to suspend the assault and place the Nez Perce camp under siege.'[38]

Miles next tried to cut off the Indians' water supply by positioning troops between the village and the river, but warriors drove the soldiers off. A howitzer was brought forward and the gun 'occasionally mouthed a shell into that seemingly deserted hollow,'[39] where the village was laid out. That night, to add to the miserable condition of the Nez Perce were in, a storm blew in over the mountains and dumped five inches of snow over the battlefield.

Miles was growing desperate. At any time Howard's column could show up and his efforts would have been in vain, his general's star a memory. Colonel Sturgis might also arrive, Miles' equal in rank, and just as desperate for a star. The Nez Perce had already sent emissaries to Sitting Bull's camp across the border before Miles had attacked, and the army officers worried that the Sioux might intervene by pouring across the line to help their former enemies. Everyone knew that upwards of 2,000 Lakota Sioux warriors were in various camps in Canada, and their intervention would have been decisive.

The next day Miles hoisted a white flag over his forward positions, hoping to lure Joseph and the prominent chiefs to peace talks. A Nez Perce who could speak English spoke with Miles, and he was persuaded to bring Joseph to meet the Colonel. White Bird and Looking Glass emphatically refused to accompany Joseph, wanting nothing to do with the white soldiers. In a display of breathtaking deceit Miles ordered Joseph seized as a hostage, but the Colonel's plan soon went awry when Lieutenant Lovell H. Jerome, believing the Indians were about to surrender, strayed too close to Nez Perce lines and was captured. Joseph was exchanged for an unharmed Jerome the following day. On 4 October disheartening news was brought to Miles – Howard and his command was approaching.

Howard dismounted, stretched his aching joints and walked up to Miles, hand outstretched, a broad smile across his face. 'Hello Miles! I am glad to see you. I thought you might have met Gibbon's fate. Why didn't you let me know?'[40] Miles made no answer except for a cold, formal greeting, barely able to disguise his disappointment and irritation at Howard's arrival. Howard was keen to pacify his glory-hunting subordinate:

> Miles, you have given me the sort of assistance I wanted, and what I expected of you. You stopped those Indians, and I intend to see you have the credit for it. I know you are ambitious for a star and I am going to do all I can to help you … We will have a surrender … and I repeat – you shall receive the surrender. Not until after that will I assume command.'[41]

Miles entire manner changed on hearing those words, and he thanked Howard for all that he had said. Turning to the situation at hand, Miles briefed Howard on the position of the Nez Perce. They were surrounded, heavily outnumbered and outgunned, and they were suffering in the appalling weather conditions that had blown up. After the situation report,

Lieutenant Wood, Howard's adjutant, spoke quietly to the General out of earshot of Miles and his staff: 'General, I am a little surprised at what you have just said, and I feel as your aide I ought to speak very freely … You have just said that you are going to help Miles to a star. I feel that is very impulsive and may lead to some feeling on Gibbon's part.' Howard listened patiently, considering the younger man's words carefully. 'He is a much older man of the Civil War than Miles,' continued Wood, 'and we have left him behind us, wounded at the Big Hole battle.'[42] The jockeying for seniority and promotion amongst the officer corps out west was legendary, and Howard well knew Miles' political connections in Washington.

In the Nez Perce camp the situation looked dire. With the arrival of 'General Two-day Behind' and his men, surrender appeared to be the only option to avoid annihilation. It rankled the chiefs greatly that they had come so far, only to be defeated within a day's march of freedom in Canada, but they had to consider their people, who were shivering in shallow holes in the snow with little to eat and subject to regular artillery bombardment. Joseph decided to parley with the soldiers. On the morning of 5 October, as a chiefs' council broke up, Looking Glass was struck in the head by a stray bullet and killed instantly. His death took the heart out of the resistance. A Nez Perce crossed the lines and delivered a speech from Joseph that he had memorised to the assembled army officers:

> Tell General Howard I know his heart. What he told me before, I have in my heart. I am tired of fighting. Our chiefs are killed. Looking Glass is dead. Toohoolhoolzote is dead. The old men are all dead. It is the young men who say yes and no. It is cold and we have no blankets. The little children are freezing to death … Hear me, my chiefs. I am tired; my heart is sick and sad. From where the sun now stands I will fight no more forever.[43]

Two hours later Joseph appeared, riding slowly towards Howard, Miles and their staff officers, accompanied by five dismounted warriors. Joseph climbed down from his horse, adjusted the blanket thrown over his shoulder, and strode towards Howard. The rifle he had cradled across his arms was now held out to the General, but Howard indicated that Joseph should give his rifle to Miles, who respectfully took it. The surrender was his, after all.

In the Nez Perce camp some hours before White Bird had begun preparations to move north, knowing that Joseph would surrender soon. Those of his band who wished to surrender were bade farewell to, while a hard core of fourteen warriors and over eighty women and children decided to take their chances and walk to Canada. During the surrender, the soldiers were distracted and relaxed, and White Bird's party was able to slip unnoticed through army lines and begin the trek towards the Canadian border, determined to find sanctuary with Sitting Bull. The army took 418 prisoners, fully half of the men being wounded, indicating the savagery of the fighting. White Bird's party faced many privations and dangers on their trip into the frozen north, and several were killed and wounded when they were attacked by Gros Ventre and Assiniboine Indians guarding the Canadian borderlands. The bleeding and exhausted survivors were eventually met by friendly Sioux sentinels just over the border and escorted to Sitting Bull's camp twelve miles inside Canada. The terrible appearance and the sufferings recounted by White Bird and his people further inflamed the Sioux against the Americans, and was a contributing factor to Sitting Bull and the other chiefs resisting American peace overtures made by Brigadier General Terry shortly afterwards at a Peace Commission.

The final cost of the Nez Perce War was heavy for a tribe that had never been numerous. They had trekked 1,700 miles through some of the most challenging country in the world and suffered 151 killed and 88 wounded. The Americans had lost 127 soldiers, and around 50 civilians.

Following their surrender, the 418 Nez Perce were taken to Miles' post at Fort Keogh, where they spent the rest of the winter. Major-General Sheridan, Miles' commanding officer, ordered that the Nez Perce be moved to Fort Lincoln in the Dakota Territory in spring 1878, and then shipped by train down to Indian Territory. Miles had promised Joseph that he and his people would be able to return to Lapwai, but he was powerless to contradict Sheridan. The excuse for the removal was the escape to Canada of White Bird and his followers, though the real reason was political. The governor and citizens of Idaho did not wish to see the Nez Perce return, so dumping them in Oklahoma seemed the best choice. The decision led Charles Wood to write presciently: 'I think that, in his long career, Joseph cannot accuse the Government of the United States of one single act of justice.'[44]

The endnote to another glorious American campaign against the Indians was the usual tale of injustice that forms the familiar background chorus of the American West. Herded onto malarial swamps in Oklahoma, a quarter of the Nez Perce captured at the Bear Paw Mountains were dead from disease within a couple of years. In 1882, and again in 1885, the government relented after a campaign to restore the Nez Perce to Idaho was launched by well-meaning whites, and the Nez Perce themselves, and most returned to Lapwai in two waves. The state government and people of Idaho refused to allow the return of Joseph, who was mistakenly believed to have commanded the Nez Perce during the war, and he lived out the remainder of his life on the Colville Reservation in Washington Territory, where he died in 1904.

White Bird died in Canada in 1882, the year after Sitting Bull and most of the Sioux, deliberately reduced to starvation by the Canadian government to persuade them to leave the Dominion, had surrendered to the Americans. Most of White Bird's followers drifted back across the border shortly after their leader's death. The Lapwai Reservation was carved into allotments in 1895, when collective tribal land ownership was eradicated following the passage of the 1887 Dawes Act. Hard times were to follow for the Nez Perce, and hard times continue for them today.

Notes

1. *Thomas Jefferson's Message to Congress requesting Appropriations for Exploration*, (University of Idaho Library), http://menolly.lib.uidaho.edu/McBeth/governmentdoc/histlewisclark.htm, accessed 1 September 2000.

2. *Report of the Commissioner of Indian Affairs 1843*, (Washington DC: Government Printing Office, 1844).

3. Ibid.

4. Ibid.

5. *Report of Brevet Major Benjamin Alvord, Concerning the Indians in the Territories of Oregon and Washington, East of the Cascade Mountains, 1853 Military and Cultural Report, Annual Message from the President and Report of the War Department 1858*, (Washington DC: Government Printing Office, 1858).

6. Francis Haines, *The Nez Perces*, (Norman: University of Oklahoma Press, 1972), 155.

7. *Chief Joseph – Quotes from Chief Joseph*, http://www.indians.org/welker/joseph.htm, accessed 20 August 1999.

8. *The Status of Young Joseph and His Band of Nez-Perce Indians Under the Treaties Between the United States and the Nez-Perce Tribe of Indians, and the Indian Title to Land, 1876, US Army, Department of the Columbia*, (University of Idaho Library), http://www.menolly.lib.uidaho.edu/McBeth/governmentdoc/statusofyoungjoe.htm, accessed 1 September 2000.

9. Francis Haines, *The Nez Perces*, (Norman: University of Oklahoma Press, 1972), 202.

10. Alvin M. Josephy, *The Patriot Chiefs: A Chronicle of American Indian Resistance*, (New York: Penguin Books, 1976), 320–323.

11. Francis Haines, *The Nez Perces*, (Norman: University of Oklahoma Press, 1972), 210.

12. *Report of the Commissioner of Indian Affairs 1878*, (Washington, DC: Government Printing Office, 1879).

13. *Grover to Delano, July 21, 1873, 1875 Wallowa Valley Report,* in *Report of the Secretary of the War, 1875*, (Washington, DC: Government Printing Office, 1876).

14. *Report of Brigadier-General O. O. Howard, 1875 Wallowa Valley Report,* in *Report of the Secretary of the War, 1875*, (Washington, DC: Government Printing Office, 1876).

15. *Whipple to Howard, August 28, 1875*, (University of Idaho Library), http://www.menolly,lib.uidaho.edu/McBeth/governmentdoc/1875wallowavalley.htm, accessed 30 August 2007.

16. *Report of Civil and Military Commission to Nez Perce Indians, Washington Territory and the Northwest,* in *Report of the Commissioner of Indian Affairs, 1877*, (Washington, DC: Government Printing Office, 1878).

17. *Report of Brigadier-General O. O. Howard,* in *Report of the General of the Army 1877*, (Washington, DC: Government Printing Office, 1878).

18. Ibid.

19. Ibid.

20. Ibid.

21. Ibid.

22. Alvin M. Josephy, *The Patriot Chiefs: A Chronicle of American Indian Resistance*, (New York: Penguin Books, 1976), 324.

23. Geoffrey C. Ward, *The West: An Illustrated History*, (New York: Little, Brown & Company, 1996), 312.

24. Francis Haines, *The Nez Perces*, (Norman: University of Oklahoma Press, 1972), 247.

25. Ibid., 249.

26. Geoffrey C. Ward, *The West: An Illustrated History*, (New York: Little, Brown & Company, 1996), 312.

27. Ibid., 312.

28. Alvin M. Josephy, *The Patriot Chiefs: A Chronicle of American Indian Resistance*, (New York: Penguin Books, 1976), 327.

29. *The New Northwest*, December 6, 1878.

30. Ibid.

31. Francis Haines, *The Nez Perces*, (Norman: University of Oklahoma Press, 1972), 274–275.

32. Charles Wood, *The Pursuit and Capture of Chief Joseph*, Archives of the West 1874–1877, http://www.3.pbs.org/weta/thewest/wpgs660/joseph.htm, accessed 14 May 2007.

33. K. Andrist, *The Long Death: The Last Days of the Plains Indians*, (New York: Collier, 1969), 310.

34. Geoffrey C. Ward, *The West: An Illustrated History*, (New York: Little, Brown & Company, 1996), 314.

35. *Report of the Commissioner of Indian Affairs, 1877*, (Washington DC: Government Printing Office, 1878).

36. Charles Wood, *The Pursuit and Capture of Chief Joseph*, Archives of the West 1874–1877, http://www.3.pbs.org/weta/thewest/wpgs660/joseph.htm, accessed 14 May 2007.

37. Robert M. Utley, *Bluecoats and Redskins: The United States Army and the Indian, 1866–1891*, (London: Cassell & Collier, 1973), 309.

38. Stephen Longstreet, *War Cries of Horseback: The Story of the Indian Wars of the Great Plains*, (London: W.H. Allen, 1970), 313.

39. Alvin M. Josephy, *The Patriot Chiefs: A Chronicle of American Indian Resistance*, (New York: Penguin Books, 1976), 338.

40. Charles Wood, *The Pursuit and Capture of Chief Joseph*, Archives of the West 1874–1877, http://www.3.pbs.org/weta/thewest/wpgs660/joseph.htm, accessed 14 May 2007.

41. Ibid.

42. Ibid.

43. Ibid.

44. Ibid.

10

THE SMALL WARS

'All we ask is to be allowed to live and live in peace ... We bowed to the will of the Great Father and went south. There we found a Cheyenne cannot live. So we came home. Better it was, we thought, to die fighting than to perish of sickness.'

Chief Dull Knife, Northern Cheyenne, 1878

Cochise was a large, muscular Chiricahua Apache who wore his black hair long in the traditional style of his people. The Chiricahua had occupied territory in the northern Mexican region of Sonora and across the border in New Mexico and Arizona for several generations. The Mexicans had tried unsuccessfully for decades to capture or neutralise them, but without success. During General Carleton's brutal campaign against the Navajo, led to a dramatic climax by Kit Carson, who sent the survivors on the 'Long Walk,' Cochise and his people had kept up a steady stream of raids on white settlements and troops.

Cochise was allied with his father-in-law, another powerful Apache chieftain named 'Red Sleeves' or Mangas Coloradas. In January 1863 the Americans had seized Mangas Coloradas after tricking him into attending a peace conference, and Carleton's subordinate Brigadier General Joseph Rodman West had ordered the chief's death, saying: 'Men, that old murderer has got away from every soldier command and has left a trail of blood for 500 miles on the old stage line. I want him dead or alive tomorrow morning, do you understand? I want him dead.' Mangas Coloradas was extensively tortured by the soldiers and then shot to death after the Americans claimed he was 'trying to escape.' His head was cut off, boiled clean of flesh and muscle, and sent to Washington DC as an object of scientific study. Cochise was furious at the Americans' dishonourable tactics and his raids continued throughout the rest of the decade, until American military pressure eventually pushed him and his warriors into the Dragoon Mountains.

From their lofty eyrie Cochise and his men kept raiding until Major General George Crook arrived in 1871, ready to defeat them. Crook cleverly decided to employ fellow Apache warriors as scouts and informants, and by this method he was able to persuade most of Cochise's men to surrender. Cochise himself was captured in September. A year later the government, ignoring the terms of a treaty they had signed with the Chiricahua guaranteeing them their ancestral lands in Arizona, instead ordered them to the Tularosa Reservation in New Mexico. Cochise and his people refused to leave, and, when it became clear that the Americans were not interested in talking, Cochise and many of his warriors escaped back into the mountains to resume their guerilla campaign against local white settlements, often using extremely barbaric methods to dispose of their enemies, and incurring the wrath and enmity of all settlers throughout the region. Eventually, Cochise was forced to negotiate surrender to Brigadier General Oliver Howard (later of Nez Perce fame), and the Americans actually relented and granted the Apache some of the terms they had requested. Cochise went quietly onto the reservation in Arizona with his people, and it appeared as though the incessant fighting that had lasted for so many decades was at last over.

In 1874 Cochise died, and less than two years later the American government, in a moment of great foolishness, decided to move the Chiricahua Apache to San Carlos Reservation. One of Mangas Coloradas' most loyal lieutenants was a warrior named Goyaale, who the Mexicans had named Geronimo after they had killed his wife, three children and mother in 1851. 'Geronimo' derived from the last utterances of dying Mexicans, 'Santa Jerome,' after they had been expertly dispatched by Goyaale's blade. After Cochise's death Geronimo, though not a band chieftain, nonetheless became a leader to be feared and respected, and was a fine warrior leader. Half of the Chiricahua complied with the government's orders in 1876, while the rest fled into Mexico with Geronimo.

In spring 1877 Geronimo and his followers were recaptured in Mexico and brought to San Carlos. In September 1881 troops began gathering at San Carlos, and this caused Geronimo to fear that he would be imprisoned for his past deeds. He fled south into Mexico once more with 700 followers, constituting a serious 'outbreak.' In April 1882 Geronimo returned to San Carlos with horses and guns, and successfully liberated the rest of the Apaches held there, leading them into freedom in Mexico.

In spring 1883 Brigadier General George Crook was placed in charge of Arizona and New Mexico, and ordered to capture Geronimo and imprison the recalcitrant Apache. He immediately pursued Geronimo into Mexico. In normal circumstances the sallying of American troops into Mexico would have constituted a border violation, but the Americans had been given a special dispensation by the Mexican government that permitted them freedom to cross the border at will. The Americans had bullied a weak President Diaz into accepting an agreement that allowed military forces to cross the Rio Grande and attack so-called 'United States Indians' who fled into Mexico, or used the country as a base to strike at the American Southwest. In 1872 Colonel Ranald McKenzie had led a punitive raid against a Kickapoo Indian village at Remolino, Mexico, and in 1877 led across another army column against an Apache group.

In 1883 Crook found Geronimo's camp in Mexico and persuaded the chief and his followers to return to San Carlos without bloodshed. Crook instituted a series of reforms at the reservation, but the local newspapers, no friends of the Apache, criticised him for being too lenient on the Indians. They demonised Geronimo in the same way that Sitting Bull and Chief Joseph had been built up by the press into figures of mystery, brutality and cunning, to be feared and despised by all whites. Most Americans believed that Arizona would be a better place once Geronimo and his ilk had been licked by the army and killed or sent away. On 17 May 1885 Geronimo, drunk and intimidated by demands for his death blatantly printed in local newspapers, escaped once more with a small following back into Mexico.

In March 1886 Crook wearily pursued Geronimo back over the border. He set up a meeting with Geronimo, but he and his people fled when the soldiers arrived, convinced that a plot to murder Geronimo and other leaders was afoot. The Indians simply melted into the harsh countryside and Crook was unable to locate them again. The War Department criticised him for his failure to control Geronimo and Crook resigned in protest.

A new officer was sent south to take command. Nelson A. Miles had gained his brigadier general's star after defeating the Nez Perce in 1877 and in April 1886 he was appointed to replace Crook. Miles went about the task of recapturing Geronimo's band in a different manner from his predecessor. Whereas Crook had relied upon hundreds of friendly Apache scouts to track down Geronimo's band, Miles employed modern military science to cracking the problem. He set up two dozen heliograph points to allow for quick communication between army units in the field. Over 5,000 troops, supported by

500 Apache and 100 Navajo scouts, along with thousands of civilian militia, were arrayed against Geronimo, who had just twenty-four warriors with him. Miles' huge force methodically combed the borderlands for Geronimo, and it was not long before the band was located and cornered.

On 4 September 1886 a detachment under the command of Lieutenant Gatewood discovered Geronimo and persuaded him and his followers to surrender at Skeleton Camp, Arizona. Miles later stole all the credit from Gatewood for the successful recapture of the Apache, living up to his glory-chasing and self-promoting reputation.

The government made sure that never again would Geronimo and his kind escape. Geronimo's group was sent to Fort Marion, Florida, where they were held as military POWs. Later they were imprisoned in Alabama. Many died at these places from disease. Apache children were forcibly taken from their parents and sent to be re-educated at the Carlisle Indian School in Pennsylvania, where about fifty died through disease and abuse. Geronimo and some others were later transferred to Fort Sill in Indian Territory as prisoners of war.

In 1909 Geronimo died of pneumonia at the age of eighty-six, still a military prisoner at Fort Sill. Only in 1912 were the Apaches finally allowed to return to the Southwest after twenty-six years' imprisonment. In an interesting footnote to the history of Geronimo, his skull, some other bones and a silver belt buckle were allegedly stolen from his grave by three upper-class members of Yale University's secretive Skull and Bones Society during the First World War, when the young men were army volunteers at Fort Sill. One of the men implicated was President George W. Bush's grandfather, Prescott Bush. According to rumours, the skull, bones and artefacts are used in ceremonies inside the society's tomb-like meeting place on Yale University campus. Harlyn Geronimo, the famous chief's great-grandson, wrote to President Bush requesting the return of the bones to the tribe for burial. The story may be apocryphal, but research conducted in 2006 has suggested that there may be some truth to the tale.

In 1877 the Bannock nation numbered around 600 people at Ross Fork Agency on the Upper Snake River in southeast Idaho. About 150 miles to the north a few hundred more Bannocks shared the Lemhi Reservation with the Shoshone and Sheepeater peoples. The Bannocks had known peace for twenty years, but in common with the Nez Perce, the region's largest nation, and many of the smaller tribes scattered throughout the Pacific Northwest, they began to experience the insatiable lust of the white man for Indian lands during the final quarter of the nineteenth century. Even lands that had been given to them by the Americans decades before now began to come under threat from settlers who were eager to reduce Indian land holdings to a minimum and free up more to exploit. The Nez Perce had been driven to war, and the Bannocks and many other Indian peoples of the region found themselves also drawn into a hopelessly mismatched struggle to retain some form of their territory and lifestyle.

With the coming of more whites it was not just a seemingly insatiable desire for land that complicated the lives of local indigenous peoples; it was also the steady erosion of wild game by white homesteaders and ranchers, eager to replace nature's bounty with tamed beasts. The disappearance of game animals, coupled with the usual problem of insufficient reservation rations to take up the slack, meant food shortages and sometimes starvation for the Indians. All of the Bannocks were aware of the drastic measures taken by the Nez Perce. The Nez Perce had even tried to leave America, so what hope was there for the smaller tribes such as the Bannocks if the Americans ratcheted up the pressure on them and tried to take their remaining lands? Most, although angry and embittered towards the whites, nonetheless knew that making war on them was a no–win situation.

Trouble first began at Ross Fork Agency in August 1877, when two whites were wounded by Bannock warriors during violent confrontations. In November a white man was murdered, and military intervention became inevitable. Local army commander Colonel John Smith marched into the main Bannock village and demanded that the person responsible be handed over for trial. When the Bannocks refused to comply trouble flared briefly, and Smith had fifty-three warriors disarmed and their horses taken away before calm was restored.

As winter clamped its icy grip over the region the Bannocks and the other indigenous peoples went into winter quarters. They debated and fumed over the behaviour of the whites through the dark winter days and nights, but they avoided talk of going to war. When spring broke the Bannocks emerged from their camps and headed out to the Camas Prairie to dig for roots, something they shared in common with the Nez Perce. They had done this for generations, but in spring 1878 they discovered instead that the whites had beaten them to this important food source. Settlers' pigs had been led up to the prairie before the Bannocks had stirred from their cosy winter camps and had eaten much of the root stock. It was another blow to Bannock self-sufficiency, and an invasion of their homeland by ignorant outsiders bent on stamping their authority over Bannock lands. Bannock patience was wearing very thin, and it would only take another incident of this magnitude to stir up some real trouble.

The catalyst for the violence that followed was the murder of two white men on 30 May by a Bannock warrior. Many of the Bannock bands that were off their reservations rushed back to the agencies in fear of American retaliation, but a significant group gathered around a revered chief named Buffalo Horn and decided to organise and launch a series of raids on their white tormentors, designed to discourage further settlement and to drive out those who were already in the region. Buffalo Horn gathered about 200 warriors to him, along with hundreds of non-combatants. Mounted and very mobile, the column set off through southern Idaho, ready to kill on sight any whites that they encountered. Ten white men were killed by Buffalo Horn's band before they appeared at Silver City on 8 June. The city's residents barricaded the streets and loopholed their houses. They fired on the Indians and eventually drove them off, killing Buffalo Horn. The Bannock party, their leader slain, drifted off west towards Steens Mountain in Oregon.

Taking their lead from the Bannocks' stand against the whites, the party was reinforced by bands of Paiute and Peigan Indians who had also left their reservations, swelling the raiding force to over 450 warriors. The army slowly woke up to a serious Indian outbreak, and began mobilising forces throughout the region once again to contain spreading Indian discontent and violence. The main forces consisted of the same units that had battled the Modoc four years earlier, primarily the 1st Cavalry, 21st Infantry and 4th Artillery. In overall field command was Brigadier General Oliver Howard, who had recently been derided by his colleagues in the War Department and his adversaries during the Nez Perce War, when the Indians had christened him 'General Two-Day Behind,' after he had been unable to capture Chief Joseph and his followers. Not all of the Bannocks were necessarily hostile to the United States, and the indecision that existed amongst the bands provided the Americans with a chance for a little more diplomacy before any real shooting war began. Sarah Winnemucca, the daughter of a friendly chief, was sent to the hostile camp to try to broker a peace deal while there was still time. She failed, and was lucky not to have been murdered.

With the failure of peace overtures Howard moved his forces towards Steens Mountain, intent on quickly and decisively defeating the Bannocks in the field. The Bannocks reacted by moving northwest across the desert towards Silver Creek, where camp was established. On 23 June Captain

Reuben F. Bernard and three companies of the 1st Cavalry discovered the village and assaulted it at once. The cavalry came charging into the encampment to the sound of a bugle, shooting at any living thing, but most of the Indians managed to run to some nearby steep bluffs, where the warriors hastily set up a defensive screen. Bernard's men tried to edge their way up the bluffs, but the warriors' fire held them back. As night fell the firing slackened off and then died altogether, and the Bannocks used the darkness to steal quietly away, keeping their lives and their freedom, but losing their camp and most of their possessions. Howard, perhaps recalling the debacle with the Nez Perce, this time kept his troops baying close at the Indians' heels like bloodhounds. The Bannocks pillaged white homesteads as they fled, with the soldiers only a few hours behind.

The Indians had to rest, and they halted atop rocky bluffs on Birch Creek near Pilot Butte. Once again the warriors entrenched themselves among the rocks and waited for the soldiers to attempt to storm their rocky eyrie. On 8 July Howard was informed of the Indian position at Pilot Butte, and the soldiers quickly launched an assault and managed to push the Bannocks off the bluffs and into a stand of timber. A flanking manoeuvre by the cavalry caused the Indians to falter, and within minutes the warriors had disengaged and fled south after their families. Howard assumed that they were heading for Nez Perce territory in the Wallawalla Valley and he hurried his forces there to entrap the hostile Indians. But it was Howard who was outfoxed, the Bannocks and their allies suddenly reversing course and trekking hurriedly north, their objective being the Umatilla Reservation, where they hoped to gather more warriors to their cause.

The Umatilla received the Bannocks and Paiutes cordially enough, but it was clear from their demeanor and speech that they preferred the hostiles to leave. Reports came in of American soldiers entering the reservation, and the hostiles hastily fled to the mountains, pursued by troops from Nelson A. Miles' command.

On 15 July a band of Umatilla warriors suddenly appeared in the hostiles' camp, wanting to speak with the acknowledged leader of the resistance, Chief Egan of the Malheur Paiutes. The Umatilla warriors said that they wanted to join him in fighting the Americans, but it was a ruse to lure the chief away from the protection of his men. Suddenly, the Umatilla warriors killed Egan, one pausing to lift the dead leader's scalp, before they fled back to the reservation carrying their bloody trophy aloft. The assassination of Egan dealt a devastating blow to the uneasy coalition of hostiles and left it effectively leaderless. Lieutenant Colonel James W. Forsyth and his command pressed the Bannock coalition, causing it to break up. The Paiutes scattered over eastern Oregon and the Bannocks headed back towards Idaho, killing any whites who were unfortunate enough to cross their path. Forsyth managed to bring the Bannocks to battle on 12 September and, after a sharp engagement, 131 of them surrendered. The war was over. Initially the Bannocks were held as military prisoners of war at Camp Brown and Fort Keogh, before being allowed to return to their reservation.

Although calm was momentarily restored to the northwest, more fighting was about to erupt on the plains. The Northern Cheyenne had been the closest and strongest ally of the Lakota Sioux in their great struggle through 1876–77 to retain control over the last buffalo-hunting range on the northern plains. The Cheyenne had fielded many of the warriors who had killed the arrogant Custer and many of his men at the Little Bighorn in June 1876, but they had paid the price for their support of Sitting Bull. The Cheyenne bands had been mercilessly hunted by the army throughout the late summer of 1876 and into the winter of 1876–77. The great alliance of Sioux and Cheyenne had broken up and the bands had scattered under their individual chiefs, all trying to stay one step ahead of a vengeful army and avoid incarceration on government reservations. The end of effective Cheyenne resistance had come on 25 November 1876, when Chief Dull Knife's band had been attacked while they camped along Bates Creek in Wyoming Territory. Colonel Ranald S. MacKenzie's force had captured many of the Cheyenne that day, put more to flight, burned 153 lodges and their contents and captured over 500 war ponies.

In the spring of 1877 those Cheyenne that had spent the winter sheltering with Crazy Horse's Oglala Sioux came in to Fort Keogh and surrendered to Colonel Miles. The government transported 972 Northern Cheyenne to Indian Territory in Oklahoma, dumping them onto the Darlington Reservation alongside their Southern Cheyenne cousins. The aim of the government was to concentrate all of the Cheyenne in one place. Darlington was a malarial and barren hell-hole, and within weeks of arriving people began to sicken and die. The government was supposed to feed the refugees, but the supplies were inadequate and of poor quality. Starvation was added to pestilence. Within two months of their arrival two-thirds of the Northern Cheyenne were sick. Dull Knife protested loudly to the agent, demanding a reservation in Montana on their old tribal territory.

The Americans refused all such entreaties from the Cheyenne, and insisted that they make a go of living at Darlington. The reservation land was worthless, there were no game animals left in the region to hunt, and even smaller animals were virtually extinct, as previous Indian inhabitants had desperately attempted to supplement their poor government rations with a little fresh meat. Malaria continued to spread, and about half of the Cheyenne were struck down by cholera as well. Others starved to death. Dull Knife was furious. He and the other chiefs had been lied to by the Americans when they had surrendered. The Americans had promised the Indians a fertile reservation, abundant with game and clean water. In August 1878 Dull Knife and another chieftain named Little Wolf pleaded with the agent, John Miles, to be permitted a reservation for their people back in Montana before things got any worse. Miles replied that it would be difficult to arrange and he asked for a year to try to reverse the government position. Dull Knife, himself shaking with malaria, replied that in a year's time all of the Northern Cheyenne would be dead. In just twelve months at Darlington half of the Cheyenne had perished from disease and/or starvation, planned genocide on the part of the American authorities. Miles could only respond to Dull Knife's vision of the future by saying that he needed more time, and that the Indians would have to be patient. But patience was not a luxury the Northern Cheyenne could afford, for it was clear to all of them that simply sitting quietly on the reservation waiting interminably for the Americans to make a decision about their future would only result in their eradication. The time to act had come and, though he himself was sick, Dull Knife rose to the challenge and quickly formulated a plan of action.

At sunrise the next morning the Cheyenne began to leave Darlington. They packed up their few belongings, the warriors loaded their few rifles and carbines, and Dull Knife led the survivors off the reservation north towards their homeland. The band numbered 92 men, 120 women and 141 children, led by chiefs Dull Knife, Wild Hog, Crow Indian, Chewing Gum, Old Bear, Squaw, Black Horse, Day, Red Blanket and Little Wolf. The band snaked through the countryside, warriors from the Dog Soldier societies providing the vanguard and rearguard, with more protecting the flanks, while scouts were far in advance checking the route, locating water sources and watching for danger. The Cheyenne would try to trek a thousand miles north to their former home in the Powder River country. They carefully avoided the white man's well-used road from Camp Supply to Fort Reno, the local military post guarding the reservation, and instead moved across country through the breaks of the Canadian River watershed and over the divide to the Cimarron River country, crossing west of Eagle Chief Creek.

Dull Knife and his followers were not reported missing at the reservation for twelve hours, even though Miles had exchanged words with Dull Knife and Little Wolf about leaving without permission. Little Wolf had told Miles: 'If you are really going to send your soldiers after me, I wish that you would first let me get a little distance away from this agency. Then, if you want to fight, I will fight you, and we can make the ground bloody at that place.' When Miles informed the local military commander at Fort Reno that he was missing several hundred Indians, army units were immediately dispatched to hunt them down.

Captain Joseph Rendlebrock gathered companies G and H, 4th Cavalry, and rode out of Reno in pursuit, his Arapaho scouts quickly picking up the fugitives' trail. Already, Dull Knife's band had killed two cowboys who they had encountered, stealing their guns and horses. As the band moved into Kansas along Sappa Creek in the northwest, they killed any whites that they came upon. The two cavalry companies closed in on Dull Knife's band on 13 September, when Rendlebrock observed through his field glasses the reported sighting of Indians slowly climbing a slope about three miles distant. The Cheyenne rearguard had already spotted the approaching horsemen and they hurried their women and children ahead to Turkey Springs and into some ravines leading away to the north. The warriors would not run. Instead, they began to hunker down behind cover atop the high ground, some scraping out shallow rifle pits, as they waited for the soldiers to attack. The Cheyenne Dog Soldiers would delay Rendlebrock's troops for as long as possible, giving the old men time to lead the women and children to safety.

Rendlebrock moved his companies forward at the trot, closing in on the Cheyenne position. When they were only 400 yards from the closest Cheyenne warriors he raised his arm and the troopers reined in their horses. Rendlebrock turned in his saddle to speak with an Arapaho scout named Chalk, and he asked Chalk to ride forward and parley with the hostiles. Rendlebrock had unwisely halted his command in an exposed position, with Cheyenne riflemen occupying the high ground, and a long distance from fresh water. Chalk rode back a few minutes later and quickly apprised Rendlebrock of the situation. The Cheyenne absolutely refused to return to the Darlington Reservation at the Southern Cheyenne Agency and if the pony soldiers tried to force them then the warriors would fight. As he was speaking with Chalk, his men drew Rendlebrock's attention to small parties of Cheyenne warriors moving down onto the cavalry's flanks. Realising that the Cheyenne could attack at any moment, Rendlebrock issued orders to his subordinate officers to dismount the companies and form skirmish order.

Hastily, troopers climbed down from their mounts and, grasping their carbines, they shook out into loose lines covering the front and flanks while, their horses were taken to the rear by the horse-holders. Rendlebrock then ordered his men to commence firing. An initial volley peppered the Cheyenne position, but the warriors returned fire with alacrity, hitting several troopers with their first shots. The soldiers took cover as best they could and for the rest of the morning and afternoon exchanged fire with the warriors on the bluffs and others on their flanks. Water was soon exhausted, and the men and horses became desperately thirsty. Rendlebrock realised that he would have to retreat, and he tried to do so during the night, but the Cheyenne managed to keep him pinned down until dawn on the 14th.

With his ammunition almost exhausted, his men and horses crazy with thirst and his rations low, Rendlebrock mounted his companies at first light and they withdrew, closely followed by the Cheyenne. Rendlebrock intended to ride ten miles back over the ground he had previously covered to a source of fresh water, but for the first three miles a running battle was fought with the Cheyenne that lasted for almost two hours. Eventually, Rendlebrock's command made it to safety, but at the cost of Corporal Patrick Lynch and two other enlisted men killed, and many wounded. The Arapaho scout Chalk was also killed during the fighting. The Cheyenne had suffered only five men wounded. After resting, watering and reorganising his command, Rendlebrock and his men started for Camp Supply on the 15th, thirty-five miles to the south-west.

Round one had most definitely gone to the Cheyenne, but the Americans remained fully committed to hunting the fugitives down. On 17 September Dull Knife's band attacked some cattle camps south of Fort Dodge in Kansas, killing several white cowboys and running off cattle that would be used for fresh meat in lieu of buffalo. Governor George T. Anthony was informed of the attacks the following day and he immediately requested military assistance from Brigadier General John Pope, commanding the department.

Pope was an interesting character, a distinguished Civil War veteran who had courted controversy in Washington by proclaiming that the reservation system would be better administered by military officers than the corrupt and inefficient Indian Bureau (he was not to be the first nor the last army officer publicly to make this point), and that the Indians deserved better and more humane treatment from the government. However pro-Indian Pope may have been, he could not stand idly by while the Cheyenne stormed through Kansas murdering and stealing. But this was exactly the attitude adopted by Pope, and much to the fury of Governor Anthony.

Of his own volition Anthony tried to take military matters into his own hands by sending arms and ammunition to Dodge City, but the Cheyenne fugitives had already passed by. Next, Anthony contacted Fort Dodge and ordered Lieutenant Colonel William H. Lewis and troops from the fort to apprehend the Cheyenne. Lewis caught up with the Indians in a canyon at Famished Woman's Fork. In the ensuing skirmish Lewis was killed and the Cheyenne slipped away once again. Anthony's office was overwhelmed with hysterical telegrams from across the state demanding military protection, but Pope still refused to act. In the meantime, Dull Knife, Little Wolf and the other leaders tried to move their people along as quickly as possible, barely pausing to fight the pursuing soldiers. They were in a race to reach their old homeland before the army mustered a sufficient force of troops to stop them. Pope's superior, recently promoted Lieutenant General Philip Sheridan, responded to the widening Cheyenne problem by ordering his most trusted Indian-fighter, Brigadier General George Crook, to take the field against the fugitives, eventually mobilising over 13,000 troops to track down and defeat only 353 Cheyenne.

For several weeks the hunt continued without success, and as the Cheyenne ploughed on northwards across the Arkansas and South Platte rivers several attempts were made to stop the fugitives, but on each occasion the Indian warriors beat off the pursuing troops, and the trek continued at a dizzying pace. Along the way the Cheyenne seized more weapons and buffalo meat from white traders. When the Cheyenne arrived at White Clay Creek in Nebraska they decided to split the party into two smaller bands and head off in different directions. They had already trekked over 700 miles from Indian Territory, an amazing accomplishment, and fought seven engagements with the US Army along the way.

Dull Knife, with the larger group of over 200 followers, decided to head for Red Cloud Agency with the intention of surrendering to the authorities and asking to be allowed to live alongside their Sioux friends. Little Wolf led the second band, numbering only 114 men, women and children, and they pressed on into the Sand Hills in west-central Nebraska. Winter was coming down fast over the plains and both Indian leaders knew that they had to find shelter for their people or die of exposure and starvation. The journey had been brutal, and the constant fighting had taken its toll among the fugitives. Iron Teeth Woman, a twenty-seven-year-old Cheyenne mother in 1878, recalled in 1945 the flight north. She was ninety-five when interviewed and one of the last adult survivors still on the Northern Cheyenne Reservation:

> We dodged the soldiers during most of the way. But they were always near us and trying to catch us. Our young men fought them off in seven different battles. At each fight, some of our people were killed, women or children the same as men. I do not know how many of our grown-up people were killed. But I know that more than 60 of our children were gone when we got to the Dakota [Sioux] country.[1]

When Dull Knife's band arrived at Red Cloud Agency they found it deserted, and so pressed on to the local army post at Fort Robinson. The fort's commandant, Captain Henry W. Wessells, took the fugitives in and informed Crook. Orders came back stating that after winter had passed Dull Knife and his people would have to return to Indian Territory. Dull Knife was horrified by the implication, and replied forcefully to Wessells: 'No! I am here on my own ground, and I will never go back. You may kill me here, but you cannot make me go back!' Dull Knife, however, underestimated Captain Wessells' resolve in seeing his orders carried out.

Wessells ordered that the entire band be locked up inside a freezing log barrack block at the fort on 3 January 1879, without food or fuel for heating. Men, women and small children starved and shivered for three days until Wessells demanded that they agree to return to Indian Territory once more. Dull Knife still refused, shouting: 'We will not go. Tell the Great Father [the President] that if he tries to send us back we will butcher each other with our own knives.' Dull Knife continued in this vein: 'All we ask is to be allowed to live and live in peace ... We bowed to the will of the Great Father and went south. There we found a Cheyenne cannot live. So we came home. Better it was, we thought, to die fighting than to perish of sickness.' Wessells again repeated his orders, and again Dull Knife harangued him: 'You may kill me here; but you cannot make me go back. We will not go. The only way to get us there is to come here with clubs and knock us on the head, and drag us out and take us down there dead.'

Wessells, dissatisfied with the Cheyenne obstinacy, ordered the water to be cut off on 8 January. By this time the chiefs and warriors had decided to act to save their people. They would try to break out of the fort on the evening of 9 January. They had managed to conceal some weapons on their women before they had surrendered and been disarmed by the soldiers, knowing that the women would not be as thoroughly searched as the warriors. The weapons were now assembled and knives were sharpened. It would be a desperate gamble, but Dog Soldier leader Little Shield and his warriors would lead the effort and were prepared to die trying. Far away in the Sand Hills the Cheyenne band under Little Wolf was settled down for the winter in a camp, after having spent time hunting the plentiful game in the region. They had effectively disappeared, for the time being at least.

At 9pm on the evening of 9 January 1878 Fort Robinson was quiet. Sentries posted outside the log barrack block where the Cheyenne were imprisoned walked slowly to and fro, their breath pluming like smoke in the freezing air. Inside the barrack Cheyenne warriors and women were poised for action. Doors and windows were levered open, and with a yell dozens of Cheyenne crashed out of the openings into the snow. The sentries were startled, but they immediately opened fire on the heavily bundled human forms that began a mass exodus out of the fort. Cheyenne warriors returned fire with their few weapons or plunged hunting knives deep into the struggling soldiers. Eleven troopers fell dead in the first few hectic minutes, but the losses inflicted on the escaping Indians were fearful. The sounds of gunshots and shouting alerted the entire garrison, who poured from their quarters and opened fire indiscriminately into the packed ranks of Indians. Around fifty were killed as they fled across the parade square and into the countryside. The bodies lay sprawled all over the fort, the pools of blood showing up black against the pure white snow in the moonlight.

Amid the shouting of the warriors and the screaming of panic-stricken women and children Captain Wessells hastily assembled some horsemen to follow the fugitives and hunt them down. A running fight developed as the Cheyenne split into smaller groups and disappeared into the darkened countryside, the cavalry hard on their heels, shooting down anyone in their path. Many of the Indians fled to nearby White River, where they desperately tried to quench their thirst, but the soldiers were quickly upon them and shot many.

For thirteen dreadful days the Cheyenne fugitives were hunted through the snow-bound landscape like animals. Terrible scenes were played out time and again. A warrior named White Antelope had taken shelter with his wife and a group of other women when the soldiers rode up. Quickly, White Antelope handed his infant child to his wife and, brandishing his only weapon, a knife, he charged towards the soldiers, yelling wildly. He was shot down before he had taken ten paces. Seeing her husband fall, White Antelope's wife ran forward, still clutching her baby to her breast. The soldiers took deliberate aim and shot both of them to death. The troopers urged their horses forward to where the other women, exhausted after running so far, were sheltering, and a fusillade of shots finished them all at point-blank range. Old Sitting Man, his leg broken, was lying in the snow, loudly singing his death song, when a trooper reined in his horse beside him. The soldier drew his revolver and, taking careful aim, blew the old Indian's brains out. A boy named Gathering His Medicine saw soldiers coming and quickly hid his younger sister under some brush. The boy bravely tried to fight the soldiers but he was quickly killed. His sister survived. Thirty-two Cheyenne warriors were trapped in a snow-covered washout at Antelope Creek, thirty-five miles from Fort Robinson. They were surrounded by 300 soldiers, who poured a devastating fire down into the position for forty-five minutes while the warriors tried to fight back. Then an officer called on the Indians to surrender. He was greeted by three rifle shots, the last bullets the remaining three warriors had left. All of their comrades were dead. The trio of warriors, all of them wounded, suddenly rose from their hiding place, and, reversing their rifles into clubs, they charged the dense mass of soldiers screaming strong heart songs. All three were riddled with bullets. Twenty Cheyenne died of their wounds or froze to death over those thirteen days. An officer mounted atop a horse came upon a Cheyenne woman dying of her wounds. Beside her was the body of a young girl, and in the woman's hand a bloody skinning knife. The woman had cut her own daughter's throat to prevent her capture by the white soldiers. The officer climbed down from his horse and tried to comfort the dying Indian woman. With her last strength she spat in his face.

Many of the Cheyenne were spared, rounded up and escorted back to the fort. Separated from the fleeing mass, Dull Knife, along with his wife and son, managed to escape. They walked through the frozen wilderness for eighteen nights, hiding by day, until they arrived at the Sioux reservation at Pine Ridge. During their epic trek Dull Knife's family had lived by eating tree bark and even their own moccasins. At Pine Ridge a friendly interpreter named Bill Rowland took the destitute family in and nursed them back to health.

Even in death the bodies of the Cheyenne were dishonoured by the Americans. The corpses were gathered and dumped unceremoniously into a mass grave, but some of the heads were taken away and donated to the Army Medical Museum for study. Eventually ending up in the Smithsonian Institution in Washington, these Cheyenne body parts were only returned to the tribe in 1993, after President Bill Clinton passed a law ordering the museum to return their huge store of Indian skeletons and bones, which numbered many thousands, for proper burial.

When the story of the Cheyenne Outbreak became known, widespread sympathy from the general public and approbation from members of the press forced the government to confront the senselessness of its actions. Trying to force the Northern Cheyenne to live in Indian Territory was abandoned, and instead President Chester A. Arthur granted them a reservation along the Tongue River in Montana in 1884. Many have credited Dull Knife with saving his people from disappearing entirely, for had they remained in Oklahoma most of them would have succumbed to disease and starvation within a few years.

Little Wolf and his people later joined Dull Knife's followers on the reservation, but Dull Knife himself did not live long enough to see his dream become a reality. The great Indian leader died in 1879. Little Wolf, who had always expected a warrior's death in battle, lived on for a long time. He worked as a scout for the army against his old Sioux allies, and in 1880 he shot and killed a fellow Cheyenne in a drunken argument over the chief's daughter. Later he settled peacefully on the new reservation and lived to a ripe old age, losing his sight, and becoming increasingly frail. He died in 1904. Today, the descendents of Dull Knife, Little Wolf and the other Cheyenne who made the trek north to the northern plains still live on the reservation in Montana.

More Indian outbreaks continued. The Sheepeater War was the last occasion when Indians and white men fought each other in the wilds of the rugged Pacific Northwest, scene of much bitter fighting with the Nez Perce and Bannocks. The Sheepeaters, or Turakina, were actually Western Shoshone and had gained their distinctive nickname because Rocky Mountain Sheep formed an important part of their diet. They inhabited the mountainous regions of western Montana, Wyoming and central Idaho, leading a nomadic hunter-gatherer lifestyle of tracking game through the Payette, Salmon, Boise, Challis, Sawtooth and Beaverhead Forests, and settling in permanent camps during the severe winters. They numbered about 300 and had first begun to have problems with white people when gold had been discovered in Boise Basin in 1862 and at Yankee Fork on the Salmon River. Gold camps had mushroomed immediately, and one at Panther Creek named Leesburg numbered over 7,000 prospectors by 1870. Leesburg was inconveniently located where the Sheepeaters liked to erect their winter quarters.

Prospectors were occasionally found dead at their diggings and the miners blamed the Sheepeaters for the murders. In summer 1878 the Sheepeaters were blamed for stealing horses and murdering three whites near present-day Cascade. In August two more prospectors were ambushed and killed as they panned in Pearsall Creek, five miles from Cascade, and in February 1879 the Sheepeaters were held responsible for the deaths of five Chinese miners at Oro Grande and for murders at Loon Creek. In May two ranchers died at the South Fork of the 'River of No Return,' as whites called the tortuous Salmon, but although everyone blamed the Sheepeaters, no one could produce a shred of evidence proving their culpability.

Brigadier General Oliver Howard was spurred into organising and dispatching a military expedition to punish the Sheepeaters at the end of May 1879. The main force was led once again by Captain Reuben Bernard and consisted of Company G, 1st Cavalry, totalling (with attached scouts and mule drivers) seventy-six men. Bernard marched out of Boise, heading for Challis. Lieutenant Catley and a small detachment from the 2nd Infantry headed south from Camp Howard, which was located at Grangeville, and Lieutenant Edward Farrow marched east from the Umatilla Reservation. All three columns aimed to converge on Payette Lake, near present-day McCall, in the heart of Sheepeater territory.

Bernard's small force soon had to cope with six-foot snowdrifts and fast-running streams in the high mountainous territory they were traversing. It proved to be very slow going, and in the appalling weather conditions the troops became separated from the pack train carrying all of the reserve ammunition and supplies. After ten days the cavalry struggled, cold, exhausted and hungry, into the mining community of Oro Grande, to find that the Indians had beaten them to it. The settlement had been largely burned and many settlers had fled. Bernard halted and rested until the pack train finally caught up five days later on 13 June. A week later, after proper rest and reorganisation, Bernard's column trekked back into the field to hunt down the Indians. They marched to Challis, then Salmon City and Warren's Diggings, but encountered no Indians. For a month the soldiers struggled up the Middle Fork of the Salmon through just about every kind of severe weather that the region could throw at them. Horses and mules perished and ammunition and other supplies were lost.

Lieutenant Catley and the men of the 2nd Infantry marched from Camp Howard and reached Big Creek Canyon near the South Fork of the Salmon River. Catley's scouts picked up signs of Indians on 28 July, but Catley stupidly disregarded the scouts' warnings to proceed with the utmost caution into the canyon itself. The young officer's arrogant contempt for his adversaries led him and his men into an ambush. Suddenly, the canyon walls reverberated with gunfire as warriors blasted Catley's column from both sides. Two of the soldiers were shot down and severely wounded, Catley withdrawing back out of the canyon followed all the way by rifle shots from above.

Catley pulled his men back about two miles out of danger, regrouped, made camp and posted sentries. The following morning the troops attempted to locate a better defensive position and ended up digging in around the base of a mountain subsequently named Vinegar Hill. The Sheepeaters had moved up from the canyon and taken up positions on both sides of Catley's men during the night and now opened fire. The Indians tried to drive the soldiers from their positions by setting fire to the surrounding brush, but the plan was thwarted when 1st Sergeant John A. Sullivan bravely fired nearby brush in order to create a fire break. Intermittent gunfire proved inconclusive, and, as darkness fell, the Indian warriors broke off and disappeared. The next morning Catley decided to return to Camp Howard, as he was short of supplies.

An Indian scout managed to rendezvous with Bernard's column, carrying orders for him to effect a link-up with Lieutenant Farrow's column, which was hot on the trail of a gang of horse thieves that he had mistaken for hostile Indians. When Bernard heard that Catley had withdrawn, he sent orders back to his post to send out more troops and supplies and to rendezvous with him at the Salmon's South Fork. Lieutenant Farrow, with two platoons and some Umatilla scouts, linked up with Bernard at the North Payette River, and the combined force set off through tough country hunting for the Sheepeaters. The soldiers were short of rations, as the supply train was unable to keep up with their advance, but on 11 August they met Lieutenant Catley and forty men fresh out from Camp Howard. The combined column soon discovered signs that the Sheepeaters were close by. Indian dwellings that appeared to have been recently vacated were discovered, along with fish traps in a nearby creek. When the column entered the area where Catley had been defeated in July the Umatilla scouts were sent on ahead. When the scouts failed to return a soldier was dispatched to them and he soon returned with the exciting news that the Sheepeaters were only about two miles ahead, and the Umatilla scouts were engaging them. Bernard immediately raced his column forward on horseback, and linked up with the scouts. The combined force crashed into the Sheepeaters' village, but found it abandoned and quiet. The Umatillas looted the encampment and then Bernard ordered it burned, after which the soldiers made camp and rested.

The following morning reports indicated that the Sheepeaters were still close by and were mounted. Catley was once again sent back to Camp Howard, as his unit was short of supplies, and Bernard dispersed the remainder of his force with orders to fan out across the steep, mountainous slopes and find the Indians. The Sheepeaters had been waiting for such an opportunity and struck the troops in another ambush when the command had been sufficiently dispersed, and also fired on the troops detailed to guard the pack train. One soldier was killed, and scattered rifle fire continued all day until the Sheepeaters once more evaporated when darkness fell.

Bernard's command was rattled by the previous day's ambush, but at first light they mounted up and gave chase. The terrain was awful, and many horses and mules gave up throughout the day. Bernard was eventually forced to abandon the pursuit due to a lack of supplies, and he led his men back to Camp Howard, ordering the Umatilla scouts to keep contact with the Sheepeaters. On 17 September Bernard's command took the field again and discovered another deserted hostile camp close by. A sweep of the surrounding country led to the capture of an Indian woman and her two children. Then, in a surprising turn of events, a half-Bannock, half-Nez Perce war chief named Tanmanmo, who was with the hostiles, surrendered to one of Bernard's patrols. The Indian promised to bring the other warriors in to surrender, as evidently the constant pursuit by the army had made life intolerable for the Sheepeaters and they were as exhausted and short on supplies as the soldiers. Lieutenant Farrow sent Tanmanmo back to his people with the assurance that they would be well treated if they surrendered.

By 1 October some sixty warriors had surrendered and been disarmed and resistance was at an end. The troops marched over 1,200 miles to Boise, while the prisoners were escorted to Vancouver Barracks in Washington

State for questioning over the murders of ranchers and miners that had precipitated the conflict in the first place. The Sheepeater warriors only admitted to the murder of two ranchers, and emphatically denied that they or their people had had anything to do with the deaths of several white and Chinese prospectors. The army sent them to the Fort Hall Reservation, with some small bands remaining in the Salmon River country.

Once again a handful of Indians had proved a costly and protracted nuisance to the American authorities, but from this point on the situation in the Pacific Northwest remained calm and the progress of white settlement and the exploitation of the region's resources was unimpeded by local Indians. The region's tribes were too small to have placed much of a delay on white immigration, and their natural antipathy towards each other meant that no real Indian coalition aping the Northern Plains Alliance of the Sioux, Northern Cheyenne and Arapaho had been possible. The Americans simply dealt with each tribe in turn, applying overwhelming military might to each small conflict until victory was achieved.

Notes

1. Thomas B. Marquis, *Reminiscences of Four Cheyennes and a Sioux* (Stockton: Pacific Center for Western Historical Studies, 1973).

11

SLAUGHTER IN THE SNOW

'The *Pioneer* has before declared that our only safety depends upon the total extermination of the Indians. Having wronged them for centuries, we had better, in order to protect our civilization, follow it up by one more wrong and wipe these untamed and untamable creatures from the face of the earth. In this lies future safety for our settlers and the soldiers who are under incompetent commands. Otherwise, we may expect future years to be as full of trouble with the redskins as those have been in the past.'[1]

L. Frank Baum, editor, *Aberdeen Saturday Pioneer*, 1891
Author of *The Wonderful Wizard of Oz*

In the decade and a half since the hated Custer had been wiped from their territory in the hot summer of 1876, the Lakota Sioux had lost almost everything. The white man's road of treaty and reservation had become a reality for all of the people, the Great Plains that was once their homeland was now divided up into fenced ranches and the once immense buffalo herds were all but extinct. Only bleached bones now littered the prairie as a reminder of the Great Father's determination to break the back of Sioux resistance by robbing them of their food source before robbing them of their lands.

Even the Great Sioux Reservation, that huge area encompassing nearly all of present-day South Dakota, was under threat from Washington. That which been given to the Sioux in 1868 following Red Cloud's victory in war, under a promise that it would be theirs forever, would now be carved into five smaller reservations, with the surplus land opened to white settlers for exploitation. Senator Henry Dawes had proposed a radical reorganisation of Indian land holdings, and the eventual 1887 General Allotment Act would attempt to 'civilise' the Indians by introducing to them the purported benefits of private ownership. The American government termed it a 'policy of breaking up tribal relationships' and 'conforming Indians to the white man's ways, peaceably if they will, or forcibly if they must.'

On the Sioux reservations each Indian family was granted 320 acres to farm. As there were insufficient Indians remaining to farm all of the reservation lands under the allotment system, vast tracts could be taken away from the tribes and returned to the public domain for settlement. 'Breaking up tribal relationships' in the case of the Sioux meant placing the separate divisions of the Lakota onto non-contiguous reservations, preventing their uniting again to resist American expansionism. They would become Indian islands in a white-controlled ocean. Ringing the new Sioux reservations were forts where the army maintained a close watch on them, ready at a moment's notice to crush any outbreaks of Indian resistance to enforced acculturation.

The purported benefits of 'civilisation' brought instead more suffering to the Lakota bands. The Indian Bureau established an agency on each reservation, from where an agent, who was supposed to care for the needs of the Indians, instead ruled like a king with a strong mandate from Washington. Behind the respectable façade of bureaucracy, many of the agents were incompetent, disinterested or downright corrupt, and this was all too evident to their unwilling charges. At Pine Ridge, the agent, Daniel F. Royer, was so uninspiring a figure that the Indians mocked him with the name 'Young-Man-Afraid-of-the-Sioux.' His purported fear of 'the Indian,' and his ignorance of their customs, would contribute to a terrible event that still colours Indian-white relations today.

When the Sioux tried to till the land the poor reservation soil in South Dakota yielded a negligible harvest. The Americans had pontificated about the Anglo-Saxon work ethic, and, believing all Indians to be inherently indigent, the government had declared that 'lazy Indians' who refused to farm were a burden. In Washington's eyes, the government had done enough to support Indians who sat around on reservations refusing to perform an honest day's labour for their victuals, and always having the gall to ask for more rations.

The wars it had taken simply to get the Indians onto reservations had been prohibitively expensive. In March 1882, the Secretary of War estimated that the total cost of the Indian Wars to the United States over the previous decade had been exactly US$202,994,506. One American general caustically commented at the time: 'It would be better as a matter of economy, to board and lodge the Indians at the Fifth Avenue Hotel, than to fight them.'[2]

The government reacted by reducing the rations imported into the Sioux reservations by half, in the hope that such a drastic step would induce the

Sioux to farm. It was a policy doomed to failure. The harvest, due to low rainfall and intense heat, was a failure. The government had failed to provide the Sioux with enough agricultural instructors or tools, and, coupled with the sudden reduction in rations, malnutrition and eventual starvation set in. The government's answer was simply to ignore the problem and to continue to blame the Sioux for the dire straits in which they now found themselves.

Local army commanders began to take a closer interest in the situation unfolding on the reservations, and many were in no doubt as to who was to blame for deteriorating relations between agents and Sioux. The commander of nearby Fort Yates (now in North Dakota), Colonel Joseph Dunn, wrote to Brigadier General Thomas H. Ruger, commanding the Department of Dakota, in December 1890. The letter was endorsed by newly promoted Brigadier General Nelson A. Miles and passed to the Secretary of War following the Wounded Knee Massacre as evidence. Dunn wrote: 'It appears … that the government has failed to fulfill its obligations, and in order to render the Indians law-abiding, peaceful, contented, and prosperous it is strongly recommended that the treaties to be promptly and fully carried out, and that the promises made … be faithfully kept.'[3]

The effects of the government starvation policy soon became all too evident to anyone visiting the reservations. The Indians soon took on a lean and emaciated look, children wandering about with starvation-distended stomachs and adults with wasted faces and sunken eyes from which all hope had departed were found begging around the agencies. Disease hounded the Sioux, striking at the very old and the very young in particular, whooping cough, measles and influenza carrying people off. The white agency doctors did what they could, but they attributed the outbreaks of disease to the poor physical conditions of the Indians. In their medical opinion, the Sioux were being systematically starved.

A group of minor chiefs and shamans had quietly left the reservations in late 1889 to travel far away to Nevada in the Southwest. They planned to meet and talk with a Paiute Indian named Wovoka, who was preaching a new gospel to all the Indians he could find, a strange amalgamation of traditional Indian spirituality and Christian teachings that was called the 'Ghost Dance.' Wovoka claimed to have been taken up to heaven and to have met with God. He had instructed Wovoka to spread the word: that the land was to be restored to the Indians if they performed the Ghost Dance; the whites would disappear, the buffalo would come back and all the people of the past would be restored to life in all the beauty of their youth.

Before the Sioux delegates had reached Wovoka, his message of Indian regeneration through Ghost Dancing had already been taken up by many other Indian peoples, who all shared the trials and tribulations of reservation life. In time, old Sioux allies and enemies alike accepted Wovoka's message to one degree or another and danced for a return to the old days. The Arapaho, Northern and Southern Cheyenne, Bannock, Shoshone and Ute peoples all danced and prayed for the good times to come. Sitting Bull is reported to have said, 'I am the last Indian.' In some sense he was right. During his lifetime the world of the Plains Indians had changed forever. The old roving life of the buffalo-hunters was over. A terrible disintegration and demoralisation had set in.[4]

Although Wovoka preached the end of the white man in North America, he did not tell the Indians to hasten his end by their own hand. They should remain at peace with the white man, for he would disappear soon enough if the Indians believed in the Ghost Dance and performed it as often as possible. It was all a question of belief, and although not all of the Sioux believed Wovoka, many nonetheless went along with the dancing just in case what he had said turned out to be true. It had been some time since Sioux voices had been united, since their drums had thundered and the people had danced proudly together.

From March 1890, and the return of the delegates to Wovoka, more and more Sioux joined in as the Ghost Dance spread from reservation to reservation, family to family. It was the perfect message of cultural regeneration at the moment of greatest collective despair in Sioux history. A host of influential chieftains accepted Wovoka's message, and permitted and sometimes encouraged their followers to take up the Ghost Dance. Sitting Bull, Short Bull, Kicking Bear, Crow Dog and Big Foot were the most prominent amongst them. The great Red Cloud remained ambivalent, and did not take part.

The starvation policy continued in spite of the fact that the Sioux were not turning to agriculture in large numbers. At Pine Ridge, Agent Royer informed the Indian Bureau in April 1890 that the monthly beef issue that was supposed to be 470,400 pounds was actually only 205,000 pounds. The reply from head office assured Royer that there was method behind the apparent administrative madness. They replied that it was better to give the Sioux half rations all year, than three-quarters or full rations for a few months, and then nothing for the rest of the year. Congress was economising with Indian lives. Sitting Bull commented, 'The white man knows how to make everything, but he does not know how to distribute it.'

Royer could hear the Ghost Dancers from his office at Pine Ridge all the time now, and their numbers grew with each passing day. The rhythmical chanting and screaming, the beating of drums and the dust raised up by hundreds of pairs of feet pounding the earth as the dancers slowly rotated in a giant circle was mystifying and frightening. Mrs Z.A. Parker observed a Ghost Dance at White Clay Creek, Pine Ridge on 20 June, writing that 'we saw over three hundred tents placed in a circle, with a large pine tree in the center, which was covered with strips of cloth of various colors, eagle feathers, stuffed birds, claws, and horns – all offerings to the Great Spirit.' Presently the dancers began to gather. 'In the center, around the tree, were gathered their medicine-men,' recalled Parker, 'also those who had been so fortunate as to have had visions and in them had seen and talked with friends who had died. A company of fifteen had started a chant and were marching abreast, others coming in behind as they marched. After marching around the circle of tents they turned to the center, where many had gathered and were seated on the ground.'[5] White observers were transfixed by this display of 'savage' ceremony. 'After walking about a few times, chanting, "Father, I come," they stopped marching,' wrote Parker, 'but remained in the circle, and set up the most fearful, heart-piercing wails I ever heard – crying, moaning, groaning, and shrieking out their grief, and naming over their departed friends and relatives, at the same time taking up handfuls of dust at their feet, washing their hands in it, and throwing it over their heads. Finally, they raised their eyes to heaven, their hands clasped high above their heads, and stood straight and perfectly still, invoking the power of the Great Spirit to allow them to see and talk with their people who had died.'[6]

To many whites, Indians only danced before they went on the warpath. Royer and other agents watched the Ghost Dancers and grew increasingly worried for their own safety. They were a few whites in the midst of thousands of 'heathen savages,' a tribe known for their warlike ways in the recent past, and now actively disobedient of the government's authority. If there was to be a war the agents knew that they and their families would be its first victims. It had happened before, and everyone knew about the Great Sioux Uprising in Minnesota in 1863, when 700 whites had perished. In the settlements surrounding the Sioux reservations panic began to spread among immigrants, and calls for strong action to be taken to stamp out the Ghost Dance cult became increasingly vociferous. Large numbers of whites packed up and left the area altogether, believing that war with the Sioux was inevitable.

Many of the male Ghost Dancers wore rifles or carbines strung over special new hide tunics called Ghost Shirts. When agents and journalists made enquiries into the purpose of the Ghost Shirt, the dancers said that they were bullet-proof. These new snippets of information and cultural misinterpretation fuelled the agents' fears. Many whites believed that the Ghost Shirts indicated the warriors were preparing for battle, as what other reason could there have been for shirts that could stop bullets? The Sioux probably wore Ghost Shirts as they rightly feared interference with their ceremonies from local army units, whose trigger-happy antics in the past had made the Sioux extremely wary of encounters with the 'Long Knives' and 'Walk-a-Heaps,' as they called the American cavalry and infantry soldiers respectively.

Stationed just outside the reservations, within easy striking distance, army units had been held in a state of cautious readiness since 1885, ready to tackle any further outbreaks of Indian resistance. The agents began to make official requests for troops to shore up their weak authority over the Sioux, and to assist in stamping out the Ghost Dance cult. Many agents believed that certain chiefs, Sitting Bull being the most prominent, were using the Ghost Dance to renew their authority over their people, which had been severely tested since the military defeats of the Sioux and Sitting Bull's failure to persuade the Canadians to grant him and his 4,000 followers sanctuary in the British Dominion. Sitting Bull had reluctantly surrendered to the Americans in 1881 after the Canadians had persuaded almost all of his followers to leave by systematically starving them for years.

The army was in no hurry to involve itself in yet another bloody Indian war, and its senior officers believed that the root cause of the trouble at the Sioux reservations was, and always had been, civilian incompetence. Agents were corrupt, they stole from the Indians, and the government refused to feed the Indians adequately, thereby breaking the terms of solemn treaties they had signed. The administrators had been storing up trouble for themselves by deliberately antagonising their charges. Senior regional commanders, including General Miles, wrote scathing letters to the government, explaining clearly the reasons for the tense situation with the Sioux, and pointing out that governmental penny-pinching was the proximate cause of any further disturbances among the Plains Indians. Nevertheless, 'Young-Man-Afraid-of-the-Sioux' Royer wired the Interior Department demanding 700 troops to calm the situation at Pine Ridge. Within days, further telegrams upped this figure to 1,000. Army commanders were inclined to view Royer as inexperienced and panicky, but when more experienced agents, such as

James McLaughlin at Standing Rock, reported that they too had lost control of their Indians, army officers began to sit up and take notice.

In a move designed to pacify the Ghost Dance crisis, President Benjamin Harrison signed a decree at the White House on 13 November 1890 that handed control of the Sioux reservations to the army. Army officers would take over the civilian agents' duties at once, ending corruption and providing even-handed and competent governance of the Indians. The army was also to arrest the chieftains the government viewed as 'trouble-makers,' a list headed by Sitting Bull, in an attempt to forestall any planned Indian rebellion before it erupted. It appeared to be an eminently sensible plan, but the Americans had overlooked one important point: there was no planned Sioux uprising in the offing. There was just Ghost Dancing, a harmless if misunderstood expression of Sioux desperation and longing for the old days.

The sudden appearance of thousands of heavily armed soldiers on the reservations would cause panic among the Sioux, who believed the soldiers had come to kill them, as they had attacked peaceful villages and massacred their inhabitants on several occasions in the recent past. Turning Hawk, a Sioux at Pine Ridge, later recalled: 'Of course, when a large body of soldiers is moving toward a certain direction they inspire a more or less amount of awe, and it is natural that the women and children who see this large moving mass are made afraid of it and be put in a condition to make them run away.'[7] The whites may have remembered the Great Sioux Uprising, but the Sioux remembered Sand Creek, the Washita and the bloody Nez Perce who had stumbled into their camps in Canada.

Within days of Harrison's order, long lines of cavalrymen rode into the reservations, bundled up in greatcoats and fur hats, sabres clinking against their saddles, the breath of men and horses hanging in the air, as the temperature dropped to freezing and a light snow powdered the ground. At Pine Ridge, 3,000 'Long Knives' were soon quartered around the neat white-painted wooden agency buildings. Some 2,000 Sioux fled the reservation at the sight of the troops, men, women and children packing up what they could carry and trekking out into the frozen Bad Lands, a region of deeply broken and difficult terrain where they believed they would be safe from the army. They camped in a remote location they named 'The Stronghold,' which afforded good protection from a sudden surprise assault by the Long Knives, and Sioux warriors guarded all of the approaches to the camp. They were soon joined by hundreds of other Sioux from the reservations, all fleeing in panic at the appearance of white troops among them.

The army viewed the Sioux exodus from the reservations to The Stronghold as an Indian outbreak. The fleeing Indians were off reservation, which was not permitted, and so the army declared them to be hostile. The army also moved to arrest the Sioux chieftains they had previously identified as spreading the Ghost Dance cult.

Sitting Bull had moved with a hard core of followers over forty miles from the agency at Standing Rock Reservation. Agent McLaughlin had been in consultation with the Interior Department and local military commanders with a view to seeing Sitting Bull apprehended without bloodshed. Various dates had been put forward, but it was a report from the Indian police that led to an arrest attempt being made on 15 December. The Indian police were former Sioux warriors who were now working for the Americans, uniformed, trained and deployed as a kind of paramilitary force to help keep order on the reservations. Naturally, many of the Sioux hated the Indian police, seeing them as turncoats and renegades who had betrayed their people in going to work for the enemy. However, even some influential chieftains viewed cooperation with the whites as the only way forward for their people, including Chief Gall at Standing Rock. Gall had fought the Americans for most of his life alongside Sitting Bull and others, but he became a judge under McLaughlin's supervision. Red Cloud had long ago accepted that white power was irresistible and determined to keep himself and his Oglala followers out of any confrontation. Sitting Bull remained hostile to white authority, and although he maintained cordial relations with McLaughlin, one of the better Indian agents, McLaughlin held the chief in some suspicion, especially concerning the Ghost Dance cult.

Sitting Bull was certainly interested in the Ghost Dance, and the philosophy underpinning Wovoka's teachings, and he permitted his Hunkpapa followers to perform the rituals at his camp. McLaughlin later wrote that 'the Messiah doctrine [Ghost Dance], which united so many Indians in common cause, was just what he [Sitting Bull] needed to assert himself as "high priest," and thus regain prestige and former popularity among the Sioux by posing as the leader of disaffection.'[8] McLaughlin was accurate in assuming that Sitting Bull had lost much of his once-huge following among the various branches of the Sioux.

To whites, Sitting Bull remained the most infamous living Indian (with the possible exception of the Apache Geronimo), a leader who had dedicated his life to preventing America from appropriating Sioux lands and subjugating Sioux peoples. Sitting Bull's long years in Canadian exile between 1877 and 1881 had not improved his view of the Americans as liars and thieves, reinforced by what he had witnessed of their management of the reservation to which he had reluctantly been assigned. The great chief remained a problem for the American authorities, and any association with the Ghost Dance may well have added undesired credibility to the cult, making it even more popular among the Lakota.

On the morning of 15 December forty-three Indian police and volunteers, including Sitting Bull's brother-in-law Gray Eagle, reined in their horses at Sitting Bull's camp, a ragged collection of log cabins and worn and patched tepees. Ten of the policemen, led by Lieutenant Henry Bull Head, entered Sitting Bull's cabin and told him he was under arrest and would be transported to Standing Rock Agency. Sitting Bull accepted the arrest and began slowly to dress, while his supporters gathered outside where the police had set up an armed cordon.

Sitting Bull's seventeen-year-old son Crow Foot began to berate his father for submitting to arrest, and the teenager's words seemed to have awakened some of Sitting Bull's old fighting spirit. He told Bull Head that he would not go with him. The police bundled Sitting Bull out of the cabin into the face of an angry Hunkpapa mob, many of whom were armed and extremely agitated. The police tried to reason with the crowd, but Sitting Bull shouted out for his followers to free him, and to kill the leaders of the police. Suddenly, two of Sitting Bull's men, Catch the Bear and Strikes the Kettle, leapt from the jostling crowd and opened fire. Lieutenant Bull Head was struck in the right side as he flanked Sitting Bull, and he swung around and shot the chief in the ribs with his revolver. On the other side of Sitting Bull, 1st Sergeant Shave Head was shot through the abdomen and, in a cloud of gun smoke and screams, all three men collapsed to the ground. Private Lone Man shot back, hitting Catch the Bear, before the fight descended into a terrible melée, with revolvers and carbines discharged a point-blank range between the 40 or so police and the over 150 enraged Hunkpapa, a group that included many women.

The fighting lasted for nearly thirty minutes, but the police managed to push the Sioux back through the scattered buildings and into some nearby woods, losing seven killed during the course of the fight. Sitting Bull died at the scene, along with his son Crow Foot and five of his followers. Sitting Bull's killer, Bull Head, survived the fighting, but died of his wound eighty-two hours later. Hundreds of Sitting Bull's followers fled from the scene of the fight up the Grand River, before elements of the 8th Cavalry arrived at the camp to relieve the police. It was somewhat ironic, as McLaughlin had dispatched the Indian police to make the arrest instead of the army because he and others felt that fellow Sioux would have been able to persuade Sitting Bull to come with them without bloodshed. And, in a further twist, Sitting Bull was reputed to have once prophesied his death at the hands of his own people.

The bungled arrest and murder of Sitting Bull served further to depopulate the reservations of Indians. Many of Sitting Bull's followers, numbering perhaps 400, fled to his half-brother, Chief Big Foot of the Minneconjou Sioux, at a reservation at Cheyenne River. Big Foot was another name on the army's list of chieftains who were to be detained, and it was only a matter of time before he too was arrested. The army was unaware that Big Foot had renounced the Ghost Dance cult, and Miles sent out orders to his subordinates that Big Foot and his followers were to be compelled to report to nearby Fort Bennett as soon as possible.

Big Foot slipped quietly out into the night on 23 December and headed south, taking with him nearly 300 Minneconjou followers who constituted his immediate band, and around 40 Hunkpapa Sioux from Sitting Bull's camp. He intended to lead his people to Pine Ridge Reservation, home to the great Red Cloud and the most powerful and numerous of the Lakota divisions, the Oglala. The Oglala had remained neutral during the Ghost Dance crisis, and had invited Big Foot to camp under their protection, and to help them restore harmony with the whites. On 28 December Big Foot and his followers were still tramping through the white landscape, blankets and buffalo robes tightly wrapped around their half-frozen bodies, women with babies and young children hurrying on while the few available warriors nervously scouted the route ahead through trees heavy with snow, carbines and pistols at the ready. Big Foot was ill with pneumonia, and lay in the back of a wagon, unable to sit up, his relatives doing what they could for him. Apart from the crunching sounds of footfalls on the frozen ground, the grind of the wagon wheels and the occasional cries of a baby, all was quiet and still, the landscape blanketed in snow. The Sioux hurried on like hunted animals, aware of every crack of a dry twig or shadow in the trees around them.

The army was looking for them, sweeping the area with mobile cavalry patrols, and it was one of these that eventually discovered the fugitives on 28 December, five miles west of Wounded Knee Creek. Major Samuel Whitside and a force from the 7th Cavalry reined in before the Sioux, and, after a few nervous moments had passed, the Indians relaxed a little, realising that the Long Knives meant them no harm. Whitside explained to the band's chiefs that he would escort their party to Wounded Knee Creek, where they would make camp.

At Wounded Knee Bigfoot's people began erecting their tepees in the snow and built fires, while the cavalrymen mounted guard over them. The regimental commander, Colonel James Forsyth, arrived at the camp with more troopers and a unit of artillerymen hauling four rapid-fire Hotchkiss guns. Forsyth had the guns deployed on a ridge above the Indian encampment, and both sides settled down to a tense night. The army officers parleyed with the Indian leaders, but their interpreter was not familiar with the Minneconjou's particular dialect, and he mistranslated much of what the Sioux had to say.

The Sioux believed a rumour that they were going to be deported to Indian Territory, where conditions on the reservations were known to be especially bad. However, because of the interpreter's incompetence, the Indian leader's speeches sounded more belligerent than they actually were. This made the officers concerned about any trouble with their prisoners on the following day when they would escort them into custody. Among the 500 officers and men of the 7th Cavalry, there were many veterans of the 1876 fight with the Sioux at the Little Bighorn who had survived the encounter because they had been with Major Reno's battalion. It has been suggested by Indian survivors of Wounded Knee that many of the soldiers became drunk that night, and that they initiated some sort of unofficial search of the tepees, looking for 7th Cavalry weapons and equipment taken from Custer's dead that still might have been in the possession of the Indians. Certainly, Major James Walsh of the Northwest Mounted Police had noted that his officers had seen 7th Cavalry weapons among Sioux who came to Canada as refugees in the late 1870s, so it was perfectly possible that a few old carbines or revolvers were among the weapons in Big Foot's party.

The suggestion, though not substantiated by any written documents, has been put forward that the tragedy that occurred the next day was the 7th Cavalry's revenge for the Little Bighorn fourteen years before. Incompetence may have a played a part in the murders that followed, and there was certainly no love lost between the 7th and the Sioux, but it was not deliberate American policy to massacre Indian villages – at least not since the 1870s.

The next morning, 29 December, was cold and bright. Forsyth ordered Big Foot's followers to assemble on some flat ground in front of their tepee camp, above which the Indians flew a flag of truce, located below the army's encampment on the surrounding ridgeline. The troops were stood to, and weapons were loaded. The men were bunched into one group under an armed guard, while the women and children stood by the tepees. Forsyth intended to have his men search the Sioux warriors and the tepees for weapons, conscious of their 'belligerent' speeches the night before. Soldiers roughly frisked the Indians, turning up a handful of serviceable rifles, carbines and revolvers, which they piled in front of the Indians, while the majority of their comrades were deployed by companies overlooking the camp, tense and ready for trouble. A shaman named Yellow Bird began to perform the Ghost Dance, reminding the Lakota that their Ghost Shirts were bullet-proof. The tension became palpable between the soldiers and the Indians, with Yellow Bird's cries being misunderstood as a call to arms. A scuffle broke out when a trooper tried to disarm a deaf Indian warrior named Black Coyote. The warrior had not heard the order to turn in his gun and assumed he was being charged with theft. At that moment a gun went off, one single shot booming out in the silent, still air, and it was like a signal to the officers commanding the troopers covering the camp. At the same moment the shot rang out, Yellow Bird threw some dust into the air. Indian bystanders said he meant it as a ceremonial gesture but the tense soldiers took it for a signal to attack. As eyewitness Turning Hawk recalled: 'When the guns were thus taken and the men thus separated, there was a crazy man, a young man of very bad influence and in fact a nobody, among that bunch of Indians fired his gun, and of course the firing of a gun must have been the breaking of a military rule of some sort, because immediately the soldiers returned fire and indiscriminate killing followed.'[9] According to Spotted Hawk, another witness to the massacre:

> This man shot an officer in the army; the first shot killed this officer. I was a voluntary scout at that encounter and I saw exactly what was done, and that was what I noticed; that the first shot killed an officer. As soon as this shot was fired the Indians immediately began drawing their knives, and they were exhorted from all sides to desist, but this was not obeyed. Consequently the firing began immediately on the part of the soldiers.[10]

The silence of the morning was broken by the crash of volley fire and the ear-splitting roar of the Hotchkiss guns. Heavy carbine bullets ripped through the densely packed ranks of Indians, killing dozens instantly, and the soldiers who had been conducting the search were similarly cut down by their comrades' fire or felled by screaming and wild-eyed Sioux warriors, who surged forward to attack the soldiers the moment the fighting began. American Horse recalled

> When the firing began, of course the people who were standing immediately around the young man who fired the first shot were killed right together, and then they turned their guns, Hotchkill [sic] guns, etc., upon the women who were in the lodges standing there under a flag of truce, and of course as soon as they were fired upon they fled, the men fleeing in one direction and the women running in two different directions. So that there were three general directions in which they took flight.[11]

Most of the Indian men tried to flee up a ravine, whereas the women and children went in the opposite direction across an open field. The women and children fared no better than their husbands and brothers as army bullets cracked through the thin walls of tepees, or felled them as they were trying to run away. American Horse recounted terrible scenes of carnage among the women and young children:

> There was a woman with an infant in her arms who was killed as she almost touched the flag of truce, and the women and children of course were strewn all along the circular village until they were dispatched. Right near the flag of truce a mother was shot down with her infant; the child not knowing that its mother was dead was still nursing, and that especially was a very sad sight.[12]

American soldiers continued to empty their carbines into women and children vainly attempting to escape the slaughter, as recalled by American Horse: 'The women as they were fleeing with their babes were killed together, shot right through, and the women who were very heavy with child were also killed.'[13]

Explosive shells from the Hotchkiss guns erupted all over the Indian camp, flattening tepees and flinging white-hot shards of shrapnel across the battlefield, killing or maiming dozens of Sioux. The survivors were pursued by bullets and cannon shells as they ran off, the wounded and dying feebly lying around in pools of blood calling for help or trying to crawl to safety. American Horse witnessed soldiers executing young children who revealed their hiding places:

> All the Indians fled in these three directions, and after most all of them had been killed a cry was made that all those who were not killed wounded should

come forth and they would be safe. Little boys who were not wounded came out of their places of refuge, and as soon as they came in sight a number of soldiers surrounded them and butchered them there.[14]

In less than an hour of sporadic gun and cannon fire, the 7th Cavalry killed at least 153 people, and wounded another 50. Many died later of their wounds, having been dragged clear of the fighting by friends and relatives. Twenty-five soldiers were also dead, and another thirty-nine wounded, some undoubtedly killed by the indiscriminate fire directed at the camp by their fellow troopers.

Their grisly work done, the 7th Cavalry descended on the battlefield, weapons at the ready, and began moving from body to body, checking for signs of life. They attended to their own wounded, and loaded up the dead soldiers to transport them to their post. The Indians they left where they had fallen, and for some time troopers moved among the bullet riddled bodies, stripping them of Ghost Shirts, moccasins and other artefacts that they took away as souvenirs. The soldiers then mounted up by companies and rode slowly away from the scene. A snowstorm blanketed the area overnight, and the following day civilians, escorted by soldiers, drew up at the battlefield tasked with burying the dead Sioux. The bodies were frozen solid in ghastly poses of violent death, and a photographer carefully took pictures of Big Foot lying on his back, almost trying to sit up in the snow, and of an officer sitting atop a horse surrounded by bodies dotted about like unwanted bundles of rags, and of a large hole dug by the civilian contractors into which the frozen bodies were being unceremoniously dumped. Grinning cavalrymen stood around the mass grave, symbolically pointing their carbines at the Indian corpses.

The day after the massacre a group of militant Ghost Dancers descended on the wooden buildings of Drexel Mission and set fire to several of them. Reports soon reached Forsyth and he immediately dispatched Company K of the 7th Cavalry to arrest the Indians concerned. When the troopers rode imperiously up to the mission, morale high after their previous day's work, the Sioux ambushed them. The troopers were soon pinned down by furious rifle fire and began to take casualties. Fortunately for the soldiers, the all-black 9th Cavalry had been following this particular group of Ghost Dancers at some distance after they had left the reservation, and now charged in to support the 7th. The warriors scattered in the face of heavy fire from the 'Buffalo Soldiers,' and Company K of the 7th was rescued. Forsyth's men had suffered one killed and six wounded in the brief skirmish. Lieutenant James D. Mann, who had been present at the previous day's massacre, was the last American soldier to be killed by the Sioux when he died of his wounds on 15 January 1891. Drexel Mission also proved to be the last time the Sioux would take up arms against the United States for eighty-two years, until trouble once more erupted at Wounded Knee in 1973.

On receipt of a report from Forsyth of what had occurred at Wounded Knee, Miles immediately relieved him of his command, and denounced him for perpetrating a cold-blooded massacre. Forsyth was later placed before an army court of inquiry, but in the whitewashing that followed, the colonel was cleared of all charges and the matter dropped. The court criticised Forsyth for his tactical dispositions but otherwise exonerated him of responsibility for the massacre. However, while it did include several cases of personal testimony pointing towards army misconduct, the court was flawed. It was not conducted as a formal court-martial, and without the legal boundaries of that format several of the witnesses minimised their comments and statements to protect themselves or their peers. Ultimately, the secretary of war concurred with the findings of the court and reinstated Forsyth to command of the 7th Cavalry.

Testimony before the court indicated that for the most part troopers attempted to avoid non-combatant casualties, which meant they tried not to gun down women and children. Miles ignored the results of the inquiry and continued to criticise Forsyth for many years after the event, believing that Forsyth had deliberately disobeyed his orders. Forsyth's perceived disobedience, as outlined by Miles, contributed to the idea that perhaps Wounded Knee was a deliberate massacre rather than a tragedy caused by poor decisions.

There was some comment in various newspapers favourable to the Indians, and many liberal Easterners were rightly outraged that such a thing could have happened, especially when it became known that among the dead were forty-four women and eighteen children. To complete the whitewash, the American government awarded the Medal of Honor to twenty soldiers who had taken part in the massacre, which remains the largest number ever issued for a single action in American military history. Lobbying efforts by the Sioux to have the awards that they call 'Medals of Dis-Honor' disallowed have failed in over 100 years. Even Miles, who had taken such a strong stance with Forsyth over his handling of the affair, nonetheless upheld the award of the medals when they were reviewed, undoubtedly anxious not to sully the reputation of the army in the process. Wounded Knee continues to poison relations between the Lakota Sioux and the American government in the twenty-first century.

Notes

1. *Aberdeen Saturday Pioneer*, January 3, 1891.

2. Captain Ernest Chambers, *The Royal North-West Mounted Police: A Corps History* (1906, reprinted: Toronto: Coles Publishing Company, 1972), 5.

3. *Commanding Officer, Fort Yates to Brigadier-General Ruger, Department of Dakota, December 7, 1890*, in *Statement of General Miles: Report of the Secretary of War for 1891*, Vol. I (Washington DC: Government Printing Office, 1891), 143.

4. Geoffrey C. Ward, *The West: An Illustrated History* (New York: Little, Brown & Company, 1996), 380.

5. 'The Ghost Dance Among the Lakota' from James Mooney, *The Ghost-dance Religion and the Sioux Outbreak of 1890*, 14th Annual Report of the Bureau of American Ethnology, Part 2 (1894).

6. Ibid.

7. 'Lakota Accounts of the Massacre at Wounded Knee' from the *Report of the Commissioner of Indian Affairs 1891*, volume 1 (Washington DC: Government Printing Office, 1891), 179.

8. 'An Account of Sitting Bull's Death by James McLaughlin, Indian Agent at Standing Rock Reservation' from James McLaughlin, *Account of the Death of Sitting Bull and of the Circumstances Attending It* (Philadelphia, 1891), Archives of the West, http://www.pbs.org/weta/thewest/resources/archives/eight/gddescrp.htm, accessed 23 August 2007.

9. 'Lakota Accounts of the Massacre at Wounded Knee' from the *Report of the Commissioner of Indian Affairs 1891*, volume 1 (Washington DC: Government Printing Office, 1891), 179–183.

10. Ibid., 179–183.

11. Ibid., 179–183.

12. Ibid., 179–183.

13. Ibid., 179–183.

14. Ibid., 183.

EPILOGUE

RETURN TO WOUNDED KNEE

'When asked by an anthropologist what the Indians called America before
the white man came, an Indian said simply, "ours".'

Vine Deloria, Junior

Wounded Knee – two words that for many Native American people have
summed up their ancestors' long struggle with the Americans. The Wounded
Knee Massacre in the closing days of 1890 witnessed the brutal slaughter of
Minneconjou Sioux gunned down in the snows of South Dakota. Eighty-
two years later, in 1973, the Sioux were still living marginalised lives. The
horses were largely gone, replaced by broken-down pickup trucks and saloon
cars, and the tepees long since replaced by cheap government prefabricated
housing that was dilapidated and lacking in many of the most basic facilities.
The old wandering lifestyle was gone, too, replaced by dirty little villages on
the reservations where crime, child abuse, drug addiction and alcoholism
were rampant, and suicide all-too common. These places were little slices of
Third World poverty in the midst of the richest nation on earth.

The former unity that had existed among the Sioux divisions had been
replaced by a murderous factionalism, as some Indians strove to modernise and
rejected everything about their culture in an effort to conform to mainstream
American society, while others clung to their identity as Indians. The reservations were hotbeds of discontent, simmering resentment and internecine
conflict, and violence was eventually ignited among one of the peoples with
the strongest record of resistance to the Americans in the nineteenth century,
the Oglala Sioux at Pine Ridge Reservation in South Dakota, who counted
Red Cloud and Crazy Horse among their honoured ancestors.

By 1973 Wounded Knee had evolved into a small town on the Pine Ridge
Reservation. It was poor, deprived of resources and funding and its residents

suffered many social problems, caused by alienation from mainstream American society. Throughout the 1950s and 1960s African-Americans had become increasingly radicalised in their struggle for equal representation and fairer treatment by the white majority. A large black population and recognisable leaders such as Martin Luther King helped to push civil rights into the mainstream of politics. American Indians, however, because of their small numbers and location on isolated reservations far from cities, had no voice. They too wanted civil rights protection and an improvement in their living standards, but successive American presidents had done little for them, because their vote was so small and insignificant.

American Indians, especially those on the plains, still inhabited, and continue to inhabit in the early twenty-first century, a nineteenth-century condition. The Indian Bureau is still in existence; reservations continue to swallow government money without real improvements; the Indians are not masters of their own destinies; they lack a national political platform; and they remain in an economic cycle of dependence. In 1968 studies discovered that Indian unemployment was forty per cent, or ten times the national average. Fifty per cent of all Indian children dropped out of high school before graduating, and 50,000 Indian families were living in dilapidated housing, even in cars, without running water and sewerage. The life expectancy of Indians lagged *twenty* years behind white Americans.

At Pine Ridge, the reservation government was under the control of Richard Wilson. Wilson was accused by many in the local community of being corrupt and abusing his authority. The FBI had already begun monitoring the situation at Pine Ridge, but President Richard Nixon's administration was more interested in rooting out potential troublemakers among those in opposition to Wilson than in healing the rifts in the Oglala community. Wilson had created a private army to protect his interests, named the Guardians of the Oglala Nation (GOONS), and this gang of hoodlums was used to intimidate and sometimes kill those who spoke out.

Over 150 civil rights complaints had been made against the tribal government by early 1973, but none were investigated by the FBI or the Indian Bureau. Those in opposition to Wilson had formed themselves into the Oglala Sioux Civil Rights Organisation (OSCRO). OSCRO members wanted the Oglala to exercise more independence from the federal government, and to force the government to honour the terms of the 1868 Fort Laramie Treaty and return to the Sioux the sacred Black Hills that had been illegally taken in 1877 as revenge for Custer's defeat.

The environment was another important issue, for Wilson and his cronies supported strip-mining of the reservation. The chemicals used in this process had entered the water supply, many people were getting sick and babies had been born with birth defects. On 26 February 1973 OSCRO held an open meeting at Wounded Knee to discuss their various grievances and try to get some help to solve them. On the following day they decided to ask members of a militant national Indian organisation to come and assist them, the American Indian Movement (AIM).

The FBI considered AIM to be a home-grown terrorist organisation, and the government moved fast to isolate Wounded Knee. AIM wanted a judicial review of the 371 broken treaties the Americans had made with Indian peoples in the past. The intention of AIM was to get back some of the land that they considered to have been stolen from Indians through unfair and dishonest treaties made by the American government. Specifically, AIM demanded that 110 million acres of land be restored to the tribes.

About 200–300 AIM members, representing Indian peoples from all over America, many of them armed, entered Wounded Knee on the 26th to join up with OSCRO. AIM picked Wounded Knee because of its symbolic association with the massacre of 1890, which they described as 'a prime example of the treatment of Indians since the European invasion.' Also, the 1868 Fort Laramie Treaty, one of the most well-known of the broken agreements made by the Americans, fired their interest. AIM believed that the original terms of the 1868 Treaty made with the Sioux had been ignored in 1876, when the government had reorganised the Great Sioux Reservation after Custer's defeat, and again from 1886 under federal allotment. This was not in accordance with the terms of the original treaty and needed to be addressed. AIM also demanded investigations into the misuse of tribal funds, GOON intimidation of Oglalas who had dared to speak out against the tribal government and a Senate committee investigation of the Indian Bureau and the Interior Department record of handling the affairs of the Oglala Sioux.

Local law enforcement agencies, the FBI and the GOONS began to cordon off the town, setting up roadblocks and arresting anyone who tried to enter or leave the settlement. Fifty US Marshals arrived, and Nixon ordered the National Guard into action.

Instead of the soldiers arriving clad in blue, armed with Springfield carbines and riding horses as in the past, the cavalry of the 6th Army arrived this time wearing khaki, toting M-16 assault rifles and riding in armoured personnel carriers. Both sides quickly erected fortifications and settled down for a long siege. Wounded Knee would be under sustained fire from the army, US Marshals and GOONs for seventy-one days. It drew media attention from all over the world and highlighted the poor relations that still existed between Indians and the federal government.

Every day the two sides traded fire, and the wooden buildings at Wounded Knee were soon peppered by rifle and machine-gun bullets. Five million rounds were fired into the settlement. The army was heedless of the women and children trapped in the town. Electricity was turned off and food supplies prevented from entering the settlement, as the government tried to starve the defenders into surrendering. Incredibly, only a few deaths occurred. On 17 April Frank Clearwater, an AIM supporter, was struck in the head by a bullet while he was sleeping and died a few days later. On 23 April twelve AIM supporters who were attempting to carry food supplies into the town simply disappeared in the countryside close to Wounded Knee. A search was conducted for a mass grave but their remains have never been located. On 26 April occupier Lawrence Lamont was shot and killed, and US Marshal Lloyd Grimm paralysed from the waist down during fighting. On 5 May a ceasefire was declared, followed by a surrender on 8 May.

The government arrested 1,200 Oglala Sioux and AIM members, but only 15 were ever convicted of any crime. The GOON squads continued to roam free from government interference and Wilson remained in charge. Between 1973 and 1976 over 300 Oglala supporters of AIM, or those in opposition to Wilson, were beaten up and harassed. Sixty-one people were the victims of unsolved homicides on Pine Ridge, and none of these murders has ever been investigated by the authorities. However, AIM and its supporters did score a minor victory in 1974, when the Indian Claims Commission, a government body, ruled that the United States had taken the sacred Black Hills from the Sioux illegally in 1877, in violation of the 5th Amendment to the Constitution. The US Supreme Court refused to hear this case until 1980, for, if indeed it were proven that the Commission ruling was right, and the court declared the historical actions of the government unconstitutional, a massive floodgate of Indian claims would potentially be opened and tens of millions of acres of land perhaps restored to the various tribes. In 1877 the Black Hills was valued at $17 million – by 1974 that figure had grown to $103 million. In 1980 the US Supreme Court agreed with the Commission and awarded the Sioux $106 million compensation, but the tribe refused the money, seeking instead the return of their land. They are still waiting.

BIBLIOGRAPHY

Books

Alexander Adams, *Sitting Bull: An Epic of the Plains* (New York: G.P. Putnam's Sons), 1973.

Gary Anderson, *Sitting Bull and the Paradox of Lakota Nationhood* (New York: Longman), 1996.

Ian Anderson, *Sitting Bull's Boss: Above the Medicine Line with James Morrow Walsh* (Toronto: Heritage House Publishing Company Ltd), 2000.

R. Andrist, *The Long Death: The Last Days of the Plains Indians* (New York: Collier), 1969.

Brian Bailey, *Massacres: An Account of Crimes Against Humanity* (London: Orion), 1994.

John W. Bailey, *Pacifying the Plains: General Alfred Terry and the Decline of the Sioux, 1866–1890* (Westport: Greenwood Press), 1979.

A. Banfield, *The Mammals of Canada* (Toronto: University of Toronto Press), 1974.

Robert F. Berkhofer, *The White Man's Indian* (New York: Alfred A. Knopf), 1978.

Black Elk (ed. Joseph Brown), *The Sacred Pipe: Black Elk's Account of the Seven Rites of the Oglala Sioux* (New York: Penguin Books), 1971.

E.A. Brininstool, *Troopers With Custer* (Omaha: University of Nebraska Press), 1989.

Albert Britt, *Great Indian Chiefs: A Study of Indian Leaders in the Two Hundred Year Struggle to Stop the White Advance* (Ayer Company Publishers (Facsimile), 1969).

Dee Brown, *Bury My Heart at Wounded Knee: An Indian History of the American West* (London: Arena), 1990.

George Pierre Castille & Robert L. Bee (eds), *State & Reservation* (Tucson: University of Arizona Press), 1992.

Edwin Chambers, *The Royal North-West Mounted Police: A Corps History* (Toronto: Coles Publishing Company), 1972.

James Clifford, *The Predicament of Culture: Twentieth-Century Ethnography, Literature, and Art* (Cambridge, MA: Harvard University Press), 1988.

J. Clifton, *The Invented Indian: Cultural Fictions and Government Policies* (New Brunswick: Transaction Publishers), 1990.

Evan S. Connell, *Son of the Morning Star: General Custer and the Battle of the Little Bighorn* (London: Pavilion Books Ltd), 1985.

Stephen Cornell, *The Return of the Native – American Indian Political Resurgence* (New York: Oxford University Press), 1988.

Vine Deloria, Jr, *American Indian Policy in the Twentieth Century* (Norman: University of Oklahoma Press), 1985.

_____ *Singing for a Spirit: A Portrait of the Dakota Sioux* (Santa Fe: Clear Light Publishers), 1999.

Raymond J. DeMallie (ed.), *Handbook of North American Indians, Volume 13, Part 2* (Washington DC: Smithsonian Institution), 2001.

Edwin Denig, *The Five Indian Tribes of the Upper Missouri* (Norman: University of Oklahoma Press), 1961.

David Dixon, *Hero of Beecher Island: The Life and Military Career of George A. Forsyth* (Lincoln: University of Nebraska Press), 1994.

Mark Felton, *The Nez Perce War 1877: An Examination of the Relationship between the Nez Perce and the United States, the Causes of the Conflict, and the Conduct of Operations of the US Army*, (MA Dissertation: University of Essex, 2000), unpublished.

_____ *Resistance in Exile: Sitting Bull and the Teton Sioux in Canada, 1876–1881* (PhD Thesis: University of Essex, 2005), unpublished.

James Finerty, *War-Path and Bivouac or The Conquest of the Sioux* (Norman: University of Oklahoma Press), 1961.

Jerome Green, *Lakota and Cheyenne: Indian Views of the Great Sioux War 1876–7* (Norman: University of Oklahoma Press, 1994).

_____ *Washita, The Southern Cheyenne and the U.S. Army* (Norman: University of Oklahoma Press), 2004.

F. Haines, *The Nez Perces: Tribesmen of the Columbia Plateau* (Norman: University of Oklahoma Press), 1972.

Kenneth Hammer, *Men With Custer: Biographies of the 7th Cavalry, June 25 1876* (Custer Battlefield Historical Museum Association), 1995.

Royal B. Hassrick, *The Sioux: Life and Customs of a Warrior Society* (Norman: University of Oklahoma Press), 1964.

Donald J. Hauka, *McGowan's War* (Vancouver: New Star Books), 2000.

Derek Hayes, *Historical Atlas of British Columbia and the Pacific Northwest* (Vancouver: Cavendish Books), 1999.

N. Hill (ed.), *Words of Power: Voices from Indian America*, (Golden, CO: Fulcrum Publishing), 1994.

Stanley Hoig, *Battle of the Washita: The Sheridan-Custer Indian Campaign of 1867–69* (Lincoln: University of Nebraska Press), 1976.

W. Hornaday, *The Extermination of the American Bison, with a Sketch of its Discovery and Life History* (1889; reprint: Washington DC: Smithsonian Institution Press), 2002.

Frederick E. Hoxie, *A Final Promise: The Campaign to Assimilate the Indians, 1880–1920* (Lincoln: University of Nebraska Press), 1984.

Alvin Hurtado & Peter Iverson (eds), *Major Problems in American Indian History* (New York: D.C. Heath & Co.), 1994.

V. Hyatt & R. Nettleford (eds), *Race, Discourse, and the Origin of the Americas: A New World View* (Washington DC: Smithsonian Institution Press), 1995.

Alvin M. Josephy, *Now That the Buffalo's Gone: A Study of Today's American Indians* (Norman: University of Oklahoma Press), 1989.

_____ *The Patriot Chiefs: A Chronicle of American Indian Resistance* (London: Penguin Books), 1993.

Robert J. Kershaw, *Red Sabbath: The Battle of Little Bighorn* (Hersham, Surrey: Ian Allan Publishing), 2005.

Patricia Nelson Limerick, *The Legacy of Conquest: The Unbroken Past of the American West* (New York: W.W. Norton), 1987.

Patricia Nelson Limerick, C. Milner & C. Rankin (eds), *Trails: Towards a New Western History* (Lawrence: University of Kansas Press), 1991.

Patricia Nelson Limerick & Richard White, *The Frontier in American Culture: An Exhibition at the Newberry Library, August 26, 1994 – January 7, 1995* (Berkeley: University of California Press), 1994.

Dean L. May, *Utah: A People's History* (Salt Lake City: Bonnerville Books), 1987.

Grant MacEwan, *Sitting Bull: The Years in Canada* (Edmonton: Hurtig Publishers), 1973.

Baron Edmond de Mandat-Grancey, *Cow-Boys and Colonels: Narrative of a Journey Across the Prairie and Over the Black Hills of Dakota* (Philadelphia: J.B. Lippincott Company), 1963.

Joseph P. Manzione, *'I am Looking to the North for my life': Sitting Bull, 1876–1881* (Salt Lake City: University of Utah Press), 1991.

Thomas B. Marquis, *Reminiscences of Four Cheyennes and a Sioux* (Stockton: Pacific Center for Western Historical Studies, 1973).

Janet McDonnell, *The Dispossession of the American Indian 1887–1934* (Bloomington: Indiana University Press), 1991.

Gregory F. Michno, *Lakota Noon: The Indian Narrative of Custer's Defeat* (Mountain Press Co.), 1999.

Marie Mitchell, *The Navajo Peace Treaty, 1868* (Mason & Lipscomb), 1973.

James Mooney, *The Ghost Dance Religion and the Sioux Outbreak of 1890*, (Lincoln: University of Nebraska Press), 1991.

Keith A. Murray, *The Modocs and their War* (Norman: University of Oklahoma Press, 1967).

Roger L. Nichols, *Indians in the United States and Canada: A Comparative History* (Lincoln: University of Nebraska Press), 1998.

D. Otis, *The Dawes Act and the Allotment of Indian Land* (Norman: University of Oklahoma Press), 1973

R. Ruby & J. Brown, *Indians of the Pacific Northwest: A History* (Norman: University of Oklahoma Press), 1981.

_____ *A Guide to the Indian Tribes of the Pacific Northwest* (Norman: University of Oklahoma Press), 1986.

Bryan Perrett, *Against All Odds! More Dramatic 'Last Stand' Actions* (London: Brockhampton Press), 1999.

Francis Prucha, *American Indian Treaties: The History of a Political Anomaly* (Berkeley: University of California Press), 1994.

J. Sayer, *Ghost Dancing the Law: The Wounded Knee Trials* (Cambridge, MA: Harvard University Press), 1997.

Dale T. Schoenberger, *The End of Custer: The Death of an American Military Legend* (Surrey, BC: Hancock House), 1995.

Francis B. Taunton, *A Scene of Sickening, Ghastly Horror: The Custer Battlefield – 27–28 June 1876* (London: Johnson-Taunton Military Press), 1983.

Erwin N. Thompson, *Modoc War: Its Military History & Topography* (Sacramento: Argus Books), 1971.

Robert M. Utley, *The Last Days of the Sioux Nation*, (New Haven: Yale University Press), 1963.

_____ *Frontiersmen in Blue: The United States Army and the Indian 1848–1865* (New York: Macmillan), 1967.

_____ *Bluecoats and Redskins: The United States Army and the Indian 1866–1891* (London: Cassell & Collier), 1973.

_____ *The Lance and the Shield: The Life and Times of Sitting Bull* (New York: Henry Holt and Company, Inc.), 1993.

W.C. Vanderwerth, *Indian Oratory: Famous Speeches by Noted Indian Chieftains* (Norman: University of Oklahoma Press), 1971.

James R. Walker, *Lakota Belief and Ritual* (Lincoln: University of Nebraska Press, 1980).

_____ *Lakota Society* (Lincoln: University of Nebraska Press), 1982.

Geoffrey C. Ward, *The West: An Illustrated History* (New York: Little, Brown & Company), 1996.

W. Washburn, *The American Indian & The United States: A Documentary History*, Volume I (New York: Random House), 1973.

James Welch with Paul Stekler, *Killing Custer: The Battle of the Little Bighorn and the Fate of the Plains Indians* (New York: Penguin Books), 1994.

Richard White, *'Its Your Misfortune And None of My Own': A New History of the American West* (Norman: University of Oklahoma Press), 1991.

R. Williams, *The American Indian in Western Legal Thought: The Discourses of Conquest* (New York: Oxford University Press), 1990.

James Wilson, *The Earth Shall Weep: A History of Native America* (London: Picador), 1998.

Charles Windolph, *I Fought With Custer: The Story of Sgt Windolph, Last Survivor of the Battle of the Little Bighorn as told to Frazier and Robert Hunt* (London: Bison Books), 1987.

D. Wishart, *The Fur Trade in the American West, 1807–1840: A Geographical Synthesis* (Lincoln: University of Nebraska Press), 1979.

Robert Wooster, *The Military and United States Indian Policy 1865–1903* (New Haven: Yale University Press), 1988.

Bill Yenne, *Indian Wars: The Campaign for the American West* (Yardley, PA: Westholme), 2005.

Reports and Treaties

Report of the Commissioner of Indian Affairs 1843 (Washington DC: Government Printing Office), 1844.

Treaty With the Nez Perce Indians June 9, 1855 (University of Idaho Library, http:// www.menolly.lib.uidaho.edu/McBeth/governmentdoc/1855www.htm, accessed 1 June 2000).

Treaty With the Nez Perce Indians June 11, 1855, (University of Idaho Library, http:// www.menolly.lib.uidaho.edu/McBeth/governmentdoc/1863www.htm, accessed 2 June 2000).

Annual Message of the President and Report of the War Department 1858 (University of Idaho Library, http://www.menolly.lib.uidaho.edu/McBeth/governmentdoc/ 1853milrept.htm, accessed 4 June 2000).

Report of the Commissioner of Indian Affairs 1862 (Washington DC: Government Printing Office), 1863.

Treaty With the Nez Perce Indians August 13, 1868 (University of Idaho Library, http://www.menolly.lib.uidaho.edu/McBeth/governmentdoc/1868www.htm, accessed 1 June 2000).

Report of the Commissioner of Indian Affairs 1869 (Washington DC: Government Printing Office), 1869.

Report of the Commissioner of Indian Affairs 1873 (Washington DC: Government Printing Office), 1874.

1875 Wallowa Valley Report (University of Idaho Library, http://www.menolly.lib.uidaho.edu/McBeth/governmentdoc/1875wallowavalley.htm, accessed 6 June 2000).

Report of the Secretary of War 1875 (University of Idaho Library, http://www.menolly.lib.uidaho.edu/McBeth/governmentdoc/1875 wallowavalley.htm, accessed 8 June 2000).

Report of the General of the Army 1877 (Washington DC: Government Printing Office), 1878.

Report of the Secretary to the War 1877 (Washington DC: Government Printing Office), 1878.

Report of the Commissioner of Indian Affairs 1877 (Washington DC: Government Printing Office), 1878.

Report of the Commissioner of Indian Affairs 1878 (Washington DC: Government Printing Office), 1879.

Newspapers and Journals

Bismarck Tri-Weekly Tribune
British Journal of Canadian Studies
Bureau of American Ethnology Bulletin
The Chicago Times
Desert
Idaho State Journal
Lewiston Morning Tribune
Lewiston Tribune
Manitoba Free Press
Montana: The Magazine of Western History
The New Northwest
New York Herald
New York Times
Ottawa Citizen
Western Historical Quarterly

INDEX